Sydney Smith compares the influence his namesake to that of Wilberforce, yet today William Smith is but a dimly remembered figure. Actually he was a man of considerable importance in several liberal and reforming movements, and the fact that his place among the early Parliamentary reformers (within the small groups that led the battles for the abolition of the slave trade and slavery, and in the Whig party) has never been sufficiently recognized is ample justification for a study of his career.

William Smith's most important contribution to the cause of human freedom —the cause which gives meaning to all his political activities—was in the extension of religious liberty. In this endeavour he stands out as a major figure in his own right. It was William Smith who directed the negotiations for the broadening of the Toleration Act in 1812; who drew up and guided through Parliament the Unitarian Toleration Act of 1813; and who presided over the final, successful campaign to repeal the greatest badger of Dissenting inferiority, the Test and Corporation Acts, in 1828. Smith dominated Dissent in what was perhaps its greatest period of achievement, and it is impossible to separate the man from the movement. This book is a study of both.

Richard W. Davis attained his B.A. in 1957 at Amherst College, his M.A. in 1958 and Ph.D. in 1969 at Columbia University, and his M.Litt. in 1962 at the University of Cambridge.

He was Supervisor in History at Christ's College, Cambridge 1960–1962; Instructor at the University of Rhode Island 1962–1964; Assistant Professor at the University of California 1964–1969; and Associate Professor at the Washington University, St Louis from 1969.

DISSENT IN POLITICS
1780-1830

WILLIAM SMITH, M.P.

from a mezzotint by V. Green
after the painting by John Opie, R.A.

Richard W. Davis

DISSENT IN POLITICS
1780-1830

THE POLITICAL LIFE OF
WILLIAM SMITH, MP

LONDON

EPWORTH PRESS

Set in 12/13pt Van Dijck
and printed and bound
in Great Britain
by W & J Mackay & Co Ltd
Chatham

SBN 7162 0154 2

Inquiries
regarding this book
should be sent to
The Distributors
The Methodist Book Room
2 Chester House
Pages Lane
London N10 1PZ

To the Memory of F.C.D.

CONTENTS

ACKNOWLEDGEMENTS

In the course of ten years I have incurred many obligations. I should like to acknowledge some of them, and I hope those I have missed will forgive me.

Professors J. H. Plumb and R. K. Webb, under whom I worked at Columbia and Cambridge, have given me invaluable advice and encouragement from the beginning. Most recently, the Rev Roger Thomas has read the manuscript and helped me to make many of my points better and to avoid many errors. My debt to all three is great.

The late Mr Philip Leigh-Smith, Miss Katherine Duff, and Mr Victor Bonham-Carter all generously turned over to me the Smith manuscripts in their possession. All the papers are now deposited in the William Smith Collection at the Cambridge University Library for the convenience of future scholars. I must acknowledge a very special debt to Victor Bonham-Carter, without whose constant help and encouragement this book would never have been published.

Sir Harry Verney gave me the first of many warm welcomes at Claydon to consult the Nightingale papers there. Joseph Travers & Sons kindly allowed me to see the Smith personal and business papers in their archives in Cannon Street. Mr and Mrs Richard Moore entertained me at Hancox, so that I could see some excellent portraits of William Smith there. Dr Mary French of Queen Mary College, London, gave me much useful information on Smith's scientific interests. The Duke University Library photostated its Smith Papers and the Cambridge University Library paid for them, for my use at Cambridge.

I should also like to thank the Trustees of Dr Williams's Library for permission to consult and quote the Belsham and Crabb Robinson papers; and the University of Chicago Press for permission to reprint substantial portions of my article, 'The Strategy of "Dissent"

ix

in the Repeal Campaign, 1820–1828', in *The Journal of Modern History*, Vol. 38, No. 4 (December 1966), pp. 374–93.

At various times my work has received financial assistance from Columbia University, the Master and Fellows of Christ's College, Cambridge, and the Regents of the University of California. The Hibbert Trustees have made a generous grant towards the cost of publication. I thank them all.

The friendship and encouragement of Miss Rosamund Heath and the Neville Temperleys have meant much to me. My late father, to whose memory this book is dedicated, gave me my interest in history and a great deal besides.

R. W. DAVIS

Washington University
8 March 1970

FOREWORD

I greatly welcome the opportunity to write a Foreword to this important book. Although my qualifications as a historian are slight, my interest in William Smith is keen, in that I am a direct descendant of his through the marriage—on Christmas Day 1816—of his daughter Joanna Maria to my great-grandfather, John Carter. The Carters resembled the Smiths in several respects. They, too, came from the Rational Dissenting tradition and became Unitarians. They had also done well in trade, in their case in brewing and distilling. Their forte, however, was local politics, for they succeeded in dominating Portsmouth Corporation over about eighty years thanks to a combination of high-pressure tactics and solid family preferment. John's grandfather was mayor seven times, his father—Sir John Carter—nine times, likewise his cousin Ned, who, to his great credit, was re-elected mayor on sheer merit after the Carter cabal had been broken by the Municipal Corporations Act, 1835. Sir John was the brave man who personally pacified the Spithead mutineers in 1797 and got them a fair hearing by the Government.

John was the first Carter to come to London. He was called to the Bar in 1819 and practised successfully until 1827, when he retired to devote himself to Parliamentary business. He was able to take this step because, as heir to his old bachelor cousin, Thomas Bonham, who died in 1826, he came into a considerable fortune in cash and property, mainly in Hampshire. The latter included Buriton Manor near Petersfield, where Edward Gibbon had written portions of his great classic, *The Decline and Fall of the Roman Empire*. In February 1827 John obtained a royal licence to 'assume and use the surname of Bonham, in addition to and before the present surname of Carter'. He thus founded the present family of Bonham-Carter.

John was elected one of the two M.P.s for Portsmouth in 1816, and held his seat for twenty-one years, until his early death at the age of forty-nine in 1838. Like cousin Ned, he got in under the bad old system, but survived under the new by reason of character and good record. Indeed, as a Whig and a Dissenter he was in the forefront of reform, but like his father-in-law he preferred to work behind the scenes. This is well illustrated by the part he played in the great Reform Bill. At the outset in 1830 he had been critical of the drafting, and when the Bill had been presented for the second time and turned down by the House of Lords in the summer of 1831, his advice was sought by Lord Grey. From then on he was in constant touch with the promoters of the Bill, from the time it was presented for the third time in December 1831 until its final enactment in June 1832. He was in the background all through the Committee stage, revising and improving the terminology, and concentrated particularly on the 36th clause which dealt with the system of registration of voters.

His interest in the franchise led subsequently to appointment as Chairman of the Select Committee, whose enquiries resulted in the passage in 1836 of Lord John Russell's two Acts, which established civil registration of births and deaths and the licensing of civil marriages. This put an end to a Church monopoly long discredited and to which Dissenters had especially objected.

By 1836 John was in the early stages of diabetes, then an incurable disease, which killed him two years later. He thus survived William Smith by only three years. They had worked together in the cause of religious and political freedom, and had witnessed the triumph of Smith's long and arduous career, when the Test and Corporation Acts were repealed in 1828. John's own contribution to Parliament, short though it was, was a fitting complement to all his father-in-law had done. They were men of similar stamp—honest, practical and energetic, caring nothing for public acclaim.

I recommend Richard Davis's discerning study with the utmost confidence.

VICTOR BONHAM-CARTER

East Anstey
North Devon
September 1969

INTRODUCTION

Thisis book is a study both of one man's political career and, in so far as it can be illustrated in the career of one man, of a movement. The man is William Smith, M.P. The movement is that of the Dissenters for social and civic equality.

Smith is a politician of whom little has been heard since his death in 1835. This is explicable in large part by the fact that Smith himself preferred to avoid the limelight. He had neither the taste nor the talents to be a leader of great popular movements. Rather he worked quietly behind the scenes. And in this he was not unsuccessful. If he was not a Wilberforce, he was one of his most valuable lieutenants. And, if the cause of Parliamentary reform owes less to Smith than it does to Lord Grey, it does owe him something for his early advocacy and for consistent support, through bad years and good, from his entry into Parliament in 1784 to his retirement in 1830. In several of the liberal and reforming movements of his day, Smith had an important, albeit not a dominating, role. None the less, his was a role which deserves recognition.

In one of the movements of his day, however, Smith was the dominant figure. This was in the struggle of his fellow Dissenters to gain what they felt to be their rightful place in English society. Almost from the commencement of his political career, Smith was the main spokesman of his co-religionists in their efforts to extend religious liberty and attain real political equality.

The Dissenters' struggle deserves more attention than it has received. Since the epochal works of Sir Lewis Namier, much time, effort, and talent have gone into the exposition of the colour, variety, and, often less successfully, the pattern of English politics in the late eighteenth and early nineteenth centuries. The history of Dissent can add much to the clarity of the exposition. Not only did the Dissenters contribute much to the colour and variety of politics, their activities also shaped some of its patterns. Religion was a constant theme in political controversy, but, more than that, it served as a fundamental basis for the emergence of a broad new division in English politics.

In retrospect, it is clear that the greatest political problem of the period roughly bounded by the American Revolution and the Great Reform Bill was the struggle between the traditionally privileged and rising new talent, ability, and wealth—between the old oligarchy based on the land and the aggressive and expanding middle classes produced by the tremendous commercial and industrial growth of the country. Dissenters were bound to be in the thick of the struggle. Partly, it was because the Church, whose members' virtual monopoly of political power the Dissenters sought to break, was an integral part of the oligarchical system in society and politics. Partly, it was because, through a close connexion between the Dissenters' religious principles and commercial and industrial success, they formed a large and influential element in the new middle classes. For both reasons, Dissenters were almost bound to be warm advocates of the reform of the oligarchical eighteenth-century system.

The career of William Smith provides an illustration both of the aspirations of his fellow Dissenters and, because he was their most influential political spokesman, of the attempts to implement those aspirations in the hard world of politics.

Smith came of a long line of Dissenting merchants who by hard work, thrift, and judicious marriages had amassed a substantial fortune. The fortune was William's, and his problem was what to do with it. Like many other young men in a similar position he chose a career in politics. But, once in politics, he found that his religious beliefs, and the political objectives derived from them, were largely unacceptable to the age in which he lived. One after another of the projects—the repeal of the Test and Corporation Acts, the abolition of the Slave Trade, Parliamentary reform—into which he threw himself were either coldly rejected or politely shelved by those in power. It is not surprising that the frustration of all his political aims caused a growing alienation from the society in which he lived and deepened his desire to reform it. Nor is it surprising that as new political issues arose, such as the French Revolution, his reaction should have been different from that of his political adversaries, thus widening the area of conflict.

Smith's experiences were by no means unique. They are mirrored in the lives of many other Dissenters, with similar results. During Smith's career in politics the foundation was laid for a division in English social and political life which was to shape the history of nineteenth-century England. This theme was one of the considerations which attracted me to the career of William Smith, and the first half of this book will deal with the movements that moulded his political attitudes.

In the second half of the book, the emphasis changes. From 1811 onwards, English Dissenters made rapid strides. Toleration was firmly established, and, with the repeal of the Test and Corporation Acts in 1828, the Dissenters' equality with Anglicans in politics was recognized. Partly, no doubt, this growing liberalism in religious affairs can be attributed to a profound shift in English social and intellectual attitudes. But this is not the whole story. The advances made during this period were also due, to a very large degree, to the political skill and adroitness of the Dissenting leadership—particularly to the astute leadership of William Smith.

To an extent generally unrecognized, political astuteness was crucial inside, as well as outside, the Dissenting movement. The movement was riven with dissension. Evangelical trinitarians and Unitarians were moving swiftly toward a definitive parting of the way. Dissent was deeply and bitterly divided on the greatest domestic political issue of the period, the question of Catholic political disabilities. To maintain unity for common ends and to suppress the religious bigotry which might have fatally marred their demands for religious liberty were critical problems for the Dissenting leadership.

More than to any other individual, the credit for the solution of these problems belongs to William Smith. He was by no means always right, and events constantly pushed him and shaped his policies. Yet both inside the Dissenting movement and in its relations with the broader political world, Smith demonstrated a remarkable grasp of what was possible, and how to achieve it. The latter half of this book will deal with the politics within the Dissenting movement and how they influenced the attainment of the Dissenters' political objectives.

DISSENT IN POLITICS

1780-1830

CHAPTER ONE

THE EARLY YEARS

The place in life to which William Smith was born on 22 September 1756 was eminently solid, substantial, and comfortable. He came from shrewd and successful Dissenting merchant stock on both sides. His forebears had risen, as his father Samuel said of himself, 'by the blessing of Providence and industry'. Samuel maintained his strong faith in both, with excellent results. Thus the background against which William lived his early life may be summed up in two words which E. M. Forster has used to describe John Thornton, Samuel Smith's close friend and neighbour at Clapham, 'prosperous and pious'.[1]

The Smiths came originally from the Isle of Wight. Indeed, William's grandfather Samuel I had been an ironmonger in Newport. Beyond the fact that he made a socially extraordinary marriage into one of the oldest and most distinguished families in the Island, the Leighs of North Court House,[2] nothing much is known of Samuel I. In any case, it was certainly not he but his bachelor brother Joseph who started the family on its rapid rise to commercial eminence and prosperity.

Perhaps Joseph was not the founder of the family grocery business in London. Tradition holds that the firm dates back at least to the Fire of London;[3] but the earliest document proving its existence is one dated 1 May 1710 in which Joseph Smith 'Citizen and Grocer of

[1] *Marianne Thornton: A Domestic Biography* (New York, 1956), p. 10.

[2] For the Leighs see Sir Richard Worsley, *The History of the Isle of Wight* (London, 1781), p. 248 and Appendix IX.

[3] *Chronicles of Cannon Street* (privately printed for Joseph Travers and Sons Ltd), p. 10.

1

London' agrees to release his brother Samuel Smith of Newport, Isle of Wight 'from all and every liability I ever had . . . from the beginning of the World unto the day of the date of these presents'. A note written by William Smith in 1800 identifies Joseph Smith and Benjamin Smith, who witnessed the document, as 'my great-uncle[s] of Cannon Street';[1] Samuel, of course, was his grandfather.

Joseph Smith's ledger, dated 'at the Sugar Loaf, Cannon Street', and running from 1728 to 1733,[2] sheds more light on the family history. Joseph had apparently become the sole proprietor of the firm, which was then in a state of transition from a retail to a whole-sale business. Some very small accounts of only a few pounds are recorded; about a dozen, one as far away as Manchester, run to several thousand; but most seem to be about forty or fifty. The ledger also reveals that Joseph served as London banker and agent for a variety of friends and relations, most of them in the Island (although one Smith had already strayed as far as the West Indies). His brother Samuel was one who benefited by these services. Joseph honoured his bills, made purchases such as an anvil for Samuel or brown silk for Mrs Smith, and doled out money to their sons in London.

Joseph also took an avuncular interest in the successful launching of his brother's children. The younger Smiths did very well. Elizabeth married Benjamin Travers, son of a wealthy London oil merchant.[3] Tryphena married William Nash, who became a partner in the wholesale grocery and subsequently Worshipful Master of the Salters Company in 1762, Alderman for Walbrook Ward from 1766 to 1772, President of St Thomas's Hospital from 1769 to 1772, and Lord Mayor for the year 1771–2.[4] Another daughter married a Kemble (not of the famous acting family), but beyond the fact that their sons subsequently became partners in the grocery nothing is known of them. Of the sons, William went to the the West Indies and became a prosperous merchant in Antigua;[5] Benjamin, the eldest, and Samuel II, the youngest and father of the subject of this biography, both entered their uncle Joseph's business.

Born in 1727, Samuel II entered his uncle's employ in the early

<hr>

[1] Photostat, Travers Papers.   [2] Travers Papers.
[3] *Chronicles of Cannon Street*, p. 23.   [4] Ibid., p. 21.
[5] See his memorandum book, Leigh-Smith Papers.

forties. In June 1750, on Joseph's retirement to the Isle of Wight, Samuel formed a new partnership with his brother Benjamin and his brother-in-law William Nash. His total capital at the time was 'one thousand pounds in money and a stock of apparell to the amount of thirty pounds. . . .' This his uncle supplemented with a loan of three thousand pounds, making him his heir for the same amount on his death in 1753. In 1754 marriage to Martha Adams brought another addition to his capital in the form of a very handsome dowry of six thousand pounds, which, Samuel recorded, 'being all in trade my affairs now stand as follows

By one third of the capital in trade	£12,601	16	4.
By balance of the Account Current	243	4	0.
By balance of my Cash Book	17	9	6.
	£12,862	9	10.'

Another balance of accounts was done in 1755, and, although he does not give the amount, Samuel notes that a third of the total capital in the business is his entire fortune 'exclusive of my household furniture, wife's jewels, apparell, which with the repairs of my house cost me about £2,500 and I now don't owe any debts to the amount of £5 that I know'. By 1757 the joint stock of the firm had reached £46,000, his share being £15,333 6s 8d., and again he notes that this comprises his whole fortune exclusive of items similar to those mentioned above and forty-two pounds in cash. In addition he owed 'to sundry about £40'.

The early years demanded careful living, keeping account of every penny, and ploughing back all profits beyond the amount necessary for the most modest existence; but by 1761 the partners felt safe, and in that year 'took out of stock and made the balance £70,000, one third of which is £23,800'. Thus 'by the blessing of Providence and industry' had Samuel Smith prospered.[1]

Samuel continued to prosper. The firm was to make a profit, in bad years and good, throughout the fifty subsequent years that the

[1] Photostats of 'Documents signed by Samuel Smith describing his entry into partnership with his brother Benjamin and the progress of his fortunes', Travers Papers, no. 30.

Smiths were to be associated with it, netting its partners a neat average of four thousand pounds per annum.[1] After 1761, with the business firmly on its feet, Samuel was able to widen his investments, particularly in real estate. And, to supplement his provision for the family's future, his bride brought, in addition to her very substantial dowry, the prospect of an even more considerable increase in the Smith fortune.

The Adamses, like the Smiths, were of Dissenting stock, but their wealth and position were of much older origin. Martha's great-grandfather, Sir Thomas Adams, had been Lord Mayor of London in 1645. Her own father, William, had a very comfortable fortune in securities and London real estate.[2] Mrs Adams was a niece of Thomas Halsey, M.P., and, on the death of the latter's daughter Lady Cobham in 1760, she inherited a large part of the Halsey estate.[3] All went, in due course, to the Adamses' only surviving heir, William Smith, assuring the latter, if he so chose, a very comfortable income removed from the risks of trade.

It was, therefore, into a family with a more than comfortable fortune and with a social position equally secure that William Smith was born. His early life was not to be without its insecurities, and its tragedies none the less. Even the well-to-do could not escape the effects of the primitive sanitation and inadequate medical knowledge of the eighteenth century. On 29 July 1759, as Samuel reverently recorded in his memorandum book, 'it pleased almighty God to deprive me of what was my greatest comfort, my dearly beloved wife. It was the first and greatest affliction that my life afforded me and I would desire to improve it'.[4] William was only three. And two

[1] From a rough capital and profit statement drawn up by William Smith in 1812, Travers Papers.

[2] His will (Leigh-Smith Papers) does not specify his holdings in cash and securities, which, except for bequests amounting to some six thousand pounds, went to his son James. It does, however, show his large real estate holdings in London and Southwark, which he left to his wife.

[3] William Adams's accounts of the Halsey estate in 1761 and 1766 (Leigh-Smith Papers) show that his wife's original share was about nine thousand pounds, which had swelled in value to eleven thousand in five years' time. The death of her spinster sisters probably increased this sum considerably.

[4] Photostat, Travers Papers.

years later his little sister, whose birth had cost her mother's life, died of smallpox.

Little William did not, however, lack for affection. His grandfather and grandmother Adams and his bachelor uncle James lavished attention on the little boy. Samuel was far ahead of them. As he wrote to William on the latter's birthday in 1770:

Since the loss of her to whom you owe your birth and which loss you were then too young to feel, you have been the first object of my affection. I have made it my study to shew it in the most convincing proofs for your happiness. I think I have always treated you as the Friend as well as [the] parent. . . .[1]

Samuel was not speaking idly. His letters to his little son at school are eloquent proofs that the stern, sober merchant who looks out of Zoffany's portraits[2] devoted infinite time and loving care to his role of father, mother, and elder brother, all rolled into one. No woman could have taken more pains than he did to see that William's boxes contained all that he could want or need; he saw to everything personally, clothes and shoes, 'Tea things, Boiler etc., Tea and Good Sugar that you may not have the trouble of breaking it', nor did he forget the special sweets and the occasional little present. If William wanted a book or a newspaper, Samuel searched until he found it. All that could be done, Samuel did, to make sure, as he said, that William would have ample 'provision for Head, Feet and Belly. . . .'

His letters also show understanding and a sense of humour. Writing to the ten-year-old William to give instructions for the latter's collection for a holiday, he assures him that

as most young gentlemen are taken with a showy Horse so John has orders to bring your *Juliett* and combe Her mane and Long tail to its advantage—the Spatterdashes, spurs and whip will also accompany her that you may be complete in appearance, all this to please spectators, but a word to please you, the Mare is very pretty and very good-tempered, steady, and safe. . . .[3]

Clearly Samuel understood little boys.

1 Samuel Smith to William Smith, 22 September 1770, Leigh-Smith Papers.
2 Now in the possession of Mr Richard Moore.
3 Samuel Smith to William Smith, 13 September 1766, Leigh-Smith Papers.

Not unnaturally the career for which Samuel intended his son was one in trade, as his own successor in Cannon Street. Prosperity had not gone, and was never to go, to Samuel's head; nor did it much alter his habits. He was still as careful with his money as he had been in his early years. Not until 1771 did he decide to lay out two thousand pounds to build a long-talked-of new house.[1] Apparently this was sufficient for the construction of what a Clapham road-book of 1790 describes simply as 'a large house built with red brick'.[2] Doubtless it was quite in keeping with the villas of his Clapham neighbours; but it can hardly have been a magnificent structure. And, if he still lived without ostentation, Samuel also worked as hard or harder. Clapham provided only a retreat for weekends, the other five days being spent in Cannon Street in rooms above the counting house.[3] He drove himself like a slave, writing to William at the end of November 1771 that he had 'not been absent a day nor to one publick diversion' since the beginning of September.[4] Such was the regimen of this large and successful merchant, and it was one which Samuel cheerfully followed until his death in 1798. He never questioned that it was a good and useful life, and he asked nothing better for himself or for his son.

Great and honourable professsion that it was, commerce demanded, in Samuel's eyes, as good a preparation as any other. He was determined that his son should get the best:

Your future destination if it should please God to grant you life and health is for Trade but learning is not incompatible with it—on the Contrary it facilitates the conducting it and gives a person a superiority in his sphere of action. To see you enter life with reputation and superior ability to what I ever possessed is my earnest desire and I hope [it] will be one of the rewards of my industry to do all in my power to contribute to it.[5]

[1] Samuel Smith to William Smith, 21 November 1771, Travers Papers.
[2] This information is supplied through the kindness of Mr E. E. Smith of the Clapham Antiquarian Society.
[3] Samuel Smith to William Smith, 21 November 1771, Travers Papers, and *Chronicles of Cannon Street*, p. 41.
[4] Samuel Smith to William Smith, 21 November 1771, Travers Papers.
[5] Samuel Smith to William Smith, 17 October 1769, Leigh-Smith Papers.

Samuel was as good as his word, providing William with one of the best educations that England at the time could offer.

In 1764, at the age of eight, William was sent off, as he later recalled, to 'the highly respectable Mr. French who had recently taken the management of a Dissenting school at Ware'.[1] Seventy years later he was most struck by the fact that he had 'never heard an oath, or a flagrantly indecent expression, uttered by one boy during the five years of my continuance at Ware'.[2] Apparently Mr French deserved his reputation for respectability. But he also had a high reputation for offering a sound basic education as well.[3] Thomas Belsham, the minister of the Essex Street Chapel and the leading Unitarian thinker of the late eighteenth and early nineteenth centuries, was another of Mr French's students, and if for no other reason than the fact that Ware gave Smith the opportunity of making Belsham's acquaintance, it would have been of major significance in his life. Belsham was six years older than Smith, and, by taking the younger boy under his special protection, laid the basis of a remarkably warm and intimate friendship which ended only with Belsham's death in 1829. Belsham's religious thought was to have a profound influence on Smith. As young men the two were to travel together the road from orthodox Independency to Unitarianism. In later years they were to co-operate closely as two of the most eminent champions of the Unitarian cause.

In 1769 Smith left Ware and followed his friend to Daventry, probably on the advice of the Rev Philip Furneaux, the minister of the Independent congregation at Clapham, and, as one of the Coward Trustees, responsible for the management of the academy. The principal of Daventry at the time was the Rev Caleb Ashworth, who had already presided over the education of Joseph Priestley and whose rigorous standards continued to make Daventry one of the finest of the Dissenting academies at a time when they were in their flower.

Daventry's rigours were considerable, In the first year students were expected to take Latin, Greek, and Hebrew, in addition to

[1] Quoted in J. Williams, *Memoirs of T. Belsham* (London, 1833), p. 5.
[2] Ibid., p. 6.
[3] Ibid., p. 5.

Euclid, Geography, and Logic. In the second, the three languages were repeated, with algebra, trigonometry, pneumatology, and 'a few lectures on civil government'. In the third and last year for those not entering the ministry, the only language required was Hebrew, with conic sections, natural philosophy, and Evidences and Moral Duties of Christians. French, which Smith took, was also taught when desired.[1] Modern in its stress on science, geography, and French, the education offered was far from deficient in the knowledge of the classics which it inculcated, a knowledge which was an absolute necessity to any cultivated person during the period. It was certainly far more useful and far more stimulating than anything offered by the Universities at this time.

Smith completed his studies in 1772. By September of that year[2] he was hard at work in his father's counting house, where he was to remain for the next nine years. The absence of any regular correspondence leaves these years largely a blank, and little but the bare facts can be recounted. After a five-year apprenticeship William became a partner on the retirement of his uncle Benjamin in 1777. He remained a partner until his own withdrawal in 1780 to make room for his cousins Travers and Kemble, with the understanding that on Samuel's retirement he should be free to assume the place at the head of the firm.[3]

Smith no longer had any pressing financial reason for remaining in trade, the death of his uncle Adams in 1779 having, as he wrote to Belsham, 'occasioned a very considerable amplification of my worldly goods and chattels. . . .'[4] His mind was already bent toward another career, for in the same letter he informed Belsham that he was 'deeper in the mire [of politics] than ever'.[5] Indeed, according to the writer of his obituary in the *Morning Chronicle*, he was being mentioned as a

---

[1] H. McLachlan, *English Education under the Test Acts, 1662–1820* (Manchester, 1931), p. 157.

[2] The date is confirmed by a letter from James Adams to William Smith, 5 September 1772, Leigh-Smith Papers.

[3] Circular of Smith, Kemble and Co., 30 June 1813, Travers Papers.

[4] William Smith to Thomas Belsham, 21 October 1779, Dr Williams's Library, London, 12.58, no. 2.

[5] Ibid.

possible candidate for London.[1] Certainly in 1780 he seriously considered standing for Worcester, but his father was strongly opposed to the idea. The grounds of Samuel's opposition are not recorded, but they weighed sufficiently with William, and he gave up his political ambitions for the time being, writing wryly to Belsham:

Whatever your partiality may lead you to conceive of me, I cannot perfectly accede to the justice of your sentiments respecting the advantages Worcester would have derived, nor think it would have been a singular felicity to the City to have been represented for a whole session by a *learner* even tho' (to put it on the *best possible* footing) that learner should have been—myself—admire my—modesty.[2]

Though disappointed in politics, William had other reasons for joy in 1780. In that year he fell in love. Frances Coape came from an old family of Dissenting gentry in Nottinghamshire, closely related to several county families, particularly the Lowes and the Sherbrookes. John and Hannah Coape having died when their three daughters were still very young, the little girls were put in the care of a guardian, Mrs Forward, a neighbour of the Smiths at Clapham. Frances received what appears to have been a remarkably good boarding-school education. She emerged something of a 'bluestocking', with a strong taste for theological disputation, and talent for it which was to win the respect of Belsham himself.[3] She also had a strong vein of priggishness which strengthened as the years passed, and which was to make her a great trial to her family of exuberant children. It is to be said to her credit, however, that her priggishness was no respecter of persons; the great as well as the small were to experience the weight of her censure. Nor, whatever others might have thought of her, can it be doubted that this plump and darkly attractive little woman always enjoyed the utter devotion and adoration of her husband. She returned both, and gave to him, as she gave to no one else, the complete and unquestioning loyalty

[1] *William Smith, Formerly Member for the City of Norwich* (Hastings, 1835), p. 1.

[2] William Smith to Thomas Belsham, 7 October 1780, Dr Williams's Library, 12.58, no. 4.

[3] His *Letters to a Lady*, written in 1797 in answer to Wilberforce's *Practical View* were directed to her (Williams, p. 483).

of her stern and unbending personality. Frances may well have been a trial in prosperity, but she was to show a cool efficiency in time of crisis and a magnificence in adversity. She was a constant aid and a strong influence in William's life.

Her letters to her future husband tell a good deal about her character, which even her conventional girlishness cannot hide. Religion was a constant theme. Deeply religious herself, she was constantly probing to find out her intended's true opinions. A certain Mr B. had apparently been playing Cupid:

B. left out *one part* of your character which *I hope* I shall find inserted, or else, all our hopes of happiness must be vain, a mere airy fiction, lighter than the wind. Not all the imaginary fabric Mr B. pretends to rear can give real felicity. He may smile and talk of virtue, but will he dare to abide by this boasted virtue? I suppose that he will answer that he will, but . . . his practice will be found far behind his theory, and so it ever must be, for he, who can have no certain hope of a future reward for his forbearance, will surely be sometimes tempted to forego his virtues when he finds inclination powerfully pleading. And methinks this appears but reasonable. But I hope better things for you. I hope he has not so poisoned your mind but you are yet *virtuous* with a particular reference to that Being, whom B. supposes to pay no regard to the actions of men.[1]

She needed to have no fears about William, and in her next letter found it 'impossible to say how happy that part of your letter made me wherein you spoke so plainly of that *most important of all Particulars*', going on to delve a little deeper:

I [have] a proposal to make, but I fear it is not possible. And yet I think I am blamable, *highly blamable*, if I do not make it. I shall then at least have done my part. Why should I fear expressing to you what I so much wish? It is being guilty of a false Bashfulness. It is deserting a *good* cause, a cause on which I ground my future Hopes. . . . I have often said I would not marry without family Prayers. Will it be possible? What think you? You see the necessity, the propriety of this Duty. The best regulated Family I ever was in, had it constantly.[2]

[1] Frances Coape to William Smith, n.d., Leigh-Smith Papers.
[2] Frances Coape to William Smith, 15 October 1780. Leigh-Smith Papers.

In this too, she had her way, and the Smiths followed the practice to the end of their lives.

But life was not all pious ruminations, and, despite her religious preoccupations, Frances seems to have lived a life very much like that of any other young gentlewoman of twenty-two. She complains about not being able to write on one occasion as 'General and Mrs. St. John dined here, and after dinner we were nailed down to cards'. And in another letter she mentions having been out riding, 'twice with the dogs. I suppose I must not presume to call it hunting, as I did not take a single leap, and never was with them but in the road and open field'. Nor was the young couple's romance entirely a matter of settling religious opinions and observances. William had descended unannounced on the young lady at Malden where she was staying with friends during a round of balls and visits, sought her hand, and been accepted, all in the course of a two- or three-day visit. The speed with which all this was accomplished shocked Frances's sense of propriety:

. . I cannot think why you came to Malden unless you supposed me partial to you. You did not surely imagine that any pecuniary consideration, you did not think your fortune. . . . But why do I torture myself thus. Had you thought thus lightly of me, you would never have thrown away a wish about me. . . . Oh tell me, why you came down, without giving me reason to expect you.[1]

Obviously, Frances was not entirely unlike any other young girl in love.

All doubts and fears were quieted, however, and the courtship continued, with the accompaniment of presents and amusing and aptly turned, if not very good, poetry raining upon the Coape sisters at Mr Forward's. All was brought to a successful conclusion on 12 January 1781, when the young couple were married at Clapham. It was an affair of some style, the bride and groom departing in 'a shell and four, with blue and silver liveries'.

Doubtless Samuel was shocked at the expense. A new generation and a new way of life had, however, been launched, and the divergences were to become ever clearer. The residence in which Frances

[1] Frances Coape to William Smith, n.d., Leigh-Smith Papers.

and William began their married life was Eagle House, on the west side of the Common. The 1790 road-book describes it as

about sixty yards from the road, a large handsome house built with grey stock bricks, except the part which connects the offices with the centre part which is of stone. . . . The house has some elegant apartments and is ornamented with a choice collection of paintings, executed by the first masters, and the gardens, plantations, etc., are consistent with the house.[1]

Life was not dull. The young Smiths danced, played cards, and went to the races, indeed did everything that young couples of fashion might be expected to have done. Sundays, of course, were different; there were no amusements, and they faithfully attended Chapel, or if they happened to be away from Clapham, and near no Dissenting place of worship, they went to Church.

William was occupied in beginning what was to become a noted collection of paintings. Travel was also a consuming interest. In the summer of 1781 they took a six-week trip to the Isle of Wight and the West Country. The next year they spent two months travelling in the Lake District and Lancashire. The arrival of children did not stop their restless wanderings. In the late summer of 1783 they set off again—as Frances recorded in her journal, 'Mr. Smith, Joanna [her sister, later Mrs Cure], myself in the phaeton, the children and maids in the chaise'—visiting their relations in Nottinghamshire, but spending most of their month's absence at Scarborough. It is not surprising that their travelling was a bit curtailed, as the children, Martha (Patty) and Benjamin, were only a year and a half and six months old respectively! Nothing, however, seems to have daunted them, or killed their enthusiasm for new sights. Sometimes their light carriage made good time, forty to fifty miles a day, on the new turnpikes, but sometimes they dragged along at a mile or two an hour in muddy ruts. Occasionally on steep and winding roads it was inadvisable to stay in the carriage at all, and they had to walk four to five miles at a stretch. But it was all worthwhile; almost everywhere they found something to interest them. If there was industry in the area, they always went out of

[1] For this information I am once again indebted to Mr E. E. Smith.

their way to see it. In Cornwall they visited the smelting furnaces and descended into the copper mines. In Lancashire, they were fascinated by the cotton mills. On a Saturday, Frances recorded, they

drove to Mr. Douglas's cotton-mills where we were very civilly treated, a gentleman attending us, who answered every question, and allowed us as much time as we pleased to examine this curious machine, where the cotton is carded, roved, and spun by one large master-wheel.

Monday. Mr. Barnes and Mr. Potter breakfasted with us and then accompanied us to see the Manchester Quilting woven, and afterwards to see the old-fashioned mode of spinning in which they can still make finer thread than they can at present in the cotton-mills: next we went to see them cut the pile of the velvets, a very pretty operation.[1]

There were also the more conventional tours of country houses, especially those with collections of paintings, and gardens, and they had perhaps a slightly more than conventional interest in the beauties of nature. If a mountain or hill promised to offer a view of interest, they ascended it, no matter what the difficulty. Caverns, rocky ravines, and cascades presented equal attraction. It was all very strenuous but apparently very rewarding.

Not strenuous or rewarding enough, however, for one of Smith's boundless energy. He needed more to occupy him than a life of leisure, no matter how active, could afford. His mind still turned to politics.

[1] 'Various Tours', I, 120 1, Leigh-Smith Papers.

CHAPTER TWO

POLITICS

The manner in which William Smith entered politics in 1784 was, if somewhat strange for a future champion of Parliamentary reform and popular rights, highly appropriate for the wealthy son of a great London merchant.

The City had been shocked to the core by the attempt of the Fox-North Coalition to revise the charter of the East India Company in the previous year. That government should contemplate appropriating to itself such a valuable piece of private 'property' as the Company's vast patronage was more than could be borne. It was natural that the great merchants and financiers of London should have rallied decisively to the King's support and to that of his new minister, William Pitt, when the hated Coalition was ousted over this issue in December 1783. As Richard Atkinson put it in announcing his candidacy for one of the City's four seats in March 1784:

When the rights of the East India Company were attacked in a way which, if successful, would have shaken the foundations of public credit, and of all property in the kingdom held under the sanction charters and acts of Parliament, I felt it incumbent upon me to withstand such fateful violence. . . .[1]

Samuel Smith shared this view and was in the forefront of those who supported the change of ministry. On 23 January 1784 he presided at a 'numerous and respectable meeting of the merchants and traders of London' at the London Tavern, which presented an address to the King thanking him for 'dismissing his late ministers, who, by countenancing an attack upon the charter and property of

[1] *London Chronicle*, 27–30 March 1784.

14

the East India Company, have jointly forfeited the confidence of his Majesty and the public'.[1] Samuel continued this active support. After the March dissolution he played a leading part in a meeting of substantial merchants held on 26 March to endorse a new slate of candidates for the City. Sir Watkin Lewes, Brook Watson, Richard Atkinson, and Samuel Smith jr (of Aldermanbury, and no relation)[2] were approved. Of the four, two, Atkinson and Smith, had been proposed by Samuel, and, in Watson's absence, it had been Samuel who had accepted for him.[3]

A more strongly pro-administration group could hardly have been found. Lewes and Watson had already proven themselves as sitting members for the City. Of particular interest are the two new candidates whom Samuel proposed. Samuel Smith jr was already a member of the government party as M.P. for Ilchester; he was also a prominent member of the 'Old' party on the Board of Directors of the East India Company. A carry-over from the days of North, whom it had likewise supported, the 'Old' party was ardently pro-government.[4] Richard Atkinson was the only candidate with no Parliamentary experience, but he too was an outstanding member of the 'Old' party in the Company, and, as a large rum contractor in the late war, had very close ties with the court. He was a particular intimate of John Robinson, North's Parliamentary manager in the seventies, and was to play a major role, under Robinson and George Rose, in the management of this election.

Samuel Smith remained Atkinson's staunch supporter throughout the London election, acting as chairman of a committee of his supporters and as his scrutineer when the results of the poll were unsuccessfully contested.[5] It is not surprising, therefore, to find Atkinson acting as political midwife to Samuel's son. In a memorandum made at about the time of the dissolution of Parliament on

[1] Ibid., 22–24 January 1784.

[2] The *D.N.B.* article on William Smith errs in confusing him with this Samuel Smith.

[3] *London Chronicle*, 25–27 March 1784.

[4] See Lucy Sutherland, *The East India Company in Eighteenth Century Politics* (Oxford, 1952), chap. XIII.

[5] *London Chronicle*, 2–4 April and *Ipswich Journal*, 24 April.

25 March, Robinson notes after Bridport:' Mr. Atkinson to learn of Sam Smith whether his son will stand or not.'[1] In the event, Smith stood for Sudbury, not Bridport, but the suggestion of his candidacy for that borough had undoubtedly come from the same source.

Sudbury was one of those very costly boroughs, beyond the range of most candidates' pockets, which governments usually urged on one of their wealthier mercantile supporters. Though Sudbury had a large Dissenting element, which probably gave Smith some advantage, neither religious nor political issues ever appear to have played a major part in elections.[2] Money was much more important. Sudbury's relatively large electorate of eight hundred freemen, being free of any preponderant interest, could largely make their own terms with candidates, and, as they were an extraordinarily greedy lot, their terms were usually very high. The borough was notorious. Indeed, it was Sudbury's advertisement for a buyer in 1761 that occasioned Horace Walpole's famous remark that 'we have been as victorious as the Romans and are as corrupt'.[3]

Elections in Sudbury were almost invariably the source of acrimonious disputes, and the two before 1784 were especially bitter. In 1774 Sir Walden Hanmer and Sir Patrick Blake, two country gentlemen of the opposition, stood against P. C. Crespigny, a wealthy ministerial lawyer, and Thomas Fonnereau, one of the small circle of bankers privileged to subscribe to government loans. The two latter had already jointly established a controlling interest at Aldeburgh and were trying to do the same at Sudbury. Initially, wealth carried the day; but Hanmer and Blake petitioned against

[1] W. T. Laprade, ed., *Parliamentary Papers of John Robinson, 1774–1784* (London, 1922), p. 115. Laprade identifies the Sam. Smith referred to as Samuel Smith, jr. in his 'Public Opinion and the Election of 1784', *English Historical Review*, XXXI (1916), 234. This is almost certainly an error. It is always the names of Atkinson and William Smith which are afterwards coupled together in the correspondence, and, as Samuel Smith, jr was already a member of the government's party in Parliament, there would have been little point in making the contact through Atkinson.

[2] Sir Lewis Namier and John Brooke, *The House of Commons, 1754–1790* (London, 1964), I, 382.

[3] Quoted in Namier, *The Structure of Politics at the Accession of George III* (2nd ed.; London, 1957), p. 158.

the result on the grounds that the mayor, who was the returning officer, had acted partially and corruptly during the poll, and that money had been distributed by the successful candidates amongst their supporters. The Parliamentary committee decided in favour of Blake and Hanmer, and they were accordingly seated.

The election of 1780 was even more spectacular, and equally unhappy for Crespigny. Blake, Crespigny, Sir James Marriott, and John Henniker jr were the candidates.[1] The election began on Friday morning, 8 September at about ten o'clock. It continued until dark when, the mayor refusing to adjourn, candles were brought and the polling proceeded all night, closing about six-thirty on Saturday morning with Marriott and Henniker declared the victors. Crespigny then demanded a scrutiny on the grounds that the tumult and disorder caused by the friends of the successful candidates had prejudiced the result in their favour. There was an adjournment until the following Friday, and the scrutiny having taken place and twenty-four votes having been disallowed, Blake and Crespigny were declared elected. This was not the end, however. Marriott petitioned, the Committee decided for him, and he took his place on 26 April 1781 in Crespigny's stead. It was for this borough that William Smith stood in 1784.[2]

Smith was perfectly suited as a candidate for Sudbury—he was wealthy. On Robinson's list of those willing to pay for seats, Smith's name appears among those willing to spend the maximum sum of £2,000 to £3,000.[3] Previous experience suggested that such sum would hardly be too much,[4] especially as Robinson considered the borough as highly unsure in 1784. In a memorandum probably

---

[1] Blake was a local landowner; Marriott an academic, the Master of Trinity Hall, and from 1778 a judge of the Admiralty Court; and Henniker came from a family of large merchants and shipbuilders.

[2] The above descriptions of the elections of 1774 and 1780 are based on C. F. D. Sperling, *A Short History of the Borough of Sudbury, in the County of Suffolk* (Sudbury, 1896), pp. 85–7.

[3] Laprade, *Parliamentary Papers of John Robinson*, p. 128.

[4] In Lord Bute's list of the House of Commons of 1761, for instance, it is noted that John Henniker had been returned for Sudbury, 'supported in his election by a very considerable sum and the Duke of Newcastle, £5,000' (Namier, *Structure*, p. 320).

drawn up in December 1783 he classified it as 'as open as the day and night too, and it is hard to say who may come, whether Marriott and Blake or Crespigny and some other person, therefore it is left doubtful'.[1] He was no more hopeful at the time of the dissolution on 25 March: 'Mr. Rose says a seat is secure through Crespigny; Mr. Robinson says there can be no contest more insecure. Crespigny says if you will not oppose he will come in himself and bring a friend for £1,500.'[2] Robinson was obviously of the opinion that there was no chance of success without a major and concerted effort, and apparently his view prevailed in the end. Crespigny retired to Aldeburgh, and William Smith and John Langston, a London banker and another of Atkinson's suggested candidates endorsed as being willing to pay the maximum amount, stood for Sudbury.[3]

Compared with previous elections, this one went off very smoothly. Neither of the sitting members, Blake and Marriott, stood again,[4] and it was not until the last minute that any new opposition arose in the person of a Captain Dickens.[5] Although

[1] Laprade, *Parliamentary Papers of John Robinson*, p. 77.

[2] Ibid., p. 117.

[3] Ibid., pp. 126–28.

[4] M. D. George classifies Sudbury as one of those boroughs in which Foxites had been defeated beforehand and says that this involved a defeat of the Crespigny interest ('Fox's Martyrs', *Royal Historical Society Transactions*, 4th series, XXI, 163). Her contention seems doubtful on both counts. Marriott does appear to have remained loyal to North. But, at the time of the dissolution, Thomas Steele, Rose's colleague as Secretary to the Treasury, was to approach Blake about standing again, which he would hardly have done had Blake been considered an enemy (Laprade, *Parliamentary Papers of John Robinson*, p. 117). And, so far as the defeat of the Crespigny interest is concerned, this would appear to have occurred when the government refused to accept Crespigny's proposals, which do not appear to have involved either Blake or Marriott.

[5] Namier and Brooke, I, 383, identify him as Francis Dickens, a Suffolk gentleman standing on the Crespigny interest. If so, his candidacy must have been a desperate last-minute move. In a letter to her husband written on the eve of the election, which took place on 1 April, Mrs Smith refers to 'this opposition which your last letter mentions to have arisen' (Frances Smith to William Smith, n.d. Leigh-Smith Papers). As they corresponded almost daily, Dickens could not have announced himself as a candidate more than two or three days before the poll.

Dickens polled 189 votes, Smith and Langston were a comfortable two hundred-odd votes ahead of him and had about a hundred more supporters who still had not voted when the contest was conceded.[1]

The manner of Smith's entry into politics was the only one, and the accepted one, for a man of his class and time. Without family interests to support them, wealthy merchants had either to buy their way into politics or stay out. This aspect of Smith's introduction into Parliament need, after Namier, no longer shock us. But, in view of the fact that Smith was to spend forty of his fifty years in politics in opposition, and with a reputation for extreme liberalism at that, those persons associated in his launching do need some comment. Richard Atkinson and Samuel Smith jr were not Courtiers simply through the necessity of the situation; they were Courtiers by conviction, having supported North in the seventies as staunchly as they supported Pitt in the eighties. Both were extremely unpopular with the London electorate, Atkinson being particularly odious for his supposed profiteering as a rum contractor during the American war.[2] Such were the men with whom Samuel Smith, and of necessity his son, had closely associated themselves. Admittedly the election of 1784 was an extraordinary one, with Pitt drawing support from all sections of opinion. And because Samuel ranged himself with Atkinson and Smith on this occasion does not necessarily suggest an identity of opinion on all past issues. It does, however, suggest a certain tendency toward conservative men and ideas. Nor was this the first time that Samuel had chosen such associates.

His previous recorded essay into politics had been in support of the candidacy of his brother-in-law and partner William Nash, for Lord Mayor in 1771. Nash could scarcely have been more conservative and less popular than he was. He had been a consistent friend of the several administrations of George III, and hence a consistent opponent of John Wilkes, throughout his political career.[3] In 1771

[1] *Ipswich Journal*, 3 April 1784.

[2] *London Chronicle*, 30 March–1 April 1784, and *Ipswich Journal*, 3 April 1784.

[3] See George Rudé, *Wilkes and Liberty: A Social Study of 1763 to 1774* (Oxford, 1962), pp. 151n and 219.

19

he stood with the ardent and unequivocal support of the Court, in opposition to two other candidates, the incumbent Brass Crosby, whom the Commons had sent to the Tower in the controversy over the printing of debates earlier in the year, and Alderman Sawbridge, the ally of that earlier and still popular idol Chatham. No set of circumstances could have been better calculated to incur the wrath of the mob—and Nash had incurred it. On the day of the election

Mr. Nash, who was the only candidate that attended on the hustings during the poll, was grossly ill treated on his return from thence . . . by the populace: and had not Mr. Wilkes taken him away in his chariot, the consequences might have been fatal.[1]

None the less, with the assistance of money and Court influence, Nash won the day. It did not take him long to clash once again with Wilkes, whose timely assistance on the day of the election had not served to make the Lord Mayor-elect any more gracious toward him. Plucking at the reliably responsive chord of Francophobia in the City, Mr Sheriff Wilkes had announced that he would serve no French wines at the celebrations accompanying the new Lord Mayor's investiture, desiring the latter likewise to refrain. To which request Nash testily replied that 'as Mr. Wilkes claimed a right of giving what he pleased, he should have no pretence to invade the privilege of another',[2] and served his claret regardless. Such a cavalier attitude toward their idol and their prejudices was not calculated to endear the new chief magistrate to the popular element in London, and highly unpleasant relations continued.[3]

Samuel may have had some private reservations about his crusty brother-in-law;[4] but, whether he had or not, he loyally supported him, and the Lord Mayor's Day celebrations, a part of which Wilkes so strongly disapproved, had his 'close attendance from 8 in the morning till 11 at night and [I had] great part in the management for which I had the thanks of the concerned and approbation of the

---

1 *The Annual Register for 1771*, p. 146.
2 Ibid., p. 148.
3 See Rudé, p. 189.
4 Samuel Smith to William Smith, 19 October 1771, Leigh-Smith Papers.

majority present'.[1] Indeed the offending claret almost certainly came from the stocks of the wholesale grocery store.

The election of 1784 was, therefore, by no means the first time that the Smiths had been associated with the most conservative elements. Nor is this strange; they were following a very ordinary course for people of their position and connexions. Recent research has demonstrated what common sense might suggest—that during the eighteenth century there was a more or less rigid division between the politics of London's middling and smaller merchants, manufacturers, and tradesmen, on the one hand, and those of the larger merchants and financiers, on the other.[2] The former often had every reason to be irritated with government. Excises and taxes, even an advance in the price of bread, affected them adversely, if not always as directly as it did their inferiors. Nor did government pay any particular attention to their wants and interests. As a result, from the days of Walpole and Bolingbroke such middling and smaller men provided the backbone of an increasing opposition in London.

The great merchants, in contrast, usually had every inducement to support the *status quo* and the existing government, whatever its composition. Government depended on them for funds, and they depended on it for loan and provisioning contracts as well as for the welfare of the great chartered companies which they dominated. The result was mutual consideration and co-operation, and the government-in-existence could usually count on the support of these greater merchants, partly from their direct interest, and also partly from the fact that those with the most to conserve had a natural bias toward the only force which possessed such scanty means of protecting property as existed during the period.

The Smiths had usually conformed to the general pattern. It does not appear that they had any direct interests which tied them to the government, although, quite naturally, some of their close

[1] Samuel Smith to William Smith, 21 November 1771, photostat, Travers Papers.

[2] See Lucy Sutherland, 'The City of London in Eighteenth-Century Politics', *Essays presented to Sir Lewis Namier* (London, 1956); Rudé, especially chaps. I and X.

relations did.[1] But provided that government fulfilled its major function of keeping order and did not trample on their special interests, the Smiths were ready to give it their active support on occasion, and their silent acquiescence most of the rest of the time. They had little cause to be dissatisfied with their lot; the existing system had always given them all they could wish for. And what was the alternative? Perhaps ideas of a new more liberal and more popular system were beginning to emerge among some of Wilkes's sympathizers, but so long as mobs raged through the streets slinging mud and breaking windows, all in the name of 'Wilkes and Liberty', it is hardly strange that the alternative remained obscure to a man like Samuel Smith.

Such was William Smith's background, solid, conservative, loyal to King and government. It might therefore seem strange to find him, immediately after his entry into Parliament, among the most liberal and reforming element of Pitt's supporters. He had promised the Sudbury electors that he would pursue 'that line of conduct, which shall appear best calculated to preserve inviolate our most excellent constitution, to maintain the chartered rights and privileges of Britain in general, and the interest of this borough in particular'.[2] No one could have questioned his means of maintaining the chartered rights and privileges of Britain; his vote for Pitt's India Bill was highly predictable. Nor, if doing such things as finding a collectorship in the excise for one constituent and a berth on a new ship for another could be called looking after the interest of the borough he represented—and it generally was so called— could he have been accused of failing in this part of his bargain. But there were those who might well have questioned his means of preserving 'inviolate our most excellent constitution'. Smith's idea of the best way to preserve it was, like Pitt's, to reform it.

Smith was deep in reform activities even before his entry into Parliament. As early as May of 1782 he attended an audit dinner of the Society for Constitutional Information, and in December of that

[1] The Traverses, for instance, had large holdings in the East India Company, of which Joseph Travers became a director in 1786 (*Past and Present in an Old Firm* [London and Aylesbury, 1907], p. 10).

[2] *Ipswich Journal*, 10 April 1784.

year he became a member of the Society.[1] Thereafter he was a remarkably faithful attendant at its weekly meetings. Apparently he early showed those capacities for hard work and the mastery of detail which were to mark his Parliamentary career. On 4 April 1783 the Society passed a resolution thanking him for 'valuable communication respecting the state of Representation in . . . the Boroughs of Newport, Yarmouth, and Newton in the Isle of Wight'.[2] And at the next meeting he was appointed a member of a committee to prepare an abstract of all the information the Society had at hand on the state of Parliamentary representation.[3]

It is doubtful that Smith ever sympathized with the Society's more extreme proposals for universal suffrage and annual Parliaments (in later years he was to take a very sceptical view of both). But he was among the Parliamentary minority of 174 (to 248) which supported Pitt's motion for the abolition of fifty rotten boroughs and the addition of 100 county members in April 1785. He was once again in the minority, in company with such stalwarts as Christopher Wyvill and Horne Tooke, which desired to press on with Pitt's plan at the meeting of the friends of reform which took place at the Thatched House Tavern on 24 May 1785.[4] And he was to continue to support the efforts of the Society for Constitutional Information, serving on committees to prepare information on the representation for publication, until 1788; though he had been inactive for two years before the Society was revived as a radical corresponding society in 1790.[5]

What was it that made a young man of Smith's background a reformer? Surely people like the Smiths could have had little reason for dissatisfaction with the existing system in England? But the fact was that not many years before, many of their kind had demonstrated

[1] 'Resolutions and Orders of the Society for Constitutional Information, April 1780 to 1783', 14 May and 13 December 1782, Public Record Office, London (hereafter cited as 'PRO'), TS11/1133.

[2] 'Resolutions and Orders of the Society for Constitutional Information, 1783–91', 4 April 1783, PRO, TS11/961.

[3] Ibid., 11 April 1783.

[4] Christopher Wyvill, *Political Papers* (York, 1794–1802), II, 460.

[5] He is last reported present on 13 June 1788 ('Resolutions and Orders of the Society for Constitutional Information', 13 June 1788, PRO, TS11/961).

a marked dissatisfaction. In the Association movement of 1779–80 large numbers of solid country gentlemen and leading commercial men had put themselves at the head of movements which expressed a distinct irritation with the government of England. One such was Christopher Wyvill's Yorkshire Association, made up of 'landed and commercial men . . . the leading elements of the "middling people" of the county'.[1] Another was the Society for Constitutional Information, which contained many leading London merchants and financiers. And with the passage of George Dunning's resolution in the Commons in 1780 that 'the power of the Crown has increased, is increasing, and ought to be diminished', it was clear that the stirrings of dissatisfaction had reached into the very bastions of the Crown's most loyal support. The cosy alliance of Crown and property that had existed up to the accession of George III was showing marked stresses and strains at the end of that monarch's first two decades on the throne. There were several reasons.

One of the main explanations for loyal support of the government had been the fact that it alone could, and generally speaking did, preserve order. This it was ceasing to be able to do. For over a decade from 1764 onwards John Wilkes was able to keep London, and sometimes the whole country, in a more or less continuous uproar—with relative impunity. And the more administrations strove to squelch the disorders, the more foolish and ineffective they looked. Rioting became almost an ordinary part of life. A letter to William, at Daventry, from his uncle Adams ends in the following manner: Your Father, Cousins Nash and Gosse are expected in town from the Isle of Wight on the morrow after an absence of eight days. Am afraid we shall not be so quiet here this night as you are like to be, tho' am not myself apprehensive of any great riot. Have nothing new of consequence to inform you of.[2]

Apparently one bit of news was as important as the other, and neither required any expansion. But the number of window panes

[1] I. R. Christie, 'The Yorkshire Association, 1780–4: A Study in Political Organization', *The Historical Journal*, III, 2 (1960), p. 148. On the Association movement, see Christie's *Wilkes, Wyvill and Reform* (London, 1962) and E. C. Black, *The Association: British Extraparliamentary Organization, 1769–1793* (Cambridge, Mass., 1963).

[2] James Adams to William Smith, 12 April 1770, Leigh-Smith Papers.

which he possessed in London and its environs must have given James Adams some cause for worry—and he was fortunate if his worries ceased with his window panes. One could hardly blame such men for not rushing into the arms of those responsible for creating the disorder, but neither could one expect them to have been entirely satisfied with those so clearly unable to suppress it.

Another reason for the complacency of men of landed and commercial wealth had been the fact that the policies of government had, by and large, not interfered with, and in some cases had even expanded, England's prosperity. With the American war this too ceased to be the case. There was little comfort to be drawn from this war; at best it could only regain a market which England had already possessed. And when even this hope paled, at least so far as physical possession was concerned, it became even harder to bear the danger and inconvenience that war brought. For those dependent on foreign commerce, and many of the propertied classes were in one way or another, the situation became ever worse. With French entry into the war in 1779 and the subsequent European league of hostile neutrality, it became almost unbearable. For the Smiths, the wholesale grocery business was already hazardous enough. The London market in sugar, tea, dried fruits and other commodities with which they dealt fluctuated considerably in the best of times, according to vagaries of wind, tide and hurricane, not to mention shifts in the East India Company's policies. War, especially one which was going badly, added another uncertainty. As a customers' circular of 1779 ruefully announced:

As we were likely to have had a large quantity of sugar at market this week, we waited in expectation of purchasing at moderate prices, and to have enabled our friends to have done the same, but unfortunately we have just received information of the loss of Grenada, one of our principal islands, which has caused an advance in raw sugar of full 4s. per cwt., and as our other islands are likewise in danger we don't see a prospect of their being lower, unless the two fleets now coming home should all arrive safe; but this in the present situation of affairs, is more than can be expected.[1]

[1] Circular of Smith, Nash, Kemble and Travers, 9 September 1779, Travers Papers.

Chatham's wars had brought an empire and naval supremacy. The American war, with all its frustrations and difficulties, promised to lose both, and the commercial prosperity that went with them. Yet it dragged on and on, kept going only by the King's blind tenacity. It is not surprising that there began to be some questioning of a system which gave one man's opinions and peculiarities so much weight, against a preponderance of opinion in the country.

It is not, therefore, strange that a man like William Smith should have been drawn into the reforming movement. The odd thing is that he should have remained true to reforming ideals at a time when interest was dwindling. By 1784 the wind had pretty much gone out of the sails of the Yorkshire Association. And after the failure of his motion in 1785, Pitt did not think it worthwhile to bring the matter up again. A number of factors combined to lull, or frighten, a great majority of men of property back to their former complacency. One was the restoration of domestic tranquillity which followed John Wilkes's transformation to respectability in the seventies, and the fear roused by the Gordon Riots that it might be disturbed again. The end of the American war removed a potent source of discontent. The bow to reform given by the Rockingham ministry's measures cutting places and sinecures was another factor, as were the reforming tendencies of the new minister himself.[1] Property therefore largely deserted the reforming movement. But a small group of men, of whom Smith was one, remained dedicated to the cause of reform into the dark years of the French Revolution and beyond. Men of property and standing in the community, they were to centre their activities first in the Society for Constitutional Information and later in the 'Society of the Friends of the People', dominated by Whig reformers like Charles Grey, and in the Whig party itself. Why was it that men like Smith, despite their secure and comfortable position, continued to advocate reform? There must have been some special reason, something which separated them from others of their kind.

There was. Almost certainly a majority of the members of the Society for Constitutional Information were Dissenters. Its member-

[1] For an important study of the critical years 1779–80, see Herbert Butterfield, *George III, Lord North, and the People* (London, 1949).

ship lists read like a roll of the most eminent Dissenting families in London and the provinces. The Rev Richard Price, T. B. Hollis, and Capel Lofft were founding members. There were Vaughans and Beaufoys, as well as several prominent Dissenting ministers, from London. Sir John Carter was one of the several members from the great Portsmouth family. The Rev Robert Robinson of Cambridge was a member. So was the Rev George Walker of Nottingham. Shores of Sheffield and several Milneses, both families also being active in the Yorkshire Association, were on the rolls of the Society. Even Samuel Smith, for all his conservative background, joined, serving as one of the vice-presidents in 1788.[1] Dissenters played a leading part in the cause of reform.

It was not a mere chance relationship. Dissenters had a very specific reason for being dissatisfied with the existing order, a very specific reform which they desired. And the source of this dissatisfaction was one which was particularly irritating to the wealthiest, best-educated, and most successful among them—the Test and Corporation Acts. Ironically, the higher a Dissenter got on the social scale, the more reason he had to be satisfied with all other aspects of his life, the harder it became to bear the legal exclusion from much of political life imposed by the Acts. For large numbers, this grievance was enough to overcome most of the conservatism natural to men of their class and position.

[1] 'Resolutions and Orders of the Society for Constitutional Information, 1783–91', 25 April 1788, PRO, TS11/961.

CHAPTER THREE

THE STIGMA OF DISSENT

The origins of the Test and Corporation Acts in the reign of Charles II, the attempt to exclude disaffected Puritans and Catholics from national and municipal offices, are well known, as is the attempt to make this exclusion a reality by the Occasional Conformity Act of 1711.[1] Their interest for us, however, really begins with the first attempt at Repeal in 1732.

The Whig government which followed the accession of the Hanoverians had been willing to re-establish the situation which had existed before 1711, repealing the Occasional Conformity Act shortly after coming to power; but it had not shown any disposition, beyond one adjustment hereafter mentioned, to go any further. Legally, Dissent remained in precisely the same position in which it had been at the time the Acts were passed.

The first of these acts, the Corporation Act of 1661, provided that every candidate for municipal office must have taken the sacrament according to the rites of the Church of England during a period of one year previous to his candidacy; otherwise his election would be void. The second, the Test Act of 1673, imposed a similar obligation on anyone receiving an office from the Crown (i.e. any office in the civil or military services[2]); in this case, however, the

[1] The Occasional Conformity Act was, of course, to prevent the practice of occasional conformity, where a Dissenter attended one Anglican service and received the sacrament, merely to qualify himself for office, and thereafter returned to his ordinary place or worship.

[2] The 'offices' covered by this act were, it must be remembered, theoretically of a very wide range indeed. As one pamphleteer complained in 1787: 'Not even a bug can be destroyed within the purlieus of the royal household but by the hallowed fingers of a communicant' (quoted in A. Lincoln, *Some*

28

sacrament was to be taken within three months *after* appointment to such office. The penalties were also much stiffer, subjecting a convicted offender to disability for suing in any court, for acting as a guardian, executor, or administrator, for receiving a legacy or gift, or for bearing any office in England or Wales, as well as to a £500 fine.[1]

It is true that, after the repeal of the Occasional Conformity Act, there was again a way around the Test and Corporation Acts: a candidate could once more comply with the letter of the law by taking the Anglican sacrament as a qualification and then ignore its spirit by returning to his own place of worship thereafter. The government of George I also made one further significant alteration in the law. By 5 Geo. 1, c. 6, the time limit for prosecution under the Corporation Act was placed at six months; thus anyone who could hold a municipal office unchallenged for six months was thereafter safe. For Dissenters elected in towns strongly sympathetic to them, and especially in corporations where election meant a lifetime tenure of office, this modification was of some importance.[2]

By the 1720s, therefore, an attempt had been made to re-establish a broad practical toleration. But there was no marked advance in the Dissenters' situation.[3] It would appear that, with the exception of those in a few strongly Dissenting boroughs, occasional conformity was still a necessity in order to hold offices and places. According to the latest authority on the subject, 'during the age of Walpole the Test and Corporation Acts were generally effective in keeping sacramentally unqualified Dissenters out of office', and therefore,

---

Political and Social Ideas of English Dissent, 1763–1800 [Cambridge, 1938], p. 240). Also, it was never quite clear whether or not the law also covered positions in such semi-public institutions as the Bank of England, the East India, Russia and South Sea Companies, and the College of Physicians, all of which derived their existence from royal charters (*Statement of the Case of the Protestant Dissenters* [London, 1827], p. 10).

[1] Ibid., p. 4.

[2] See R. V. Holt, *The Unitarian Contribution to Social Progress in England* (London, 1938), p. 320.

[3] It may be thought that the occasional Indemnity Acts passed during the period constituted such an advance, but see below, pp. 42-3.

'when Dissenters were office-holders or members of Corporations they were almost nearly always occasional conformists'.[1] To a scrupulous Dissenter, and indeed to anyone who took the sacrament seriously, this was far from a satisfactory situation. Apart from this, with the persecution of Queen Anne's reign still vivid in everyone's memory, there was felt to be a danger that even the practical toleration which existed might be swept away whenever a new whim took Parliament and the country. Dissenters were at one in wanting the offending statutes abolished once for all; this, they felt, was the only just and safe solution to their problem. The conscientious had had enough of what Daniel Defoe called 'playing bo-peep with Almighty God',[2] and the more flexible wanted a surer protection for their offices than an easily altered convention provided.

In 1732, following the earlier example of the Quakers,[3] the Dissenters organized to achieve their aims, founding the Dissenting Deputies to direct a campaign for a repeal of the Acts. The Deputies consisted of two representatives from each congregation of Presbyterians, Independents, and Baptists (the 'Three Denominations') within ten (afterwards extended to twelve) miles of London. The real direction of the movement, however, lay in the hands of a committee of twenty-one members elected from among the whole body.

The Deputies, as it was in their interest to do, elected their most influential members to the Committee; and the composition of the first Committee gives some idea of how far the spirit of the Test and Corporation Acts, if not their letter, was avoided. Of the eighteen members that can be identified no fewer than six were directors of the Bank of England, and another was soon to become one; there was also a director of the South Sea Company. Samuel Holden, the Chairman, was, besides being a director of the Bank, Governor of the Russia Company. All these semi-public offices had considerable political significance. The Committee also possessed in Sir Thomas

[1] N. C. Hunt, *Two Early Political Associations: The Quakers and the Dissenting Deputies in the Age of Sir Robert Walpole* (Oxford, 1961), p. 127.

[2] Quoted in Holt, p. 318.

[3] Besides his more extensive work cited above, see N. C. Hunt's 'The Quakers and Dissenters', *The Listener*, 20 October 1960.

Abney, a future justice of the Common Pleas and, in Viscount Barrington, politicians of the first rank.[1]

There were difficulties as well as advantages in placing the direction of the campaign in the hands of men such as these. In 1732–3 Walpole was in serious difficulties over his Excise Bill, and in deference to his wishes, the Deputies postponed their agitation, over the strong and vocal opposition of the country Dissenters and some of their own membership. This split on tactics illustrated very clearly the mixed advantages of placing leadership of the campaign with the London Dissenters, and especially with their most distinguished representatives. The advantages were obvious—the ease with which the Deputies could be gathered together at a time of crisis and the influence which the powerful men among them could exert. But the interests of London and the country could differ—and were to do so again. In this case the leaders of London Dissent, already high in the favour of government, were naturallly reluctant to give offence and thus disturb existing good relations; it was inevitable that their method should be to win Walpole's support, rather than to press their own campaign regardless of the opinion and interest of the administration.

Yet it is impossible to doubt that in this case the personal interests of the London leadership actually coincided with those of Dissent as a whole. By this time Walpole had such a firm personal grip on government and was so dominant in the House of Commons that the only possible means of achieving success was to gain his support. It was not the Committee's fault that this was impossible. Walpole's whole policy was one of not arousing unnecessary controversies, of letting sleeping dogs lie. He would not risk raising another cry of 'the Church in danger!' merely to salve tender consciences or make timid natures more easy. As a result, when the Committee did wage campaigns for Repeal in 1736 and 1739 it met crushing defeats in Parliament. It was to be fifty years before the Dissenters tried again.

The results of defeat on Dissent during the intervening years were profound. One was that the more ambitious drifted away. It

[1] See N. C. Hunt, *Sir Robert Walpole, Samuel Holden and the Dissenting Deputies* (London, 1957), pp. 23–34.

was a natural and predictable result, for it was an obvious fact that, although one might succeed in attaining office and favour as a Dissenter, it was much easier to succeed if one was not. Lord Barrington's sons became Anglicans, one a bishop. Others followed the same course; by the eighties none of the names of the Committee of 1732, Holden, Abney and the rest, were among those of the Dissenting leadership. When the 1787 campaign for Repeal was launched, the last of the old Dissenting peers, Lord Willoughby of Parham, had been dead for six years.[1] The strong pull of ambition deprived Dissent of its most powerful and influential members.

Those who did not conform resolutely turned their backs on politics, and, for the most part, seem to have found an outlet for their energies and abilities in commercial pursuits. Large numbers prospered exceedingly. Heywoods in Lancashire, Milneses and Shores in Yorkshire, turned their already considerable landed and commercial wealth into large and successful banking ventures. Newer Dissenting families, like the Smiths of London and the Carters of Portsmouth, rose to join them in the ranks of the wealthy and commercially prominent.

But business could absorb such families for only a certain length of time, usually a generation or two at most. A new generation which had not tasted defeat began once again to yearn for the things so natural to men of their class—for office and place, for professional and social advancement. It was only natural.

Education—or, in this instance, the circumstances of education—was another factor. The wealthier Dissenters placed a high importance on education, and the excellent Dissenting academies, such as Daventry and Warrington, were established to meet their needs. But the very excellence of the academies attracted others besides Dissenters; and many gentlemen of the Established Church, as well as wealthy West Indians, also sent their sons there. As a result, young Dissenters often rubbed elbows with the same class of fellow-students, and sometimes even lived much of the same kind of life, as they would have done at the Universities. The maintenance of a horse for his son at Daventry was not considered an extravagance by

[1] *The Monthly Repository*, n.s. I (1827), 249.

even such a provident father as Samuel Smith.[1] And life at Warrington became so riotous that the academy was eventually forced to close its doors in 1785. As Dr William Enfield, its last principal, lamented, there was among the student body 'an idle waste of time, a coarse and vulgar familiarity, a disposition towards riot and mischief, intemperance, and in some instances gaming, profaneness and licentious manners. . . .'[2] It might have been a description of Oxford or Cambridge during the same period, largely because it had come to draw the same kind of people. Admittedly this was the situation at its worst; but it was not one that had grown up overnight.

New associations and new ways of life naturally bred new ambitions. Some young Dissenters went on to the Universities and to the Inns of Court.[3] Benjamin Heywood's two sons went from Warrington to Cambridge and thence to the Bar. Edmund Calamy and Samuel Yate Benyon, scions of other old Dissenting families, followed the same course. Samuel Shore jr substituted two years at Geneva for Cambridge, but then read law at Lincoln's Inn. Other wealthy young Dissenters, Henry Beaufoy, William Smith, and Benjamin Vaughan used their wealth to secure entry into Parliament.[4] Naturally, these young men went into the professions and into politics for the same reasons, and with the same expectations, that other young men did. The Test and Corporation Acts were bound once again to loom large on the Dissenters' horizon.

There was a difference, however, between the ambitious Dissenters of the seventies and eighties and their predecessors of the twenties and thirties. The Dissenters of the later period were not of a sort, by and large, who were willing to sacrifice conscience to ambition. As has been seen, Samuel Shore jr altogether avoided

[1] Samuel Smith to William Smith, 17 October 1769, Leigh-Smith Papers.

[2] Quoted in McLachlan, p. 224.

[3] The great majority went to Cambridge, where there was no test imposed for matriculation. But even there subscription to the Thirty-nine Articles was necessary to obtain a degree. With the exception of Gray's Inn, tests were generally not imposed at the Inns of Court.

[4] With the exception of Smith, all were educated at Warrington (see Joshua Toulmin, 'A Biographical Account of Students Educated at Warrington Academy', *Monthly Repository*, IX [1814], *passim*).

Cambridge and its test for a degree. Samuel Yate Benyon left after two years, thus avoiding the difficulty. And though Samuel Heywood went up to Trinity Hall in 1771[1] and spent three years there, he refused to qualify himself for a degree.[2] Men like these would not find occasional conformity an answer to their problem.

The explanation of the new inflexibility lies partly in the fact that the defeats of the thirties had rid the Dissenting body of those weakest in principle, leaving a hard and unyielding core behind. But it is also to be explained by the fact that the principles themselves had become tougher and less pliable. This latter development was intimately connected with the profound impact of rationalism on Dissenting thought. It was an impact that had wide implications for the Dissenting movement, internally as well as externally, and some attempt must be made to understand its nature.

The history of rationalism in the Dissenting movement—at least of its major exponents—has been brilliantly traced elsewhere,[3] and it is only possible here to suggest very inadequately some of its main outlines. The exaltation of human reason in the philosophy of John Locke and the science of Isaac Newton did not fit easily into the traditional Christian scheme. Their ideas and accomplishments suggested that man had considerably more control over his destiny than the Calvinist doctrine of election allowed, strengthening an already existing tendency toward Arminianism, or the doctrine that salvation is attainable by all who choose to accept it. And, particularly, Newtonian science with its divine Author of Nature at least implied a questioning of trinitarianism. Both the new rationalism and the heterodoxy which could spring from it early found fertile ground among the Dissenting intelligentsia, and early gave rise to important internal differences.

As Roger Thomas has demonstrated, the Salters' Hall controversy of 1719 was decisive in beginning the process of separating

[1] He is the unidentified Heywood in J. A. Venn's *Alumni Cantabrigiensis*, Part II (Cambridge, 1947).

[2] M. W. Woolrych, *Lives of Eminent Serjeants-at-Law* (London, 1869), II, 711.

[3] C. G. Bolam, Jeremy Goring, H. L. Short, and Roger Thomas, *The English Presbyterians* (Boston, 1968).

34

those who placed a major stress on reason from those who did not. The controversy centred on free inquiry in the interpretation of scripture, and the main line of division was between those who were willing to accept free inquiry and such consequences as it might bring and those who insisted on maintaining the hard line Calvinist orthodoxy of traditional Dissent by the imposition of creeds. There was a difference of opinion within the denominations, but the two Funds for supporting ministers divided on the question. The Congregational Fund commenced a policy of refusing grants to non-Calvinists, while the Presbyterian Fund deliberately continued to make grants to orthodox and heterodox ministers alike. The consequences for their respective denominations were profound.[1]

By committing their denomination to Calvinist orthodoxy, the Congregationalists, or Independents as they were usually called, were to find themselves in a peculiarly favourable position to profit from the great burst of religious enthusiasm generated by the evangelical revival. And the same was true of the Particular Baptists, who shared their Calvinist orthodoxy. Initially at any rate, though lines blurred as time went on,[2] the activities of George Whitefield had greater significance for traditional Dissent than those of John Wesley. One reason obviously was that Whitefield was a Calvinist, while Wesley was an Arminian (though his Arminianism was, of course, drawn from an older Anglican, rather than the newer rational, tradition). More important perhaps, as nice theological distinctions were probably lost on many converts, was the fact that, unlike Wesley, Whitefield paid little attention to organizing those whom he had converted. From 1740 onwards these flocked in ever increasing numbers to the doctrinally congenial atmosphere of orthodox Dissent.[3]

The Presbyterians, for their part, were set on a very different course. At the time of Salters' Hall they represented a wide spectrum

[1] Ibid., pp. 151–74.

[2] For a more extensive consideration of the impact of the evangelical revival, see below pp. 153-4.

[3] Henry W. Clark, *History of English Nonconformity* (New York, 1965), II, 235 and R. Tudur Jones, *Congregationalism in England, 1662–1962* (London, 1962) pp. 148–52.

of religious opinion, from orthodox Calvinism to Arianism, but at that time they committed themselves to the twin principles that all religious truth is embodied in scripture and that reason should be unfettered by human formulations in the pursuit of that truth. The consequence was almost bound to be religious heterodoxy, for human formulations provided the only clear authority for both Calvinism and trinitarianism, and the prevailing rationalism militated against both. Practical considerations worked in the same direction, for their tolerant attitude made Presbyterianism the refuge of the unorthodox. Though many of the original Presbyterian causes, particularly in country districts, fell away and threw in their lot with the Independents, by mid-century Arminianism had captured the denomination. Arianism—the belief that Christ is inferior to God, but still divine—had also become widespread. Thus at just about the same time that their Dissenting brethren were being infused by a new spirit of Calvinist militancy, the Presbyterians had completely rejected Calvinism and had begun to acquire ideas which by the end of the century brought them to Unitarianism, ideas which were anathema to all orthodox Christians.

The result was to shatter what was has been called the 'catholicity' of the old Dissent, a spirit of mutual tolerance and forbearance which insisted little on sectarian divisions. But 'catholicity' broke down at different times in different places. It lingered longest in the Dissenting academies—and, as a consequence, much longer still where those they had educated exercised a dominating influence. Before 1750 rational inquiry had been the prevailing approach to religious studies in all the more eminent academies. And though after 1750 the Independents and orthodox Baptists felt impelled to establish new institutions where their future ministers would be educated in sound orthodox doctrine, those academies which particularly catered for laymen, like Daventry and Warrington, continued true to the rationalist tradition.

Daventry, where Smith was educated, provides an example of the kind of atmosphere that prevailed. Recalling his own student days in the fifties, Joseph Priestley described the academy as 'in a state peculiarly favourable to the pursuit of truth, as the students were about equally divided upon every question of much importance.

. . . The tutors were also of different opinions; Dr. Ashworth [the principal] taking the orthodox side of every question, and Mr. Clark, the sub-tutor, that of heresy, though always with the greatest modesty'.[1] Others, educated in a very different tradition, were to remember Daventry in a less kindly light. The Rev Robert Hall, the great Baptist divine, called the academy in retrospect a 'vortex of unsanctified speculation and debate', adding that 'the majority of such as [were] educated there became more distinguished for their learning than for the fervour of their piety or the purity of their doctrine'.[2]

From the evangelical point of view, Hall's was doubtless a stricture well warranted. The majority of those educated in the rationalist tradition would certainly not have held the strict Calvinist views of the great bulk of evangelical Dissent. Many would have acquired anti-trinitarian views as well. But it is important not to anticipate the polarity which fast began to emerge at the very end of the century, in which rational Dissent became largely synonymous with Unitarianism, and the other Dissenting denominations became identified almost exclusively with trinitarianism of the evangelical variety. Before the nineties, when lines began to be drawn more sharply, the state of opinion within Dissent was far more complicated. At least, it was considerably more complicated among the educated elite, particularly in London where they naturally tended to cluster. Rational religion was not yet the monopoly of the Presbyterians, or Rational Dissenters as they were significantly coming to be called, but was fairly widespread among the educated of all denominations. And there was no uniformity of religious opinion among those who believed in rational religion.

What did unite the Dissenting *élite* was a deep conviction that free inquiry in religious matters is the inalienable right—indeed the Christian duty—of every individual. Such a belief lay at the very foundation of the system in which they had been educated. And it was this conviction that gave a new universality and a new intransigence to their arguments. Nowhere is the importance of the new attitudes made clearer than in the campaign of the 1770s to free

[1] Quoted in McLachlan, p. 153.
[2] Quoted in ibid., pp. 163–4.

Dissenting ministers of their legal obligation to subscribe to those of the Thirty-nine Articles which dealt with doctrine,[1] the success of which William Smith later cited as a significant encouragement to Repeal efforts in the eighties.[2]

It was not, in fact, the Dissenters, but a small group of Anglican clergymen who shared their rational views, the Feathers' Tavern petitioners of 1772, who first brought the issue of freedom of religious inquiry into politics. Under the leadership of Theophilus Lindsey, Dean Blackburne, and John Jebb, they led the way for the Dissenters by demanding the abolition of compulsory subscription to the Articles by clergymen and University men. Parliament did not look favourably on this request, but some of the arguments against it seemed to suggest that, while such a boon was not appropriate for clergymen, it might be for Dissenters. Thus encouraged, shortly after the failure of the Anglican petition the General Body of Ministers of the Three Denominations (the clerical counterpart of the Deputies) decided to make a similar application on behalf of Dissenting ministers. Twice, in 1772 and 1773, their petition was approved by the Commons, only to be rejected by the Lords.

The reason was nothing less than the opposition of the King himself. His objection was his usual one:

. . . Are we to have no other object but to be altering every rule our ancestors have left us? Indeed this arises from a general disinclination to every restraint.[3]

So far as religious affairs were concerned, he was certainly right. The arguments which the Dissenters used in the controversy bore him out.

In the Repeal campaign of the thirties the Dissenters' case had

[1] Under the Toleration Act, Dissenting ministers were freed from the necessity of subscribing to those sections of the Articles which dealt with form, ceremony, and church government, but remained obliged to subscribe to those dealing with doctrine.

[2] 'Minutes of the Dissenting Deputies', City of London Library, Guildhall (hereafter cited as 'Minutes'), 7 March 1823.

[3] Quoted in J. Steven Watson, *The Reign of George III, 1760–1815* (Oxford, 1960), p. 156.

been based upon the contention that the Protestant Dissenters, specifically, had a natural capacity for, and a right to, offices and places. There had been no attempt to expand the arguments to include the cases of other excluded groups, such as Catholics and Jews, and, as far as can be told, no desire to do so. Implicit in the whole campaign was a reservation which one pamphleteer made explicit in contending that the Acts, 'never *were* necessary, neither at the time of making them, nor since, I mean so far as they extend to *Protestant Dissenters*'.[1] It was a significant qualification.

The petitioners of the seventies scorned such qualification. It was on the broad ground of principle that they took their stand, on the principle of religious freedom. Philip Furneaux, their out-standing leader and the Smiths' minister at the Independent congre-gation in Clapham (who exercised a great influence on William) set the tone:

. . . Upon what principle can [we] maintain, that the Jewish rulers did wrong in attempting to suppress the teaching of the Christian religion; or that the Apostles did right, in disobeying their injunc-tions: upon what can [we] plead for liberty of preaching Christianity under a Mahometan government, or the Protestant religion under a Popish: upon what principle can [we] do this, which will not warrant the liberty of professing and teaching any religion . . . under a Christian and a Protestant government?

Against the claim of the Establishment that it was protecting the eternal truths of Christianity, Furneaux contended that 'reason and argument are the only methods which God hath appointed, and which, in their own nature, are calculated for the propagation of true religion'. The evidence and truth of doctrines must be left to 'every man's own conscience' to decide.[2]

The principle from which the petitioners argued had very wide implications, and neither the principle nor the implications were generally acceptable. It was not until 1779 that their prayers were answered, and then not on the ground of principle, but of expediency. With serious difficulties both at home and abroad, Lord North's

[1] *A Letter to a Member of Parliament, Concerning the Repeal of the Corporation and Test Acts* (London, 1739), p. 19.

[2] *An Essay on Toleration* (London, 1773), p. 40.

government was anxious to attract all the support it could get and let it be known that it would look favourably on a renewal of the question. Thus in that year an act was passed substituting a declaration of the sufficiency of scripture so dear to the rationalists for subscription to the Articles as the necessary qualification for protection under the Toleration Act (though it should be noted that the Dissenting Ministers were opposed even to this limitation).[1] But if it was thought that the Dissenters would be content with this concession, it proved to be a wrong assumption. The King had been right; the demands of the petitioners had sprung from a general opposition to every restraint in matters of religion. And one very important restraint remained—the Test and Corporation Acts. Nor could anyone who could not stand the positive requirement of subscription to a creed stand the Acts any more easily. It mattered little whether the State forced subscription, on the one hand, or withheld office, on the other; both implied a coercion of religious opinion, and a coercion of religious opinion was something that those who spoke for Dissent were no longer prepared to accept.

The position of Dissent in the eighties was so different from that of the earlier era in which Repeal had been agitated that it is necessary to survey it anew. Indeed it was so different that one might well wonder why the Dissenters found it necessary to move at all. While in the days of Walpole the Acts had been sufficient to exclude from office most of those who had not qualified themselves, this had largely ceased to be the case by the time of the new agitation. It is difficult to get accurate information on how many Dissenters who held office had, or had not, qualified themselves by occasional conformity. Where information is available, however, it strongly indicates that many were not doing so, choosing rather to accept 'office with hazard', to use a term the very currency of which is

[1] On the whole agitation against subscription, see the excellent account in R. G. Barlow, *Citizenship and Conscience* (Philadelphia, 1962), chap. IV. So far as opposition to the new subscription was concerned, as Mr Thomas has kindly pointed out to me, it sprang at least in part from the Calvinists as well as from the rationalists. The main cause of concern with the Articles from the rationalist view was their Calvinism (i.e. the objection was an Arminian rather than an anti-trinitarian one), and the Calvinists objected that the new subscription suggested that Calvinism was not scriptural!

indicative of the new situation. This, for instance, was the course adopted by John Howard, the prison reformer, when in 1773 he was nominated for High-Sheriff of Bedfordshire.[1] Similarly, Samuel Shore, member of the Yorkshire Association and the Society for Constitutional Information, having been High-Sheriff of Derbyshire in 1761 and for some years a magistrate in the West Riding, resigned the latter office in 1787 *not* apparently because he had ever qualified for it or expected to have to, but simply as a protest when the bill for Repeal was thrown out.[2] The holding of 'office with hazard' seems also to have been the practice of the Carters in the Corporation of Portsmouth,[3] as well as of numerous other Dissenters in places like London, Bristol, Norwich, Nottingham, Bridport, and Bridgwater.

Nor would it appear that failure to qualify was really very dangerous. The Dissenters were able to produce only one contemporary instance of prosecution under the Acts, and that, of William Smith (no connexion of the subject of this book), Mayor of Nottingham, was not undertaken until January 1790,[4] almost three years after they themselves had once again drawn public attention to their legal position. It is true that the convention, generally followed by both sides in the controversy, of discussing the Acts as if they were still in full operation obscures the fact of their abeyance. But Samuel Heywood, the most eminent lawyer among the Dissenters, though devoting a substantial pamphlet to an analysis of their legal position, indicates quite clearly on occasion that the Acts had fallen into desuetude. As, for instance:

. . . It may be laid down as a sound maxim in politics, that laws applicable to ordinary cases ought to be repealed when they become dormant, when the government of a country dare not, or from motives of expediency do not choose, to put them in execution. The

---

[1] Lincoln, p. 241.

[2] Lady Stephen, *The Shores of Sheffield and the Offleys of Norton Hall*, p. 8, reprinted from the *Transactions of the Hunter Archaeological Society*, V, 1 (January 1938).

[3] Victor Bonham-Carter, *In a Liberal Tradition; A Social Biography, 1700–1950* (London, 1960), p. 19.

[4] Lincoln, p. 258.

Acts of Indemnity, which pass annually, now are become absolutely necessary for the peace and orderly government of the state, and to save almost the whole nation from penalties and disabilities.[1]

This abeyance of the Acts was a major change in the position of Dissenters since the thirties. And it may have been due partly to the one significant change in their legal position since that time, the annual Indemnity Acts mentioned by Heywood. But these acts were probably more important for the tolerance they suggested than for the legal protection they afforded. Heywood and other advocates of the Dissenting cause pointed out some of their inadequacies, and they were doubtless aware of more than they thought wise to reveal. Certainly the protection they afforded was full of ambiguities and loopholes.[2] At least two proved to be of some practical importance. The acts did not, and could not possibly, have affected disqualification for election to offices in corporations on account of not having taken the test, since the candidate never got the office in question and hence there were no penalties to be waived! Only detailed local studies can reveal how often the Corporation Act was invoked at elections, but it certainly was on occasion in later periods and very likely in this one.[3] And that the acts did not provide clear protection even after the assumption of office was proven by a prosecution as late as 1824. Arguments in the Court of King's Bench in that year illustrated that, while the title suggested that the acts protected only those who had failed to qualify *previous* to the date of passage, the enacting clauses suggested that it protected those who failed to qualify *after* the date of passage as well. The specific argument against the Mayor and four Bailiffs of Berwick was that, as there was in their case still a month of jeopardy left under the 1719 modification of the Corporation Act at the time of the passage of the 1824 Indemnity Act, the latter did not cover them. Though the Court decided in favour of the defendants, the case showed some of the holes in the protection afforded.[4] It is

[1] *The Right of Protestant Dissenters to a Compleat Toleration Asserted* (London, 1787), p. 85.

[2] For discussions of some of these inadequacies, see Hunt's several publications and Barlow, p. 73ff.

[3] See below p. 124.

[4] *Monthly Repository*, n.s. 1 (1827), 30.

clear, then, that there was ample opportunity in this legal tangle for anyone who wished to prosecute Dissenters, but, as has been seen, there was vitually no disposition to do so.

What then were the Dissenters complaining of? Apart from their very practical grievance under the Corporation Act, it was again a matter of disposition—in this case of a disposition not to appoint them to office. And this too marked a distinct change in their position since the thirties. As the contemporary historians of Dissent put it:

In the eventful reign of George the third, the dissenters have not retained that high degree of favour with the court which they had enjoyed ever since the accession of the House of Hanover. They had before been treated with the highest confidence; but now they began to be viewed by many members of the administrations with jealousy and suspicion, if not with aversion and disgust.[1]

And it was an inescapable fact that the Abneys, Barringtons, and Holdens were no more, nor had others arisen to take their places. Though Dissenters might continue to flourish in some localities, they had ceased to occupy positions of power and influence in national affairs.[2]

Such a situation inevitably brought Dissenters back to the Test and Corporations Acts, 'to the operation of penal statutes', as William Smith was later to maintain in much more serious difficulties, 'which marked out particular descriptions of people as odious,

[1] D. Bogue and J. Bennett, *History of Dissenters* (London, 1812), IV, 146.

[2] The careers of former students at Warrington and Daventry, two academies which might be expected to have produced some eligible candidates, are of interest here. Apart from several High Sheriffs and J.P.s (and the former office was hardly sought after), there are only two certain instances of Dissenters achieving office, and these after the period under consideration. Samuel Heywood was made Chief Justice of the Carmarthen circuit in 1807; and Samuel Benyon was Attorney General of the County Palatine of Chester at the time the biographical accounts appeared in 1814. Two are also queried as having received some minor office under the Shelburne administration. (Toulmin, *Monthly Repository*, IX, *passim*.) Daventry could boast only one officeholder, a former Baptist minister who became Secretary of the Legation at Paris in 1801 (*Monthly Repository*, XVII [1822], *passim*).

and as objects of persecution'.[1] It could be argued that there were no longer very many Dissenters of a social position such that they could expect to obtain offices of honour and profit under the Crown. But this was hardly a satisfactory explanation of the fact that there were virtually none, and, in any case, the rejoinder to such an argument was—why? The Dissenters' answer was that, operative or not, the mere fact that the Acts continued to exist suggested a prejudice, and perpetuated it. So the Dissenting leadership reasoned, and so in 1787 they once again moved for a repeal of these badges of their inferiority.

It was in the Repeal campaign of the eighties, quite appropriately, that William Smith first made his mark in political life. Before 1787 he had had little to say in Parliament, satisfying himself with quiet but loyal support of Pitt's policies. But in the debates on Repeal Smith was a very active speaker and a not ineffective lieutenant to Henry Beaufoy, the Dissenting member[2] who moved the motions of 1787 and 1789, and later to Charles James Fox, who moved that of 1790. Also, Smith, though not yet a member of the Deputies' Committee, was naturally, as one of its Parliamentary spokesmen, a prominent member of the larger 'Committee to conduct the Application to Parliament'.[3]

The Application Committee appeared to have good reason to hope for success at the beginning of the campaign. One reason, already mentioned, was the recent success of the Dissenting Ministers' petition. Also, though the Committee no longer included important officeholders, there were a number of men of prominence and influence connected with it: three Dissenting members of Parliament, Sir Henry Hoghton, Bart., besides Beaufoy and Smith; others emi-

[1] *The Parliamentary History of Great Britain*, XXIX, 1395.

[2] Beaufoy came from an old Quaker family, and though he was now probably nominally an Anglican, his closest associations were always with the Rational Dissenters.

[3] For the composition of this committee, formed in January 1787, see Barlow, p. 227, n. 12. Barlow's is the only extensive modern account of the campaign of the eighties—and a very good one—but Ursula Henriques, *Religious Toleration in England, 1787–1833* (London, 1961), pp. 59–67 is a most useful supplement.

nent in the professions, like its chairman, Dr Edward Jeffries of St Thomas's, and Samuel Heywood; and still others, like Samuel Shore and Capel Lofft, who were substantial gentlemen of wide connexions. There were other reasons for confidence. Fame and fortune seemed to continue to smile on the rational religion which most of these men espoused. The failure of the Feathers Tavern petition had caused an accession to their ranks. It had been followed by the secession from the Church of several clergymen, and in 1774 Theophilus Lindsey had founded an avowedly Unitarian chapel in Essex Street. Its purpose, reflected in a service closely modelled on the Anglican service, was to draw out sympathizers from the Church. This it did, and very eminent ones, but the bulk of its support from the beginning came from Dissent. Thus in the Essex Street congregation (of which William Smith was later a member and Belsham the minister), old Dissenting families like the Shores rubbed elbows with the Dukes of Grafton and Richmond and Lord Le Despencer (better known as Sir Francis Dashwood).[1] The Dissenters were not represented by complete unknowns. And there was reason to believe that these representatives would have weight with government, both because of their personal standing and their support of the ministers and because of the fact that Dissenters generally were widely believed to have given Pitt strong support in the previous election.[2] At worst, it was believed, he would be neutral, and this alone would be sufficient to allow Dissent to carry the day. On the eve of the campaign in 1787 there appeared to be no clouds in the Dissenters' sky.

In the campaign of 1787, as in those of the thirties, the Committee relied primarily on its influence with Parliament and the administration. The first move after its initial meeting on 29 December 1786 was to seek an interview with Pitt himself. He received the Committee's deputation politely, but requested time for consideration. Thereafter, the Committee concentrated on adding prominent men

[1] On the founding of the Essex Street Chapel, see Alexander Gordon, 'Theophilus Lindsey', *Addresses Biographical and Historical* (London, 1922), pp. 265–9.

[2] According to Lord John Russell, for instance, 'in 1784 they had acted heartily and efficaciously in support of Mr. Pitt' (*Memorials and Correspondence of Charles James Fox* [London, 1853], II, 361).

to its own number and on circularizing other leading politicians. The Committee included some prominent country Dissenters, but almost all had their own private reasons for being in London during the season. It circularized a few more. There was, however, certainly no attempt to rouse Dissent as a whole to a vigorous campaign.

In the event, the Committee was proved to be over-sanguine in two important respects. In the debates of 28 March 1787, Pitt not only did not support the Dissenters, he openly opposed them. Though not much information exists as to his motives, it is fairly safe to speculate. The bishops had already indicated their firm opposition to the measure and the King's adverse views were well known. And, as Mr Barlow has emphasized, though the champions of the established order had been willing to make a concession in 1779, it was on the grounds of expediency, not of principle. They saw no reason to make a concession now, and the motion was lost by 176 to 98.

The second respect in which the Committee erred was in its judgement of its own constituents. No serious attempt had been made to arouse the country Dissenters. But the Committee certainly did not expect the reaction that it got. The general Dissenting response to its effort had been not only infinitesimal in volume but apparently in some cases openly hostile, leaving the cause open, as the Committee complained, to the charge that 'the Dissenters at large were neither earnest in their exertions, nor unanimous in their wishes for redress'.[1] In the thirties it had been the country Dissenters who had been most ardent in the cause of Repeal and London which had appeared to drag its feet. Now the situation was completely reversed.

There are several explanations for the reversal of roles. In the thirties the wealth and talent of Dissent had been in the actual enjoyment of offices and places. Now it was on the outside thirsting for those places of power and influence. It was only natural with this changed situation that the sense of oppression under the Test and Corporation Acts should be in direct proportion to the wealth, education, and talent of the Dissenters involved, bearing hardest on

[1] Quoted in *Sketch of the History of the Protestant Dissenting Deputies* (London, 1813), p. 48.

those at the top. London had the greatest concentration of the wealth, education, and talent of Dissent. For these reasons London also had the greatest concentration of Rational Dissenters and those who sympathized with their outlook, that is, of those intellectually most incapable of bearing the restraints imposed by the Acts. The combination of these two factors, the social and the intellectual, was to make London the leader in the movement for Repeal throughout its subsequent history.

The attitudes of country Dissenters were more complicated. Clearly 'country' is a broad term; and in the larger towns where a situation similar to that in London existed on a smaller scale, there were similar results. 'Country' Dissenters like Priestley, for example, made even the ardour of London look pale in comparison.[1] But the great bulk of Dissent, increasingly under the sway of the evangelical revival and growing ever larger as a result, was not drawn from those classes most intimately and obviously concerned with the Test Acts. Many lower-class Dissenters, in country districts or at any rate outside established towns, would have been removed from the influence of those socially and educationally their superiors. And, in any case, very different approaches to religion might well have weakened that influence. Thus many country Dissenters doubtless saw little to interest them in the campaign. Beyond this, some seem to have felt that to divert Dissent's energies into a political controversy would weaken its religious unity and zeal. Indifference and a narrow religious fervour combined to put a serious obstacle in the way of the objects of the London leadership.

It was by no means an insuperable obstacle. It was not difficult to make a convincing argument that every Dissenter, no matter how humble, had an interest in Repeal. The petty persecutions which had continued throughout the century were constant reminders that Dissenters were a class apart, and there was force in the contention that all their troubles could be traced 'to the operation of penal statutes which marked out particular people as odious, and as objects of persecution'.[2] Smith, while admitting that some Dissenters might be sceptical of the campaign, denied in the

[1] Barlow, p. 238.
[2] William Smith, quoted above, pp. 43-4.

1787 debates that there was any serious division on the matter: 'there were hardly any dissidents upon this subject, though the most rigid of them conceived, that, by a repeal of the Test Act, the bond of Union would be taken away'. And he claimed that had the Committee encouraged them 'the table would not have contained all the petitions that would have been sent up'.[1] His boast was justified by events, but only after strenuous exertions by the Committee and its allies.

The Dissenting leadership had not been unduly distressed about defeat in 1787 and remained convinced that the spirit of the times and a demonstration that Dissent was serious about the issue would finally carry the day for them. Their efforts during the next three years were bent toward proving the latter point. Between the motion of 1787 and that of 1789 they did not, however, so much change their methods as intensify existing ones. More prominent country Dissenters were added to the Committee. Efforts were made to obtain the name of every Dissenting minister in the country, so that the Committee's propaganda would reach every congregation. And, finally, moves were made to mobilize the electoral power of Dissent. Lists of the division on Beaufoy's motion were circulated and Dissenters were urged to put pressure on their M.P.s.

For two years the Committee and its allies laboured, and when Beaufoy moved a second time for Repeal in 1789, these labours appeared to have borne fruit. Despite the fact that Pitt remained opposed to the measure, this time the Commons rejected it by only twenty votes, 124 to 104. This was an advance indeed, redoubling the Committee's efforts. More important, as it proved, the Committee's methods also changed. Following their second defeat, which occurred in May, the Dissenting leadership decided to adopt a form of organization closely modelled on the Parliamentary reform movements of the earlier part of the decade, with all the paraphernalia of a network of local associations throughout the country, the promotion of county meetings etc.[2] This was hardly a surprising development as many of the Dissenting leaders, Capel

[1] *Debate on the Repeal of the Test and Corporation Act, in the House of Commons, March 28th, 1787* (London, 1787), p. 51.

[2] Henriques, p. 63.

Lofft, Samuel Shore, Beaufoy, and Smith, among others, were no strangers to this form of organization, having played a prominent part in the earlier movement. It is indeed somewhat surprising that they had not adopted this form of organization earlier, but this may well be explained by the fact that they had relied on the various meetings and societies for commemorating the Revolution of 1688, in which Dissent always took an almost proprietary pride, to do their work for them. And, if so, they were probably not far wrong, for the centenary celebrations had very often served as a platform for Dissenting propaganda.[1]

During the summer and autumn of 1789 and the spring of the following year the new Dissenting organization flourished, setting up a swelling demand for Repeal. The new activities appeared to have provided the final justification of Smith's assertion in 1787 that 'amongst the Dissenters, there were hardly any dissidents upon this subject. . . .'[2]

The Committee had been successful, startlingly successful, in organizing Dissenting public opinion behind the cause. It had been invited to show its teeth, and it had done so, dramatically repudiating the aspersion that 'the Dissenters at large were neither earnest in their exertions, nor unanimous in their wishes for redress'. It was not because of any failure in this respect that Fox's motion on 2 March 1790 was lost in a very full House by the overwhelming majority of 294 votes to 105. Rather the failure sprang from exactly the opposite cause—the efforts to arouse Dissent had been much too successful, striking terror into the hearts of their opponents. One adverse pamphleteer looked at the 'general and vehement bustle' among Dissenters and claimed to observe 'delegates . . . hastening together from East and West, from North and South for the purpose of subverting the constitution'. He ended with the warning that the Dissenters' real purpose was 'to dismantle our fortifications' and 'lay things open as in France' where justice 'allowed only seven minutes to prepare for death before one is hanged up by fish-women at a lamp iron . . .!'[3]

[1] Barlow, pp. 241–3.
[2] *Debate on the Repeal of the Test and Corporation Act, 1787*, p. 51.
[3] Quoted in Barlow, p. 253.

The relationship between the Repeal movement and the French Revolution which coincided with its last stage is by no means a simple one, and consideration of the question will be reserved for the following chapter. But there can be no doubt that events in France ended the Repeal question as a live issue in Parliament. Though the Dissenters maintained their optimism, and even further perfected their organization, into the nineties,[1] the motion of 1790 was to end attempts at Repeal for another thirty years.

The political implications of this defeat and its effect on the political orientation of Dissent were to be momentous. Robert Hall contended that the Dissenters' zeal for freedom could not 'be imputed to any alliance between their religious and political opinions but to the conduct natural to a minority'.[2] It is doubtful, however, whether such a distinction is very useful. So far as the Dissenting leadership was concerned, the rational approach to religion was the only principle they held in common. And it was this principle which had first pricked them to political activity and which, in large part, sustained that activity. It was, in turn, the course of their agitations and the support they aroused among Dissenters generally which drew attention once again to the fact that Dissent was a minority and to the determination of the majority to keep it in that position.

In the thirties Dissent had been divided in its interests; office and place had bound many of its leaders closely to the existing political system. Such was no longer the case. Dissenters were now united in their apartness, and exclusion bore equally—indeed much more—heavily on the wealthier and more successful Dissenters who constituted its leadership. This is a more than sufficient explanation of the restlessness and frustration of men like William Smith, and of their desire to reform a social and political system which perpetuated their exclusion. In all respects but one they were similar to other men of equal wealth and position in society—but this one difference was enough irrevocably to separate them, placing a firm bar to normal expectations and ambitions. They could not bear this restriction easily. As Smith said in the debates of 1789, they

[1] See ibid., chap. VII.
[2] *Christianity Consistent with the Love of Freedom* (London, 1791), p. 23.

held it to be highly improper in itself, and injurious to society, that religious opinions should be made the Test of fitness for the discharge of civil offices or of admission into them. They held, that every subject of the state, willing to give the requisite proof of his fidelity to the *civil* Constitution and Government, and unconvicted of any crime, was entitled to the participation of every civil right, among which was to be reckoned, the *Capacity* of holding offices, though not the *actual possession* of them; and therefore that to incapacitate a whole body of such subjects was to inflict on them an injury, of which they had a right to complain, and to seek redress as a matter not of Favour, but of Justice.[1]

There is an intransigence here, a sense of deep injustice keenly felt, which was more than enough to shatter every other reason for complacency and satisfaction with the existing system which Smith and others like him may have had.

B. L. Manning distinctly discounts the reforming tendencies of the Dissenting leadership during this period. He particularly cites an address presented by the Deputies to the King in April 1789, finding in it evidence of what he calls 'perfervid affection for the King and the Constitution'.[2] The fact that its point was to congratulate the King on his recovery from his first bout of insanity and was personally presented at a levee at Windsor might be argued as a mitigating circumstance. But, as a matter of fact, its language was no more effusive than was usual at this time and for a long time to come in the formal and highly stylized addresses to the Throne. There is, however, some significance in the conclusion of the address:

It shall continue to be our sincere prayer that the Divine Mercy thus displayed may be continually exerted in preserving your Majesty's reign over a free, loyal and united people to the last period of human wishes.[3]

[1] *The Debate in the House of Commons on Mr. Beaufoy's Motion for the Repeal of Such Parts of the Test and Corporation Acts as Affect the Protestant Dissenters, on Friday, the Eighth of May, 1789* (London, 1789), p. 53.

[2] B. L. Manning, *The Protestant Dissenting Deputies* (Cambridge, 1952), pp. 455–6.

[3] Minutes, 18 April 1789.

'A free, loyal, and united people'—was this a statement of fact or desire? It could hardly have been the former. The whole point of the campaign for Repeal, of which they were then in the midst, was that English liberties were deficient in one crucial respect, that far from being united, the English people were arbitrarily and unjustly divided.

Could a people not free and not united also be a loyal people? The answer proved to be that traditional concepts of loyalty, indeed of King and Constitution, would be revised, and that Dissenters would be in the forefront of those advocating reform and revision. George III had complained that the Dissenters' demands arose 'from a general disinclination to every restraint'. By denying them the easing of one particular restraint, he and his government had done a great deal to make this come true.

CHAPTER FOUR

THE FRENCH REVOLUTION

S mith's new absorption in politics did not make his private life any less strenuous or active. Quite the contrary: with his new position in the political world, there was a natural expansion of his style of life and of his social horizons.

In 1785 he had acquired a country seat, Parndon Hall, near Harlow in Essex. It was a fine, large red-brick house built in the early sixties, sitting atop a medium-sized hill, known in the family as 'The Mount'. There was a large walled garden and the surrounding pleasure grounds, dotted with big old firs, stretched on all sides to the base of the hill. The estate connected with the house was not large, only about two hundred acres, but there was ample room to provide good shooting and a little of that contact with agricultural pursuits so necessary to a gentleman of the period. As lord of the manor of Little Parndon and patron of its church living, which in not unusual fashion he filled with a relation,[1] Smith lived and entertained very much like any other country gentleman.

Parndon, however, did not take up all the Smiths' time during the summer and autumn months when Parliament was not in session. They had not by any means lost their taste for travel. In 1786 there was a five-month tour of Scotland, a large part of the time being spent in the Highlands. It was a gruelling journey, as it was bound to be before any extensive road construction had been undertaken, but the Smiths were not easily put off. They poked everywhere with their customary thoroughness, breaking their trip by visits to acquaintances or those to whom they had letters of introduction. They were given a warm reception, enjoying the

[1] *Norfolk Chronicle*, 28 March 1812.

53

hospitality of the Dukes of Argyll, Atholl, and Lennox and Gordon, Lord Breadalbane and Lord Seafield, as well as a number of lesser lights. Mrs Smith had the opportunity to strike a blow for the decencies of the Sabbath at Inverary: 'In the evening I grieve to say the family went to cards, as is their usual practice, but neither Mr. Smith nor I would play, which broke the Duchess's whist table and reduced them to play cribbage. . . .' Smith received the freedom of six Scottish boroughs, including Glasgow and Edinburgh. And the next year he was given further recognition by being elected to the Highland Society of London, on the proposal of Captain Colin Campbell and the second of Lord Breadalbane. It was a pleasant and instructive trip, beginning an interest in Scotland and its affairs which Smith never lost; it was useful as well in broadening his contacts in the political world.[1]

In 1788 the Smiths took a three-month trip to the continent, partly to see the sights and partly to buy pictures for Smith's growing collection. A large part of their sightseeing was done in France, with which they were not at all favourably impressed, Mrs Smith being heartily 'thankful we were born in a more enlightened land. . . .'[2] Her ideas were to change radically before many years were out, but neither she nor anyone else could have known it at the time.

Their family was also expanding. Indeed it seems only to have been the birth of children which restrained their restless peregrinations. Patty had been born in 1782. Benjamin followed the next year. Then there were two summers of travelling through northern England and Wales. Anne came next in 1785. The next summer was spent in Scotland. In 1787 another daughter was born, but died after four months of inoculated smallpox (which did not, incidentally, shake their faith in the practice). Frances (Fanny) came early in 1788, early enough for the trip to the continent not to be interfered with. In 1789 William Adams was born. Smith went alone to Paris the following summer, only because he considered it unwise to take his wife in the prevailing political situation. Joanna's birth

[1] 'Various Tours', I, 220–408, Leigh-Smith Papers, and Lady Stephen's MS, chap. I, p. 30.

[2] 'Various Tours', I, 418, Leigh-Smith Papers.

followed in 1791. And so on, with Samuel in 1794, Octavius in 1796, Frederick Coape in 1798, and finally Julia in 1799. Smith's political life was lived against the background of a thriving domesticity.

In the meantime, a change of the greatest significance for his future career had taken place in Smith's religious convictions. He had become a Unitarian sometime in the years immediately preceding 1791. There is no record of just how or when this took place. Smith had probably been moving slowly toward this position since Daventry. Shortly before his death, when his evangelical friends were making the last of many onslaughts to save his incorrigible soul, he suggested to Zachary Macaulay that he had early revolted against the doctrines of the Assembly Catechism.[1] His friend Belsham had not only abandoned his strict Calvinist views, but had become a Clarkean (or Arian) at Daventry.[2] Whether Smith had moved so far so early, it is impossible to say. But it is safe to assume that the strongest influence upon him in his spiritual pilgrimage was Belsham. Enough of their correspondence survives to show that the two maintained a regular, and very intimate, exchange of letters before Belsham came up to London after he resigned the principalship of Daventry on becoming a Unitarian in 1789. Smith's letter approving the motives which led to his friend's resignation, which Belsham gratefully noted in his diary,[3] shows no surprise at the intelligence and indicates no disapproval of the opinions which prompted it. There is only the—to a biographer—maddening, 'I purposely defer entering into the subject till I have the pleasure of seeing you here', and the enigmatic remark that 'I trust that tho' you in a certain sense, "have cast your bread upon the waters", you will find it again after *not* many days'. Then the letter trails off into politics, upon which subject Smith loved to play the mentor to Belsham![4] But whether or not Smith agreed with Belsham's religious

---

[1] Zachary Macaulay to William Smith, 26 August 1833, William Smith Collection, Duke University Library, Durham, North Carolina (hereafter, 'Smith Collection [Duke]').

[2] Gordon, 'Thomas Belsham', *Addresses*, p. 288ff.

[3] Williams, p. 383.

[4] William Smith to Thomas Belsham, 28 February 1789, Dr Williams's Library, 12.58, no. 8.

opinions in 1789, he clearly did by 1791 when he threw in his lot with the militant Unitarian Society, at a time when the Society was under violent criticism.[1]

While these changes were taking place in Smith's personal life and in his religious opinions, his political life was growing more busy. Besides his immersion in the affairs of the Dissenters, he was also deep in the activities of those who opposed the Slave Trade. It was not strange. The circles in which Smith moved had long been deeply concerned with the plight of the negro. The Thorntons were old friends and neighbours at Clapham, and, as early as 1784, the Society for Constitutional Information began publication of materials denouncing negro slavery.[2] According to Thomas Clarkson, Smith was the first outside the original Abolition Committee to enter the lists against the Trade:

When our Committee was formed in June 1787, it received several letters from individuals promising support. . . . The very first of these came from Mr. Smith.[3]

Probably it was this same letter which occasioned the resolution of the Abolition Committee dated 5 July 1787, thanking

William Smith Esq. for his interesting letter of the 1st Instant assuring him of the satisfaction they receive from the coincidence of his views with their own. That they feel much pleasure from the zeal he expresses in the cause of the oppressed Africans: and will be glad to avail themselves in future of his assistance and support in the attainment of the common object of their wishes.[4]

Unfortunately, Smith's letter does not survive;[5] but his actions prove his passion for the cause.

In the following year he gave strong support to Sir William Dolben's measure for a regulation of the Trade. Once again he was

[1] See below, pp. 63-4.

[2] 'Resolutions and Orders of the Society for Constitutional Information, 1783–91', 11 June 1784, PRO, TS 11/961.

[3] Thomas Clarkson to T. F. Buxton, 25 September 1833, Clarkson Papers, Huntington Library, San Marino, California, CN 75.

[4] Smith Collection (Duke).

[5] I am informed that there are no letters of William Smith, either in London or at Rhodes House, Oxford, among the papers of the Anti-Slavery Society.

thanked by the Committee, which also requested permission to publish some detailed observations which he had made on the evidence brought to light by the debate.[1] Unfortunately, these too have vanished. But it is certain that very few other M.P.s, besides Wilberforce himself, devoted such careful attention to mastering the facts of the case.

This is illustrated in the part Smith played in the investigations of the Trade which the Commons undertook in the years 1789–91. In his *Letter to Wilberforce* in 1807 Smith claimed that in these investigations he had taken 'perhaps a larger share than almost any other individual, yourself and Mr. Clarkson . . . excepted'.[2] Wilberforce himself bore testimony to Smith's services in later years. Writing to Smith in 1832 of his distress that the government had granted yet another West Indian request for an investigation he remarked:

As if you and I had not superseded that application forty years ago. You cannot any more than myself have forgotten the weeks after weeks, rather the months after months in which our chief tho' not most cherished companions were that keen, sour Stanley [Smith notes, "John S., the West Indian agent"]—that ponderous, coarse, Jack Fuller-like (a very graphical—to use the style of the day—epithet, if you remember the man) Franklin.[3]

Nor is contemporary evidence lacking of the high esteem in which Wilberforce held Smith and of the close co-operation in which the two men worked. In June 1790, in the middle of their investigations, Smith lost his election for Sudbury. He and John Pardoe had stood in the government interest against Crespigny, now in opposition, and John Coxe Hippesley, recently returned from Bengal and the new Recorder of Sudbury.[4] It was an extremely hot contest, with two electors dying in drunken accidents; but the Foxites

1 8 October 1788, Smith Collection (Duke).

2 *A Letter to William Wilberforce, Esq., M.P. on the Proposed Abolition of the Slave Trade, under the consideration of Parliament* (London, 1807), p. 21.

3 Wilberforce to William Smith, 5 May 1832, Smith Collection (Duke).

4 Both Crespigny and Hippesley were to appear with Fox in the list of the opposition on the Oczakov ultimatum, in which Pitt, fearing Russian expansion in the Balkans, had strongly protested against the seizure of the Turkish port (*Parliamentary History*, XXIX, 1000–01).

carried the day, Smith being nineteen votes behind, with 352 to Hippesley's 371.[1] Wilberforce immediately sent his condolences from York, 'with every good and affectionate wish for your present and future usefulness', and begged him 'not to form any plans for your time, place etc. etc. till we meet'.[2] Smith departed for Paris shortly after his defeat, and on 3 July Mrs Smith informed him of another letter from Wilberforce desiring 'you to let James Philips know that he hopes to be in Town on Saturday next, that he may summon Clarkson, Dickson, etc. etc., that you may lay your Plan for the conduct of the Slave Trade'.[3] He wrote again shortly thereafter to say that he had decided to stay in the country for a while, unless, as Mrs Smith informed her husband, he could '*be of any personal use to yourself in the neighbourhood of London.* . . .'[4] He wrote again on 12 July to let Mrs Smith know that he would 'be in London by the middle of next week at the farthest, when we may hope to see Mr. Smith again at Clapham. . . .'[5] If these letters show nothing else, they show that Wilberforce had no intention of allowing a valued lieutenant to slip through his fingers.

He had no need to worry. Smith had no thought of abandoning his Parliamentary career. In January 1791 the death of Sir Samuel Hannay left vacant a seat at Camelford. There was no question of a contest there, as the borough's seventeen voters were firmly in the pocket of its patron Sir Jonathan Philips. Camelford could be had by anyone who could pay the price, in this period usually about £2,000 for each seat.[6] As it was still early in the session, Smith probably

[1] *Ipswich Journal*, 26 June 1790.

[2] Wilberforce to William Smith, 26 June 1790, Smith Collection (Duke).

[3] Frances Smith to William Smith, 3 July 1790, Leigh-Smith Papers.

[4] Frances Smith to William Smith, 13 July 1790, Leigh-Smith Papers.

[5] Wilberforce to William Smith, 12 July 1790, Smith Collection (Duke).

[6] In 1780 and 1784 Camelford had been a government borough, Robinson having paid Philips £4000 and then collected £2000 from each of the successful candidates (Laprade, *Parliamentary Papers of John Robinson, passim.*). In 1784 Philips had returned himself and James Macpherson, shortly thereafter vacating his own seat for Sir Samuel Hannay. Both Macpherson and Hannay ratted on Pitt over the Regency Question, but they were none the less returned in 1790. Then, with Smith, Philips returned a fairly consistent Pittite in the following year.

paid about this sum and was duly returned, in a manner which he himself was later to admit 'perhaps . . . would not be sanctioned by the public approbation'.[1] He was therefore back in the House in time to take his place with Wilberforce in the Slave Trade debates in April.

The Slave Trade was not, however, to be Smith's major political preoccupation during the next several years, and despite their continued intimacy and their co-operation on this one issue, Smith and his Clapham friends were soon to differ on most others. It was natural enough, and once again the explanation was the peculiar position which a Dissenter was forced to occupy in English society. For, if its defeat on Repeal had underlined Dissent's position as a minority group, events were soon to make it once again a persecuted minority, driving Dissenters still further away from the existing system in politics.

The Dissenters' difficulties arose directly from their vigorous campaign for Repeal and the bitterly hostile response it evoked. A great deal of the hostility can doubtless be explained by the fact that the period of Dissent's greatest vigour and organization, from the early summer of 1789 to the spring of 1790, coincided with the first violent stages of the French Revolution. Certainly the adverse pamphlet literature during the campaign demonstrated a fertile imagination in drawing parallels between the two movements.[2] But it would be wrong to over-emphasize the importance of events across the Channel in shaping attitudes on either side of the controversy.

So far as the Dissenters are concerned, as Fox pointed out in the debates of 1790:

. . . The situation in France had neither excited the attempts nor raised the hopes of the Dissenters for the accomplishment of their wishes. A similar motion . . . was submitted . . . three years back, when no person could have predicted the singular events which have occurred on the Continent.[3]

True, the Dissenters had not fully perfected their organization

---

[1] Quoted in W. P. Courtney, *The Parliamentary Representation of Cornwall to 1832* (privately printed, London, 1889), p. 352.

[2] Barlow, pp. 251–3.

[3] Quoted in ibid., p. 265.

three years previously, but it can hardly be argued that this owed anything to French inspiration. Nor did that organization do anything beyond promoting such respectable activities as county meetings to petition for Repeal. The Dissenting leadership derived both their ideas of organization and of its purpose from the earlier Parliamentary reform movement they had themselves helped to organize.

The attitude of the Dissenters' opponents is more complex, but here too at least a great part of the hostility had little to do with events in France. As Mr Barlow has shown, there was little indication that the defenders of the established order would have been willing to grant the Dissenters' demands before the upheaval in France.[1] Nor, though it was a proof of the effectiveness of the Dissenting organization and doubtless stirred their adversaries to greater efforts, was the great gain made in the Commons between 1787 and 1789 necessarily such an indication. M.P.s had often before found it convenient to accede to pressure from their constituents; but, as the fate of the Ministers' petition in the early seventies had shown, what was done in the Commons was easily undone in the Lords. And the breadth and depth of opposition to the Dissenting demands suggests that politics closer than those in France moved a great many. It stretches credulity, for example, to believe that the Mayor, Recorder, Aldermen, and Burgesses of Barnstaple were thrown into panic by the fall of the Bastille.[2] Similarly, this seems an inadequate explanation of the strenuous activities of the supporters of the close Corporation of Leicester, who formed the Constitutional Society in 1789 for the purpose of resisting the Dissenting demands.[3] Or, again of the ministerial party in the Norwich Corporation who rejoiced after the defeat of the 1790 motion that

> . . . the sons of Schism
> Were most completely ditch'd.[4]

[1] See ibid., chaps. V and VI.

[2] Barlow, p. 257. For a selection of the responses of public meetings to the Dissenting demands, see ibid., pp. 257–60.

[3] A. Temple Patterson, *Radical Leicester* (Leicester, 1954), pp. 64–5.

[4] Quoted in the chapter on Norwich below, p. 124.

The examples might go on. The point, however, is that at least a large part of the hostility the Dissenters aroused would seem to have sprung from local rather than from international considerations.

The conflict between the Anglican Corporation of Leicester and the Dissenters pre-dated 1789 and it was to continue, in times violent and quiet, for a long time. The same was true of Norwich, though there the battle was within the Corporation itself. And very probably similar situations existed in a great many other places. It is perhaps significant that, though pamphleteers on both sides talked a great deal about the French Revolution, local meetings do not appear to have done so—at least, their resolutions do not give evidence of it. Rather, Dissenting meetings talked about civil and religious liberty,[1] and those of their opponents talked of preserving inviolate the existing establishment in Church and State—though sometimes the latter harkened back to an earlier revolution which had 'nearly effected the ruin of our church and monarchy. . . .'[2]

Both sides talked in very English and very traditional terms—indeed sometimes in terms hoary with age! The Dissenters were not responsible for the fact that the French chose to use terms very similar to theirs, and to put their professions into practice by abolishing civil disabilities on account of religion. It is true that Dissenting publicists often claimed the credit, which undoubtedly further alarmed their opponents and provided them with ammunition, then and in the future. Dr Richard Price, for instance, in his famous *Discourse on the Love of our Country*, which roused Edmund Burke to such eloquent fury (but first delivered, it will be remembered to the London 'Society for Commemorating the Revolution in Great Britain'), called upon his audience to 'behold kingdoms, admonished by you, starting from sleep. . . .'[3] Dissenters welcomed the French Revolution as another manifestation of the growing spirit of liberty, for which both as Englishmen and as Dissenters they took a great deal of the credit. But the Revolution wrought no basic change in their attitudes.

[1] See, for example, the resolutions of the Suffolk meeting at Stowmarket, *Ipswich Journal*, 5 December 1789.
[2] Quoted in Barlow, p. 259.
[3] Quoted in ibid., p. 251.

It is also doubtful that events in France were the basic reason for the opposition to the Dissenting demands. The eighteenth century system in society and politics was founded on a complex network of oligarchies national and local. The Church was an important part of the oligarchical system, and the laws which protected its privileged position provided a kind of moral justification of that system. This was probably the basic reason why oligarchs great and small, at this time and long after, rallied so enthusiastically to support the establishment in *both* Church and State. The Dissenters were clearly recognizable as outsiders demanding entry. Those on the inside were determined to keep their pleasant preserves for themselves. Considerations very close to home were at the heart of much of the hostility the Dissenters' vigorous efforts aroused. The French Revolution certainly hardened the hostility, and spread it. But it would probably not be far wrong to see the Repeal campaign as preparing the way for increasingly violent reaction to events in France, arousing passions, drawing lines, and sowing the seeds of bitterness which were to grow and blossom with events abroad. In Thomas Walker's opinion, the campaign of 1789 marked the 'commencement of party violence'[1] in Manchester. Manchester was by no means unique.

There can be no doubt that Dissenters hailed the first stages of the French Revolution with enthusiasm. Mrs Smith, who two years before had been thankful she had not been born in so unenlightened a land as France, waxed almost ecstatic in 1790. As she wrote to her husband soon after his departure for Paris:

Improvement I consider as the motive that induced you to leave me—to learn the state of a Kingdom, now more than our *sister*, after so great, so happy a revolution. . . .[2]

Smith himself had said as much in reply to Burke during the debate on Repeal on 2 March sneering

that the virulent and severe abuse thrown out against the respectable body of Dissenters, would have had more effect on his mind, had not

[1] Quoted in Frida Knight, *The Strange Case of Thomas Walker* (London, 1957), p. 38.
[2] Frances Smith to William Smith, 3 July 1790, Leigh-Smith Papers.

the same gentleman indulged himself in still more unqualified imputations against a whole nation, that had nobly delivered itself from a state of ignominious bondage, and had recovered the just inheritance of freedom.[1]

It was an understandable reaction. The difficulty was that, having welcomed the Revolution with open arms, it was very hard to explain one's position when the noble venture began to turn itself into something quite different, when Burke's warnings began to appear increasingly justified. Unitarianism, for instance, had publicly launched itself early in 1791, and the first meeting of the Unitarian Society in April had combined religion and politics, with warm and fervent toasts to France's new liberty, in what proved to be a very dangerous fashion. The results were plain a year later in May 1792, when Fox introduced his measure for the relief of non-trinitarians. France had by now set herself on the path of aggression, and the Jacobin Club was howling for the King's head and a republic. When Burke rose on 11 May to oppose Fox's bill his opinions had considerably more basis than they had had two years before. Once again it was Smith who answered him, but now it was a Smith very much on the defensive.

. . . The right hon. gentleman had assumed that all who approved of what was done in France on the 14th July, approved likewise of every abuse that had since occurred in that country. This was an argument against the Unitarians, as uncandid as it was unjust and untrue. . . . The right hon. gentleman had charged the society with being a set of men not fit to be countenanced by this country; if so why had not the hon. gentleman come forward and prosecuted them for their conduct? He challenged Mr. Burke to show, from any documents which he had, any just grounds for charging that society with a correspondence with the Jacobin Club in Paris. If the right hon. gentleman could find, in any of their books, any plan for the subversion of the country, he should be very much obliged to him; as in that case he should take the advice of the right hon. gentleman, and withdraw himself from the society.

Referring once again to the meeting, he contended that whatever

[1] *The Debate in the House of Commons, on Tuesday, the 2nd March 1790, on the Motion of Mr. Fox, for a Repeal of the Corporation and Test Acts* (London, 1790), pp. 54–5.

the existing situation in France, 'its state at the period when the meeting took place, was, in his opinion, a state far more happy than that which the kingdom of France had ever known under the old form of government. . . .' He declared his adherence to the Unitarians, in all they had done and written, ending with the ringing assertion that 'as long as his name was William, he would stand up for the principles he then maintained, and would support them to the utmost of his ability'.[1] And so he would, but, as he himself must have known, not without leaving himself open to a most serious misunderstanding of his position.

That position was essentially very moderate. Smith's background and the temperament which grew from it were far indeed from those of a revolutionary. He loved order and he had a deep inbred dislike of an unrestrained populace. On his trip to Paris in July 1790 the people with whom he associated were hardly the most radical. He several times dined with the Duc de la Rochefoucauld, whom he found 'a quiet, honorable man—not formed to take the lead in such times'. La Fayette was another acquaintance. Perhaps Condorcet and Brissot are not quite in the same category, but they were certainly of a class and type with which he could feel at ease, and, in any event, his great interest in them was the hope of advancing a common end—the abolition of the Slave Trade. These were the people he met and from whom he drew his impressions. As for the people themselves, he remarked that they were

in a great ferment—much Idleness—much Zeal and more attention to Politics than to Business and tho' they don't seem disposed at all to *mischief*, yet they may do something extravagant.[2]

Nor did he think much of the ceremony of swearing to the new constitution, which he viewed with Lord Gower from the Ambassadors' section. He liked the 'respectable appearance of the *Electors* of Paris, and the National Assembly'. But the whole impression left upon him was unfavourable. He disapproved of the 'want of Discipline in the Guards and Deputies. . . .'

[1] *Parliamentary History*, XXIX, 1396.
[2] 'Old Tours chiefly [with] My Uncle B. S. and Kept out of respect to his Memory', p. 7, Leigh-Smith Papers.

The (seeming) want of a proper feeling of their situation; viz. of who they came to represent; for what purpose they were come; the behaviour suitable to the occasion, and especially considering the number and *Character* of the Spectators and the Impression intended to be made on Paris, France, and even Europe by the Exhibition—which must suffer much from the Levity and puerility shown by great Numbers.[1]

All this is not to suggest that Smith secretly disapproved of the Revolution itself or what it had accomplished. Nor does it suggest any dislike of the populace, in its proper sphere. He was greatly impressed by its obvious support of the new system:

The Zeal shewn in the preparation for this ceremony has convinced every one how much the Hearts of the People are in the Revolution and that no Fear need be entertained of any counter attempt. . . . The new doctrine (here) of Egalite des hommes is on ye whole triumphant.[2]

Smith saw the Revolution as one would expect the quiet, sober, liberal English gentleman that he was to have seen it. Far from begrudging the French their liberty, he gloried in it. He simply hoped that the new wine would not be too strong, that the French people would settle down to a quiet and sober enjoyment of their new freedom, under their natural leaders. Government, he thought, was the business of people not unlike himself; the business of the people was business.

Smith clearly did not see the French Revolution as a Jacobin saw it, as he was suspected of doing. But neither did he see it as the great majority of his fellow countrymen saw it. The excesses, though hardly to be admired, he found explicable in terms of the oppressive regime that had preceded it. Added to this was his firm conviction that, by and large, the Revolution was immensely popular with the French themselves, who were, to his mind, the only ones who had any need to be concerned with it. If the Revolution was aggressive, it was, he thought, because it was itself threatened with aggression by the European despots. None of this was England's affair. It was inevitable that Smith should have found

[1] Ibid., pp. 16–17.   [2] Ibid., pp. 4–5.

himself among the small minority of Englishmen who opposed the war with France, supporting Fox's contention in the House on 13 February 1793 that

it was not for the honour or the interest of Great Britain to make war upon France, on the account of the internal difficulties of that country, for the purpose either of suppressing or punishing any opinions or principles which may prevail there, or of establishing among the French people any particular form of government.[1]

It is, of course, arguable that this was not the point of the war, that its aim was no more than the preservation of eternal British interests. Undoubtedly this always was the point in Pitt's mind. But what of Burke, of Grenville, and of Windham? Before one is too harsh toward Smith's point of view it is well to remember that there was a thesis to which it posed an antithesis. Doubtless Smith was wrong, but no less wrong, perhaps, than some of his opponents. But, right or wrong, his was an assessment of the situation which differed radically from that of the vast majority of his fellow-countrymen, whatever their reasons. Most Englishmen came to see the French Revolution as a great and terrible threat to their national interest, and to their way of life. Smith never could, and the result was profound. For him and a great number of Dissenters like him, the war with France ended the slow process of alienation from the existing system in society and politics, and fixed their position in the new political orientation which was taking place.

In 1802 Christopher Wyvill wrote of Smith that his

merit as an advocate for a radical Reform of Parliament on temperate principles, and his ability as a Public Speaker, are but too well known to need the Editor's commendation. Suffice it to observe that Mr. Smith's first political attachment was to Mr. Pitt, the friend to peace and popular rights; and one of his most affectionate friendships was that which has subsisted without interruption, personally, to Mr. Wilberforce, from the earliest period of his manhood. Yet when the great, but inconsistent Statesman plunged his country into a war with France, and deferring the cause of reform, attacked the Rights of the People, with daring hostility, Mr. Smith did not hesitate to become

[1] Quoted in *William Smith, Formerly Member for the City of Norwich*, pp. 4–5.

the opponent of the Minister, and, as a public man, to abandon the too partial friend who still adhered to him. With little change the adage may be well applied to this firm and consistent patriot, Amicus Pitt, Amicus Wilberforce, Magis Amica Libertas.[1]

Unlike Sir Norman Moore in the *Dictionary of National Biography* and the writer of Smith's obituary notice in the *Morning Chronicle*, who both ascribe the break with Pitt to the clash over the Test and Corporation Acts in 1787, Wyvill was right. It was over Reform and the French war that Smith broke with his former leader in 1792, and not until then. On 1 March 1791, after Pitt had three times opposed, and Fox had three times supported, the cause of Repeal, Charles James Fox still remained to Smith 'the right hon. gentleman on the other side of the House'.[2] And as late as March 1792 Smith's name is not to be found among the minority on the opposition motion censuring Pitt for his aggressive protest to Russia after its seizure of the Turkish port of Oczakov.[3]

An open break did not occur until April when Smith's name appears among the founders of 'The Friends of the People', an organization which his friend Samuel Shore had hesitated to join because of its almost exclusively opposition complexion.[4] This was followed by Grey's motion for Reform on 30 April, which Pitt opposed. To him Windham's picturesque argument, 'Who would repair their house in a hurricane?'[5] was conclusive. To Smith, who stubbornly refused to recognize the fact that there was a hurricane, it was irrelevant. He continued to argue, as he always had and always would, that 'he had long been persuaded, that if the country were fairly represented in that House, the general interest could not fail to be promoted'.[6] This was more than a difference of opinion, it was a complete lack of contact on the most basic issues. And when, for similar reasons, Smith supported Fox's resolutions against the warlike Address from the Throne on 13 December, and against the

[1] Wyvill, V, 224–5.
[2] *Parliamentary History*, XXVIII, 1376.
[3] Ibid., XXIX, 1011.
[4] Wyvill, V, 38.
[5] Quoted in Steven Watson, p. 302.
[6] *Parliamentary History*, XXIX, 1338.

war on 18 February 1793,[1] the break with Pitt was clinched, the long and painful process of alienation was over, and Smith was firmly and irrevocably a Foxite.

It is hardly strange that the process took so long. England was just beginning to emerge from its long period without parties, a situation which had prevailed for the greater part of the eighteenth century. The reason for the absence of party had been the absence of a series of interconnected and persisting issues on which political men could divide. The American war and the concurrent problems in Ireland had made a beginning in providing such issues. But during the eighties the issues of the preceding twenty years receded into the background, and politics resumed for a time their previous factionalism, became again a struggle for power without a marked difference in principle.[2] In so far as there was any progressive leadership it came, not from the opposition, but from government. For a man of Smith's background of conservative loyalty, on the one hand, and his own reforming interests, on the other, it was the best of all possible worlds. Unfortunately it did not last. In the process of the struggle over Repeal, Reform, and the French Revolution, principles were sorted out once again, producing what in time were to become the new Whig and Tory parties. Merely one issue certainly would not have brought the new situation about, and no eighteenth-century politician, or government, would have considered a man who went into opposition over one issue anything but mad. It took a complex of issues, long-term and interconnected, to make the new parties. The complex which created the Whigs and the Tories left the Dissenters little choice; they almost had to be Whigs.

A great deal more study in local history would undoubtedly be necessary to prove conclusively the political orientation of Dissent. But such studies as have been done clearly point to the fact that the reforming interests of Dissent continued and expanded, while the rest of the country became more conservative, that Dissenters ranged themselves in a liberal Whig position and leftwards. Among

[1] *Parliamentary History*, XXX, 59–60 and 453.

[2] This is not, of course, to argue that the idea of party disappeared in the period (see Donald Ginter, ed., *Whig Organization in the General Election of 1790* [Berkeley and Los Angeles, 1967]).

the more radical were those who participated in the activities of the Manchester and Leicester Constitutional Societies of 1792.[1] Samuel Shore's correspondents claimed that another of these societies in Sheffield had the support of large numbers of 'Methodists' (probably meaning lower-class evangelicals generally) and even of Quakers.[2] Such societies, demanding universal suffrage and distributing the works of Tom Paine, without doubt deserve the term 'radical'.

Such was not the case with the Dissenting leadership, with Smith and others of the same sort who dominated the London organization. But it can be said with some certainty that, though they were clearly not radicals, they were quite definitely among the more moderate of the reforming elements. Their preference is shown by the relatively large number among the founders of 'The Friends of the People', a society which, though it ostentatiously dissociated itself from the more radical societies of 1792, was none the less pledged to pursue Reform on what Wyvill would have called 'temperate principles'. Besides William Smith, Thomas Christie, T. B. Hollis, Samuel Rogers, R. S. Milnes, Samuel Shore, Samuel Shore jr, J. T. Rutt, Francis Kemble, the Rev Dr Kippis, J. C. Bentley, John Towgood, and the Rev Dr John Towers—there may have been others—were among those who signed the first declaration as resident members, with William Belsham of Bedford (brother of the Rev Thomas Belsham) and James Milnes signing as non-resident members.[3] Even Capel Lofft, though personally favouring universal suffrage, joined the Society shortly after its founding.[4]

The Dissenting Deputies themselves, though for good and obvious reasons they generally eschewed pronouncements on politics where the interests of Dissent were not clearly involved, left little doubt of their position on the rare occasions when they did speak. One such occasion was in December of 1792. It was a most crucial time for English Dissent. The country was fast moving towards

[1] Knight, *passim*, and Temple Patterson, *passim*.
[2] Wyvill, V, 48.
[3] Ibid., III, Appendix, p. 128.
[4] Ibid., V, 88.

war with France; and the loyalist associations, founded shortly before,[1] were in full halloo, and bitterly hostile to Dissent.[2] Feeling ran so high that a statement of the Dissenters' position seemed imperative, and a meeting was therefore called 'for the special purpose of declaring their sentiments on the British Constitution'. The meeting duly expressed its 'firm attachment to the Constitution of Great Britain' and pledged itself 'to contribute our best endeavours to maintain and preserve by all the means in our power, the present Constitution of this kingdom consisting of King, Lords and Commons. . . .'

At the same time we rejoice as Britons, that one great merit of the invaluable Constitution is that it contains within itself the means both of reform and improvement.

And the statement ended with a bow to 'the Glorious Revolution of 1688 which we consider as the basis of the Constitution and which happily conduced to the establishment of the present Royal Family on the Throne'.[3] At a time when reform and revolution were both damned in the same breath, the Deputies might be expected to have omitted to affirm their commitment to the former, and to remind the Royal House of its origins in the latter. But they did not; they could not.

It is true that their statement was moderate to a degree, but a situation was fast developing in which even a moderate position

[1] See Austin Mitchell, 'The Association Movement of 1792–3', *Historical Journal*, IV, 1 (1961), pp. 56–77.

[2] In a letter to the Chairman of the Deputies, dated 18 December 1792, John Reeves, the leading spirit in the loyalist associations, denied that they were anti-Dissent. He admitted that an early manifesto had contained 'some harsh reflections [in particular that the American Revolution had been brought on "by the Dissenters, there and here"]; these we disapprove and we accordingly left them out'. The Deputies, however, were unconvinced. Edward Jeffries, the Chairman, replied in a letter dated 21 December and approved by the General Meeting of that day, that 'I am authorized by the the body unanimously to say that they consider the expression as it stood in the first edition a gross calumny and the alterations since made so trifling as scarcely to merit attention, the allusion still remaining the same' (Minutes, 21 December 1792, and *Sketch*, pp. 54–7).

[3] Minutes, 12 December 1792.

aroused deep suspicion. The great majority of Englishmen felt very differently on the issues of reform and revolution than Dissenters were able to do; and they felt as well that everyone who was not wholly with them was against them. Thus Dissenters, whether moderate or radical reformers it mattered not, were lumped together as suspect, as men who were in all likelihood traitors to King and Constitution.

In such a situation moderation became unacceptable. However moderate and qualified one's approval of events in France, however careful one's advocacy of reform, the interpretation was bound to be damning. Such was the situation in which Smith found himself at the beginning of 1793. He was bent on a moderate middle course and on it he remained, but few besides himself could see its moderation; he was bound to be misunderstood. Nothing better illustrates the difficulty of Smith's position, and for similar reasons, of that of the whole Dissenting interest, than a notorious spy case in which he became involved at the beginning of 1794.

William Stone was a member of a family of Dissenting chemical manufacturers in London and a former member of the Society for Constitutional Information. In the early months of 1792 his brother, John Hurford Stone, had gone to France to establish a sal-ammoniac manufactory. J. H. Stone remained in France after war had been declared and became a French citizen. Early in 1794 he provided a French agent, an Irish-American clergyman named William Jackson, with a letter of introduction to his brother in London.

Sometime in March 1794 William Stone approached Smith at a meeting of 'The Friends of the People' at Freemasons Hall. He told Smith that his brother feared a French invasion of England. Smith scouted the idea, whereupon Stone suggested that strong representations of the disadvantages of such a course, by those whose opinions might be expected to have weight in Paris, would be of the greatest assistance in avoiding a calamity.[1] Smith had known the Stones for some six years and was a close friend of the poetess Helen Maria Williams, with whom J. H. Stone was living in Paris. There seemed

[1] *A Complete Collection of State Trials*, compiled by T. J. Howell (London, 1818), XXV, 1241–8; the Treasury Solicitor's brief, PRO, TS 11/1793, Box 555.

nothing disloyal in the scheme, and he therefore agreed to set down his impressions in a letter to William Stone.

Smith's letter was cautious and moderate, nor is there any reason to believe that it was not genuinely his own careful assessment of the situation in England.

I was a good deal surprised the other day, at the degree of credit which you appear to give to the rumour of a French invasion, but as I know many are of your opinion and many more affect to be so, I feel desirous of stating to you the reasons why I cannot but disregard any such apprehension. In the first place, nothing appears to me more certain than that those who are now at the head of affairs in France, are too wise to make such an attempt without prospect of some advantage, adequate to the risk which must be incurred by both the army and the fleet employed in the service; and this advantage, I should think, must be something more than merely the burning of a few towns and villages (supposing even that to be accomplished) or the creation of a temporary alarm. From general history too, and yet more strongly from their own recent experience, must they be aware of the difficulty of a hostile army's making any lasting impression on a people un-willing to receive them, and especially on an island in possession of a superior navy, and which can at any time call other fleets to its assistance.

If all this be true, it is scarcely reasonable to expect such attempt, unless the French flatter themselves with the hope of co-operation on this side; an expectation, as far as I am able to judge, still less likely to be realized, than even that of success without it. That numbers here are disgusted with the war, I have no reason to doubt, but no symp-toms have yet appeared of any general disapprobation of government; on the contrary, ministers seem to have been successful in raising a strong spirit of attachment to every branch, I might almost say to every abuse of the constitution. . . .

Up to this point, Smith's letter was no more than an unimpas-sioned, and an undoubtedly accurate, assessment of the chances of success of a French invasion, and of the English response which could be expected to such an attempt. The balance of the letter is far more personal, an attempt to make clear the views of one who was, with qualifications, sympathetic to the French cause. In his opinion no other effect could be expected from an invasion than an almost universal rising of the people to defend themselves against an attempt, which they would consider as levelled at their constitution and liberty, and which they would, therefore, execrate and resist, as much as the French did the duke of Brunswick's irruption.

Much has been said of the progress of French principles here; if by this be meant no more than that at one time the opinion was rapidly spreading of the French Revolution having a favourable aspect on the happiness of Europe, and of mankind, I firmly believe it, and I believe also that a pretty general persuasion also prevailed of the existence of abuses in our own government, as required a reformation speedy and effectual; partly, however, from natural causes, and partly from artifice, I am convinced that these opinions have much decreased both in force and extent, and that, though the tide may turn, yet that it is not by an invasion that such a revolution would be brought about; we should only wrap our cloak tighter around us, like the man in the storm, and refuse every offer of fraternity, which came in so questionable a shape.

Sincerely wishing for peace, and thinking that these rumours of invasion are industriously circulated with a view of exasperating the people, and of rendering them more in earnest for the war, I should be very desirous of stating publicly in parliament every idea I have communicated to you, if I did not know that my general attachment to the cause of liberty, and the satisfaction which I have repeatedly expressed at the overthrow of despotism in France, have rendered me, to a very considerable degree obnoxious, and expose my sentiments to misrepresentation of the most invidious kind. I trust, however, that a more pacific and liberal temper will prevail.[1]

Smith made it perfectly clear that his sympathy for the French Revolution ended at Calais. Such drastic medicine as the French peddled might possibly be a necessary antidote to the European despotisms to the east, but it had little applicability to England. All he desired there was a 'speedy and effective reformation' of specific abuses. This comprised the extent of his desire for a 'revolution' in England. He desired peace so that both France and England could progress in their own, separate ways. There was obviously nothing traitorous here; and, though Smith was summoned before the Privy Council and questioned well into the night

[1] Howell, pp. 1186–8.

on 3 May, when Stone and Jackson were apprehended, he was released and no charges were made against him.

On the other hand, however, there were circumstances in the case which could hardly fail to do the very thing which he himself complained of, 'expose my sentiments to misrepresentations of the most invidious kind'. In the first place, though Smith had no reason to know that they would be, his impressions were not transmitted directly to an acquaintance in France, but to a French spy, Jackson, who used them as he used other sources of espionage. True, there was nothing in his letter which told the enemy anything which they could not easily have observed for themselves. Smith had carefully guarded against giving any specific information, and he had strongly advised his friend Benjamin Vaughan, also implicated by a letter in William Stone's possession, against such 'exceptionable' passages as:

terror pervades the friends of liberty; who would soon shew a different appearance, if they were countenanced by the majority of the people *seeing that there are no regular troops in England but militia, and a few cavalry who are stationed near the coast only.*

The italicized section had been hastily scratched out before being sent to Stone, but what remained was ill-advised enough. Vaughan was probably wise to flee to France after his own examination by the Privy Council; but his hasty departure certainly did not improve the position of those that he left behind. Vaughan was a close friend of Smith's, had been his travelling companion to Paris in 1790, and was a Dissenting colleague in Parliament. Even though there was a vast difference between the sentiments expressed by Smith and Vaughan, the latter's flight inevitably made the whole connexion look more sinister.

The affair was not settled until 1796. Then, in two much-publicized trials Jackson was convicted and hanged and Stone was acquitted as an innocent accessory.[1] Smith was a witness at Stone's trial, and upon its favourable conclusion a friend wrote congratulating him on Stone's acquittal.[2] In a sense, it was true that Stone's

[1] Ibid., pp. 783–1438.
[2] John Longley to William Smith, 31 January 1796, Smith Collection (Duke).

74

acquittal was also an acquittal for Smith, but the case had dragged on for so long, the connexion had been so well publicized, and suspicions had been so much aroused, that the final conclusion did little to undo the damage already done. Those who wished to believe the worst were not shaken in their belief, and as late as 1802 when he first stood for Norwich, Smith's 'treasonable correspondence' was still being thrown in his face.[1]

In later years, Patty Smith remembered attending Priestley's farewell sermon at Hackney early in 1794:

My F[ather] said, 'We shall soon see you here again.' Dr. Priestley replied, 'Or I you in America' and went away, my Mother saying to me the instant after, 'Now mind you never repeat that,' and un-doubtedly I never did.[2]

Many Dissenters followed Priestley's example and fled the country. Had Smith been a man of weaker nerve, and less convinced of the moderation of his own position he might have done the same. As it was he preferred to stay and fight.

There is no question, however, that his position, and that of the rest of Dissent, was critical and dangerous. The feeling against Dissenters was deep, and it was cleverly fanned by their enemies. The loyalist associations are one example, and the *Anti-Jacobin* is another. As late as 1800 the latter was still proclaiming that

the descendants of the puritans are still found among us, in great numbers; they retain the same principles which in England and America have produced so much disturbance; they take care, by their offspring and their seminaries, to transmit those principles to their posterity; and they have, with few exceptions, admired, ex-tolled, nay, even encouraged and promoted, to the utmost of their power, the French Revolution, because it was founded upon their own principles.[3]

Clearly these were only half-truths, but there was enough truth in them to make them extremely damaging.

[1] 'A Friend to Loyalty and Honesty', *Norfolk Chronicle*, 3 July 1802.
[2] 'Notes dictated by Patty Smith', p. 47, Leigh-Smith Papers.
[3] Quoted in F. K. Brown, *Fathers of the Victorians: The Age of Wilberforce* (Cambridge, 1961), p. 169.

Nor did it take much to convince many of their fellow country-men that Dissenters had a treasonable taint. The century's first decade had witnessed violent rioting against Dissenters. Then the mobs had turned their attention mainly to Jews and Catholics. Now, in the last decade of the century, there were once again to be violent riots against Dissenters. The clock seemed to be going back-wards. And there were those who seemed intent on turning it back still further—Leveller and Regicide were epithets more common to hurl at Dissent than Jacobin.

To such a point had the interworkings of principle, politics, and prejudice brought Dissenters by the nineties. The Repeal and Parliamentary reform campaigns and the relevance to both which they saw in the French Revolution had divided them from the great majority of Englishmen on the great issues of the day, and those issues were such that the minority opinion was bound to be execra-ted, especially when held by those whom religious prejudice marked out as suspect. The result might have been disastrous.

CHAPTER FIVE

DISSENT ON THE DEFENSIVE

The Dissenters' position in the nineties was full of dangers, real and potential. How low a point they had reached is perhaps indicated by the fact that during the period Dissenters replaced Catholics as the favoured scapegoats of the mob. Measures easing Catholic disabilities much more extensive than those which had given rise to the Gordon Riots in 1780 passed quietly in the following decade. Thus in 1791 the benefits of the Toleration Act were extended to Catholics, with hardly a murmur of disapproval.[1] The Dissenters were much less fortunate. In the same year the Gordon Riots were reproduced on a smaller scale, this time in Birmingham and aimed against Dissenters. For several days in July a 'Church and King' mob reigned supreme, burning the two principal Dissenting meeting houses and the property of prominent Dissenters, including the house and laboratory of Joseph Priestley. Order was finally restored by troops sent at the insistence of the King himself. But George III noted: 'I cannot but feel better pleased that Priestley is the sufferer for the doctrines he and his party have instilled, and that people see them in their true light. . . .'[2]

It might be argued that it was Priestley who was primarily responsible for bringing this disaster on the heads of Birmingham Dissenters. He was always a controversial figure and not only were his doctrines very radical, they were also often advanced with a good deal of asperity and sometimes without a great deal of judgement. But the case of Thomas Walker, around whom events very similar to those in Birmingham were to centre in Manchester in the

[1] See Barlow, p. 282.   [2] Quoted in ibid., p. 285.

following year, was rather different. His principles were perhaps not much different from Priestley's; he was also a Unitarian and the president of the local Constitutional Society (i.e. an advocate of radical Reform). But heretofore Walker had been a leader in the affairs of the town, a magistrate, and generally a popular and respected figure.[1] This, however, did not stay the violence of the Manchester mob in 1792.

The Birmingham and Manchester cases were the most notable, but there were many others. Yet, considering the antipathy which they aroused and the amount and skill of the propaganda launched against them, it is surprising that Dissenters did not suffer more than they did. The striking fact is that such persecution as there was remained, as it had always been, local and sporadic.

Had effective action not been taken to stem it, there can be little doubt that the persecution would have been much greater, and perhaps have reached major proportions. But effective action was taken. The credit must be divided between those who took the initiative, the quietly efficient organization which represented Dissenting interests in London, and those who rendered this initiative effective—that seemingly unlikely organization for the protection of Dissenters, the government of William Pitt. Not once during the nineties did the Dissenting Deputies turn to government without receiving kindness, consideration, and assistance.

One might point to three characteristic examples of such assistance. In each William Smith played an important part, although it is impossible to say precisely what part, for the Deputies' Committee functioned as a unit. It is necessary, therefore, to speak more of the unit, and less of the individual. Still, although it is the Committee's activities which will be discussed here and in later chapters, it must be remembered that, not only did these activities take up a great deal of Smith's time and constitute one of his contributions to the protection and advancement of religious liberty, but also, and increasingly as time went on, his position, his connexions, and his prestige gave him a dominating part in determining the group's strategy.

The Dissenting Deputies, as has been seen, had originally been

[1] On the situation in Manchester, see Miss Knight's study.

organized in 1732 to direct the Repeal campaign. But when the first campaign had finally failed in 1739, they had remained in existence 'as a permanent guardian of the civil interests of the Dissenting Body: to which recourse might be had for assistance in procuring redress of injuries suffered in consequence of their religious professions. . . .'[1] The arena of Parliament was exchanged for that of the courts of law, and their methods from those of public appeal to the quieter ones required to conduct a prosecution, or, if possible, to avoid the necessity of one. Their longest legal battle and their most striking success, was the famous Sheriffs' Cause. The matter was the constant concern of the Deputies for twenty-five years—1742 to 1767—and it took their Committee thirteen years of litigation—1754 to 1767—to establish the justice of the Dissenters' position. But they were successful, and more than successful; for they emerged from the controversy armed for the future with Lord Mansfield's definition of Dissent as a positive legal right, acknowledgement of which was more than worth the long and arduous battle.[2]

The Sheriff's Cause was the most important, but only one of scores of cases in which the Deputies extended their protection, and in the process slowly but steadily clarified and solidified the Dissenters' position in law. During the period between 1740 and 1812, the Committee dealt with forty-five cases of unjust demands and prosecutions, thirty-eight cases of riots, assaults, and disturbances, twenty-seven cases of magistrates refusing to execute their office (e.g. administering the oaths required by the Toleration Act),

[1] Minutes, 7 March 1823.

[2] See the chapter in Manning, and *Sketch*, pp. 25–39. Briefly stated, the question was whether the City of London had the power to elect Dissenters to offices from which they were excluded by law, and then, upon their refusal to serve, to fine them for neglecting their civic responsibilities. The Dissenters argued that they could hardly be punished for not assuming offices from which they were barred by the Corporation Act, while the City of London contended that non-conformity, itself a legal offence, could not be pleaded as an excuse for refusal to do their duty as citizens. The issue was carried to the highest court in the land, Lord Mansfield deciding in the Lords that 'bare non-conformity is no sin by the common law; and positive laws inflicting any pains or penalties for non-conformity to the established rites and modes, are repealed by the Act of Toleration; and Dissenters are thereby exempted from all ecclesiastical censures'.

forty-two cases of a similar refusal by clergymen (e.g. marriage, baptism, and burial), twenty-four parochial disputes, and sixty-five private disputes.[1] Individually, the cases were most of them minor, but, taken as a whole, they were extremely important. Every time a clergyman was forced to marry, baptize, or bury a Dissenter, it became better established that these were legal rights, and easier to deal with the next case of refusal.

So the Deputies continued their slow and quiet, but effective, way until 1787, when, as has been seen, they launched themselves once again into the cause of Repeal, with a result which was not only unsuccessful, but disastrous. It would be a long time before they would risk burning their fingers with public agitation again. Instead they reverted to their old tactics, not now to extend their rights but, as it might well have seemed, to fight for Dissent's very existence.

It was at this point that William Smith became one of their number, being elected a Deputy from Clapham and a member of the Committee at the annual meeting in December 1791.[2] It is perhaps surprising that he had not been elected before (although the family had been represented by his father as a Deputy since 1789). But Smith had, of course, been active in the most important business of the period, as a member of the broader Application Committee for Repeal; and it is improbable that before 1791 the routine work of the Deputies' Committee would have been such as to attract a busy and rising young politician.

By 1791 the situation had changed. The routine business of the Committee had assumed much wider implications. The broad acceptance by the rest of the community which had apparently been achieved during the course of the eighteenth century was suddenly shattered, and the Dissenters seemed on the verge of becoming once again the suspect and detested outcasts which their grandfathers had been under Charles II. It was no longer a matter of slowly and painstakingly building an ever stronger edifice in law, but of stemming a tide of persecution which threatened to engulf the whole structure.[3]

[1] *Sketch*, pp. 123–44.   [2] Minutes, 23 December 1791.
[3] In the period 1780–9 the Committee had dealt with fourteen cases of

In the new situation which confronted the Committee the kind of assistance which Smith could give became invaluable, for the aid of government became more and more necessary as the cases of violence and disorder increased. A politician of some prominence and of broad contacts was needed to manage negotiations with the ministers; Smith had both.

It seems likely that the first mission that Smith undertook on behalf of the Committee was his trip to Birmingham in July 1791, before he had become one of their number. True, neither the Minutes nor the *Sketch* mentions the riots, but a letter from the Deputies to Priestley[1] proves that they did, in fact, take an interest in the matter; and the fact that Smith was accompanied by a barrister and that all the evidence was taken in the form of sworn affidavits would indicate that the trip was not taken solely for his own information.[2] It all sounds very much like the careful preliminary probing of the Committee before it undertook a case. That it did not, in the end, do so is doubtless explained by Samuel Whitbread's adoption of Priestley's cause. The Committee could have desired nothing better than a full Parliamentary airing of the whole affair.

Others were not so fortunate, and it was to these unknown sufferers that the Committee's protection was extended. Smith was first recorded present at a special Committee meeting on 1 February 1793, at which he read a letter received from John Wood of Rothwell, Northamptonshire, to the following effect:

That on 25th December 1792 about ten o'clock in the evening the Meeting House of Guilsborough in Northamptonshire was discovered to be on fire and in a few hours was entirely consumed. That there were many circumstances attending it which made it extremely

---

persecutions of various sorts. From 1790–9 it dealt with twenty-eight, and these did not include the more spectacular cases, like those of Birmingham and Manchester (see above, pp. 77-8) which were never formally considered.

[1] J. T. Rutt, ed., *The Theological and Miscellaneous Works of Joseph Priestley* (London, 1826), XIX, 568.

[2] The results of the inquiry were made available to the House of Commons on the occasion of Whitbread's motion for an investigation of the matter on 21 May 1792 (*Parliamentary History*, XXIX, 1431–69).

probable that it was not done by accident but by design, particularly some conversations of one Butlin that passed soon afterwards at a public house in the neighbourhood about the King and the Constitution, and Paine and the Dissenters, who used several threats respecting destroying Meeting Houses, as one Haddon who heard it would have sworn but that he found four or five others who would have contradicted him, which persons are supposed in combination with Butlin and are enemies to the Dissenters, [and] by whom some things reflecting on Dissenters have been said which increases the probability of its being set on fire by the pretended Friends of Church and King.

That the Dissenters from Guilsborough are far from having been distinguished as the advocates of [Thomas] Paine but have manifested merely a favourable regard to a reform in Parliament and a repeal of the Test Laws.

The Committee moved cautiously, resolving

that the Chairman be requested to write to Mr. Wood desiring him to furnish the Committee with the most exact account which can be procured of the circumstances attending the fire and the discovery thereof, regularly attested on oath before a magistrate but carefully omitting every thing which might tend to *fix a suspicion* on any individual as the perpetrator of the action, and informing Mr. Wood of the opinion of this Committee, and on the receipt of such authenticated statement of the transaction, an application to his Majesty's Ministers to offer a reward for the discovery of the offender will be an advisable measure.

It was part of the Committee's effectiveness that it closed every possible loophole and built up a case as airtight as it could before acting. Because the Committee rarely went off half-cocked, it was rarely ineffective. The Committee prepared to act at the earliest opportunity however, resolving 'that upon the affidavits arriving from Mr. Wood, the Chairman, William Smith Esqr., and Sir Henry Hoghton Bart. be requested to act in the case as they shall think proper'.[1]

The required evidence arrived, and Smith and the Chairman waited on Dundas, then Home Secretary, requesting that a notice

[1] Minutes, 1 February 1793.

be published in the *London Gazette* offering a reward by the government for the apprehension of the incendiaries. In the *Gazette* of 9 March a notice duly appeared offering the substantial reward of two hundred pounds. At the next Committee meeting the Secretary was ordered to insert an advertisement of the reward in 'several county newspapers'. He did not ignore his instructions, publishing it in thirty-seven county publications![1] Had the aim merely been the discovery of the perpetrators of the crime at Guilsborough this would have been rather excessive, but quite obviously such was not the sole aim. As the *Sketch*, of which Smith was probably the major author, notes:

. . . the vigilance of the Committee, and the prompt attention of His Majesty's government to their representations, were probably the means of preventing further outrages in other parts of the kingdom.[2]

Guilsborough was a very ordinary sort of place, a small rural community (even today its population is less than 500) in a relatively remote corner of Northamptonshire; nor was there apparently anything extraordinary about its Dissenting congregation. The minuteness of the Committee's instructions to them and the fact that they were thereafter recommended to the charity of other Dissenting congregations in the rebuilding of their chapel, would indicate that they were neither particularly sophisticated nor particularly wealthy. It is their very ordinariness that makes them interesting. Humble Dissenters though they were, they had been reached by the Repeal and Reform campaigns; and their equally humble neighbours had been reached by the wave of reaction, and had responded accordingly. It was the kind of thing that might have happened all over England. The Committee was well aware of this, which is why it acted so decisively. But its efforts would have been in vain without Dundas's co-operation. The real importance of the

[1] Ibid., 23 March 1793.

[2] *Sketch*, p. 57. Manning, p. 14, surmises that Smith had a large part in the writing of the *Sketch*, which was published in 1813. I agree. Certainly Smith was not the only author. Generally, the prose is more direct than his. But some of the passages are almost his verbatim reports to the Committee, and there can be no doubt that the whole work is dominated by his point of view.

affair was that the Committee was able to get such quick and effective action from the government, a tangible sign of its disapproval of the persecution of Dissent.

The affair at Guilsborough was a relatively spontaneous outburst of violence, the kind of thing that no authority, local or national, no matter how well-intentioned, was capable of preventing in the eighteenth century. More serious, and more difficult to deal with, were cases in which the local authorities themselves openly or tacitly encouraged violence. One such case was initiated by a riot at Woodstock in the early summer of 1794, in which some recruits forcibly broke up a Dissenting service and severely injured some of the congregation. Smith brought the matter to the attention of the Committee at its 30 May meeting. A deputation including the Chairman, Smith, Sir Henry Hoghton, and three others was appointed to wait on Dundas and request government action. They acted swiftly, and on 2 June the meeting with the Home Secretary took place, the latter promising to send an agent to Oxford especially to look into the affair.[1]

Here the negotiations became lost in the government reshuffle of July in which Dundas became Secretary of War and the Duke of Portland took his place as Home Secretary. Edward Jeffries, the Chairman, reviewed the whole affair in a letter to Portland, dated 13 March 1795:

My Lord Duke,

In consequence of a riot at Woodstock last summer, attended with alarming circumstances in molesting and injuring nigh unto murder a society of Protestant Dissenters in their religious worship, application was made to the Right Honable. Mr. Dundas by a Sub-Committee of the Deputies from the several congregations in and near London for defending the Civil Rights of the Dissenters, accompanied with paper testimonials, who very readily and politely offered every relief in his power and did actually send a person to Oxford to enquire into the circumstances of the case. . . . Upon further application by letter requesting to know the intention of his Majesty's Ministers with respect to it I (as Chairman of the Committee) received an answer dated 24th August—informing that the matter was now

[1] Minutes, 12 December 1794.

transferred to your Grace's Department and [making] no doubt of our having proper information. A long interval in the meetings of the Committee has been the chief cause of not sooner seeking for this information.

So much time having elapsed, the injured persons rather wish to drop all judicial proceedings, even supposing the offenders could now be found which is not very likely. The Reverend Mr. Hinton residing at Oxford and well esteemed by many gownsmen there, . . . the Minister officiating at Woodstock and personally very much hurt, has had an intimation from respectable magistrates, that it might be unsafe to appear there again, and though the outrage was chiefly committed by some military recruits, long since removed, yet it is very notorious that the Peace Officers at Woodstock were very remiss in not offering protection and assistance, though perhaps not sufficient to ground a criminal charge.

The Committee beg leave to submit to your Grace whether some intimation from authority may be conveyed to the Peace Officers at Woodstock stating that such an outrage has been represented to his Majesty's Ministers at the same time enjoining them to be watchful in preventing the like again.

The Committee cannot but view the matter in a light which appears to them sufficient for requesting such an interposition or any other mode your Grace may please to adopt, or if your Grace should deem it necessary the Committee will readily wait on your Grace at any time you may please to fix.[1]

Portland replied on 16 March, politely but firmly declining to follow the Committee's suggestion.

The protection of the Protestant Dissenters in the peaceable and legal exercise of their religious worship will always be an object of the attention of Government.

I am apprehensive however that the request contained in your letter of the 11th instant 'that in consequence of the riot which happened at Woodstock in the last Summer, an intimation from authority should be conveyed to the Peace Officers of that town enjoining them to be watchful in preventing a similar disturbance for the future' might have the effect of renewing a subject by this time probably in great measure forgotten; and as the persons principally

[1] Ibid., 29 March 1795.

concerned in that unpleasant affair have long since left the place I am inclined to hope the ordinary protection of the law, and the authority of the magistrates, will be found fully sufficient to prevent a repetition of such interruptions in future.[1]

Had this answer come eight months previously, Portland might be charged with wilful evasion; but coming when it did, it is difficult to make such a charge. It was no longer a matter of punishing the offenders—what had been done to the recruits does not appear—but of admonishing the Woodstock justices concerning an event almost a year old. Nor was it clear how they were to be admonished, as no charges were to be levelled against them. What the Committee was asking was, in effect, that Portland should administer what could not have failed to appear a gratuitous slap on the wrists. This he was naturally very reluctant to do. It must always be borne in mind that throughout the eighteenth century the fear of popular disorder was very great, and the means of controlling it very inadequate, the burden resting almost solely on the justices of the peace. The justices, in their turn, were largely dependent on their position and personal standing in local society to keep their subordinates in order; they could rely on little else. Government would always have been reluctant to do anything which might weaken that position, and at a time of acute external crisis, Portland was bound to be doubly reluctant.

Indeed, there is some question whether the Committee itself seriously expected any action. After the long delay caused by the government reshuffle, the matter is not mentioned again until 30 January 1795, when the Secretary was instructed to inform Hinton that 'the Chairman will write to the Duke of Portland as he requested'.[2] It would appear, therefore, that no further action would have been taken without prodding from Oxford, and such action as was taken may well have been to satisfy constituents, rather than from any expectation of success. The fact was that the Committee had already achieved a large measure of success. Dundas had responded quickly to its initial representations with a special investigation, which, if there was cause for it, may well have given the magistrates

[1] Minutes, 29 March 1795.
[2] Ibid., 30 January 1795.

pause. At any rate, Hinton, an eminent Baptist divine, did not desist from his activities in the area—and he had no further difficulties.

There is certainly no hint of a feeling of betrayal in the Committee's Minutes. Quite the contrary, it seems to have been convinced of the government's good faith throughout the period of acute tension in the nineties. Smith himself, at a time when he was in bitter opposition to almost all of its policies, went out of his way to testify to the co-operation which he had received in safeguarding the Dissenting academies from the strictures of the Seditious Meetings Acts. In an acknowledgement of a resolution of thanks passed at the General Meeting of the Deputies of 18 December 1795, he stressed the fact that

the conduct of both the Attorney and Solicitor General to me on this occasion was so perfectly candid and liberal and they both showed so much readiness to comply with such alterations as I suggested that I should feel gratified in being empowered to transmit to them some expression of the sense the Committee entertains of their behaviour.

The Committee promptly passed, and sent to Smith, a resolution of thanks to Sir John Scott (later Lord Eldon) and Sir John Mitford.[1]

In view of the dark picture which is usually, and correctly, painted of Dissenting affairs in the nineties, the co-operative attitude of government is worth stressing. Neither Dundas, nor Portland, nor Eldon is noted for liberal opinions, and Pitt at one time—January 1800—was considering an amendment to the Toleration Act which would have severely limited the freedom of Dissenting preachers and teachers.[2] But, whatever the personal prejudices of its

---

[1] Ibid., 18 December 1795.

[2] The precise nature of this intended legislation remains unclear. The Committee seems to have been under the mistaken impression that it was to explain and amend the Act 'with regard to the burial of infants' and Smith was requested to watch the business when it came before Parliament (ibid., 31 January 1800). According to Dr Thomas Coke, it 'would have destroyed itinerant preachers, root and branch' (quoted in R. I. and S. Wilberforce *The Life of William Wilberforce* [London, 1838], III, 512). And F. K. Brown p. 223ff., believes that it would have endangered the activities of the Evangelicals. In any case, Wilberforce opposed the projected legislation, and successfully.

members, the fact is that the central government, unlike some of its representatives in the localities, and a large number of the people over whom it ruled, did not succumb to those prejudices. There is certainly nothing in the proceedings of the Deputies' Committee to indicate that when Portland stated that 'the protection of the Protestant Dissenters in the peaceable and legal exercise of their religious worship will always be an object of the attention of Government', he was speaking with his tongue in his cheek.

The fact that during the time of greatest stress—and long afterwards—the government was the Committee's firmest, most consistent, and often its only, ally, was not lost upon the Committee of the Deputies. William Smith and his friends had seen the fear and hatred which their agitation for Repeal had aroused; they had been profoundly disillusioned to see popular execration of their cause, instead of the support which they had expected to follow the public airing of their grievances; and they had been impressed by the speedy assistance government had given in the protection of their rights. They drew the obvious—if in future not always the correct— conclusion: safety lay in keeping quiet, progress in discreet negotiation. It was a conclusion which was to have the profoundest effect on Dissenting strategy in the next thirty years.

CHAPTER SIX

SMITH AND THE WHIGS, 1793–1804

Whatever tactics Smith chose to adopt as a member of the Deputies' Committee, his personal political life showed a marked and consistent adherence to the most liberal Whig principles. Nor was he the kind of man who was content merely to voice his opinions in Parliament; he strove to implement them with all the energy and influence at his disposal. His energy cannot be doubted, and his influence was growing. While Smith was coming to be the most important Dissenting politician, and was advancing to a position of considerable standing within the Whig ranks, he retained his place within the small inner circle of the Anti-Slave Trade party in Parliament. He had a foot in several camps, which allowed him considerable manoeuvrability. This situation he did not fail to exploit.

Smith's essay into personal diplomacy in the Stone affair was not an unqualified success. He was not, however, without a somewhat more successful precedent. Pitt is usually given great credit for having negotiated to the end in an attempt to avoid war with France—it was Smith who was mainly responsible for arranging those negotiations.

It was an extremely complicated business. The Marquis de Chauvelin, the former French Ambassador, had ceased to be recognized by the British government on the deposition of the King, but he had remained in London as the agent of his government. There was strong reason to believe that he was engaged in stirring up what disaffection he could, and no doubt that in a short time he had rendered himself *persona non grata* to the ministry. There was no chance either of negotiating or of arranging negotiations through

89

such a representative; but Chauvelin's powerful friends in the Jacobin Club made his recall a political impossibility. P. M. H. Lebrun, the French Foreign Minister, was therefore forced to have recourse to special secret agents to by-pass the official agent. Two of these, Morgues and Noël, were in close touch with W. A. Miles, a confidential agent of Pitt; and Morgues got so far as to have several interviews with Charles Long, joint Secretary to the Treasury. But both their relative insignificance and the close connexions which they were at the same time establishing with Fox, made it impossible that they should get any further. It was at this point, November 1792, that Hugues-Bernard Maret (later Napoleon's Foreign Minister and Duc de Bassano), an official of the Foreign Office, and a close friend of Lebrun, arrived in England, apparently on private business for the Duc d'Orleans and without any official status.[1]

But on 29 November Maret wrote Lebrun that

. . . M. William Smith, ce membre du Parlement qui avait déjà eu une conférence avec Noël, demande avec instance à parler à quelqu'un qui tienne au gouvernment francais. *On m'a proposé de le voir*. . . . Je me suis décidé à défferer mon départ, qui devait avoir lieu aujourd'hui, presqu'à l'instant *même* ou cette ouverture m'a été faite. J'irai donc demain chez M. Smith.[2]

What made Smith's demand so worthy of attention was the fact that he offered a prospect of seeing the Prime Minister. Pitt had apparently already sanctioned the idea of Smith's conducting preliminary negotiations, and had arranged to keep himself informed of the results through Charles Long.

The two men accordingly met on 30 November. Smith demanded information on the intentions of the French government on three crucial points. Was there any plan to invade Holland? Could some compromise be reached with regard to the opening of the Scheldt? Did the decree of 19 November, promising French aid to other peoples in overthrowing their governments, apply to England? Maret gave his strong assurance with respect to the first and third points, and hinted at the possibility of some arrangement over the

[1] J. Holland Rose, *William Pitt and the Great War* (London, 1911), p. 79.
[2] Le baron Alfred Auguste Ernouf, *Maret, Duc de Bassano* (Paris, 1878), p. 89.

Scheldt at a future date. Smith, on his side, was able to assure Maret that Pitt was more opposed to war than many members of the opposition. He admitted that there had been negotiations for an alliance with Spain, but denied that Pitt had played any part in them. And, although he dismissed the possibility of immediate recognition for the new French regime so soon after its recent provocations, he was very definite in not ruling out the possibility at a future date. The results of this interview were striking and immediate. Several hours after it had terminated, Maret was informed that Pitt would be happy to receive him.[1]

Pitt was greatly impressed with Maret at their meeting on 2 December, and expressed a willingness to receive him officially if the French government was willing to provide him with proper credentials. This would have been a step forward of no small importance. It was not to be, however. When Chauvelin learned of the interviews, he was able to raise such a stir in Paris that Lebrun repudiated Maret and insisted that only the former ambassador was qualified to negotiate. This news arriving on 13 December, Maret immediately sought out Smith with the request that he arrange another interview with the Prime Minister. Once again, Smith was able to produce an almost immediate response. Pitt agreed to receive Maret the next day. It was in vain—he would have nothing further to do with Chauvelin under any conditions.

This was not quite the end of the business. After the execution of the King in January, the French government rather belatedly decided to send Maret to London as its *chargé d'affaires*. Upon his arrival he again sought out Smith at Parndon, with yet another request for assistance. This time Smith was not successful; matters had gone too far. It is perhaps surprising that he had been successful so long as he had, but Patty Smith gives the clue to that success in her remembrance of this last visit. Maret, she said, came to Parndon 'to know if my father could thro' Mr. Wilberforce once more obtain him audience of Mr. Pitt. . . .'[2] Patty can certainly be trusted on this point; she accompanied her father and mother on their trip to

[1] H. B. Maret to P. M. H. Lebrun, 2 December 1792, *A Collection of State Papers relative to the War against France* (London, 1794), pp. 220–1.

[2] Patty Smith to Mrs Thomas Malthus, n.d., Duff Papers.

Paris in 1802 when they saw a great deal of the Duc de Bassano, and must have heard the whole affair discussed in detail. Nor can there be any other explanation of this strange situation in which a member of the opposition conducted negotiations for a Prime Minister. Smith's closeness to Wilberforce placed him in a unique and very useful position.

Certainly Pitt had no reason to love Smith for himself alone, and was to have ever less reason. No voice was to be louder in the cause of freedom, peace, and Reform than that of the member for Camelford.

At the special request of James Muir, who was a customer of the family firm, Smith undertook the cause of his son, the radical attorney sentenced in 1793 to fourteen years in Botany Bay for his activities in connexion with the Scottish Convention.[1] In Parliament he defended Muir and his fellow sufferer the Unitarian minister Thomas Fysshe Palmer, and besides this used all his influence with Wilberforce to gain the latter's intervention with Pitt.[2]

The Treason and Sedition bills of 1795 also occupied his attention for a broader reason than their already noticed implications for Dissent. He was active in the organization of public meetings in and near London to oppose them, and pressed his friends to be likewise active in their localities.[3] But the incident in the whole controversy which provided the real test of Smith's principle occurred when the Whig leaders attempted to apply the rod of persecution to an opponent's back. Charles Sturt, in the process of introducing a petition from the London Corresponding Society (which represented radical and largely working-class reformers) turned attention to some of the more extreme publications of John Reeves in which it had been stated that 'the kingly government may go on in all its functions, without Lords or Commons . . .; but without the king, his parliament is no more'. On the basis of this Sturt moved that Reeves be prosecuted for a libel on the House of Commons. Fox, Grey, and Erskine took up the theme; but Smith, though he had less cause to love Reeves than any of them, would have none of it:

[1] James Muir to Messrs Smith, 11 December 1793, Smith Collection (Duke).
[2] Wilberforce to William Smith, n.d., Smith Collection (Duke).
[3] Wyvill, V, 306–7.

. . . He was averse to prosecution in general for publications, unless they tended to some overt act of a breach of the peace. However absurd, false, or unconstitutional a book might be, he should only wish to meet it with refutation and exposure.[1]

This was precisely the point of the argument against the Treason and Sedition bills, and nothing could persuade Smith to stray from it.

But though he took a firmly liberal line, Smith was never to be pushed to a point where the more extreme radical ideas had any appeal for him. This was shown clearly in the part which he played in hammering out a Reform programme for the moderate Whig reformers represented in 'The Friends of the People'. Early in 1795 two plans were laid before that Society, one drawn up by Philip Francis, the other by Wyvill. Francis's proposed a uniform household franchise, single-member constituencies, and the payment of members out of the public revenue. In the event that all these conditions were met, and not otherwise, the plan called for more frequent elections, which

might be triennial, biennial, or even annual, as they were in former times. Members of Parliament, who acted faithfully, would generally be re-chosen, but it is neither safe nor constitutional to leave any Representative very long out of risk with his constituents.[2]

Wyvill's plan was, on the whole, more moderate. He suggested that, instead of a uniform franchise and single-member constituencies, 'a competent number of little venal and enslaved boroughs in England, not less than the number proposed by Mr. Pitt in the year 1785, should be disfranchised'. The right of representation thus obtained should be transferred to the counties, parts of the Metropolis, and to Sheffield, Birmingham, Manchester, and Leeds. Householders and copyholders of the value of forty shillings should be added to the electorate throughout the kingdom. The plan agreed with Francis's on the payment of members. But there was a sting in the tail. The final proposal came down strongly for annual Parliaments.

Wyvill forwarded a copy of his proposal to Smith, and the latter's

[1] *Parliamentary History*, XXXII, 676.   [2] Wyvill, V, xviii–xxiv.

comments are most revealing. He generally agreed with Francis's plan, but with very significant qualifications. What appealed to him most was the provision for a uniform household suffrage. This would be the 'most effectual and radical Reform'. But he was very explicit in not wishing to go further. The suffrage was to be '*by no means Universal. . . .*' He was extremely sceptical of the idea of paying members. The only reasons he could see for it were to 'mark dependence on the constituent' and 'to secure attendance on duty'. It is hardly strange therefore that he considered it an unnecessary expense. Even more significant was his reaction to annual Parliamentary elections. He preferred every 'three years, or if one, a proportion only to go out in rotation'. But he was 'very doubtful' of the whole idea of making Parliaments shorter.[1] Smith wanted a selective franchise, and he wanted only a limited dependence even on these select electors.

But though Smith wanted to go just so far, that distance he was firmly determined to go. He saw no reason to place his aims lower than what was, to his mind, the essential point of household suffrage. As he told Wyvill:

On *your hypothesis, that more cannot be done*, I should be much disposed to agree with you on almost every point, could it be proved that *so* much could be accomplished; but I fairly own that, as yet, I expect nothing, and [that I am convinced] that more may be done when the nation shall be sufficiently awake to the importance of the subject to call imperiously for some Reform, without which it will, I fear, never be given. An uniformity of qualifications, unembarrassed by charters and other partial privileges, throughout the whole Kingdom, does appear to me a most desirable object in every point of view—so highly important that, in my present way of thinking, I would willingly wait some years longer to attain this point.[2]

Therefore Smith continued to support Francis's plan and presided at the meeting of the Society on 31 May 1795 which finally adopted it.[3]

It was not until May of 1797 that any programme was placed before Parliament. Then, the bill which Grey proposed had dropped most of the plan's provisions, except the one which most appealed

[1] Wyvil, V, pp. 269–73.   [2] Ibid., p. 269.   [3] Ibid., p. xvii.

to Smith, the household franchise which was, he said, 'the most obvious test of property on the one side and of selected population on the other'.[1] He gave the bill his heartiest support, demonstrating in the process the moderate aims which prompted that support. Smith still thought very much in the traditional terms of a balanced Constitution. The great question involved in Reform he defined thus:

It was of no account to examine whether the landed representation had the superiority over the commercial, or whether the commercial was greater than the landed; the question was whether the crown had not a domineering influence over both?

In his mind, there was no doubt of the answer. The problem then was to restore the independence of the Commons:

He demanded to know, whether, if the choice of representation was as free and popular as it ought to be, it would be either probable or rational that the people of England should delegate a number of persons in the pay of the crown to watch, examine, and control the expenses of the crown? Was it likely that, when they were creating a barrier between themselves and their rulers, they would choose the hired servants of government to constitute their barrier.[2]

The use of the term 'barrier' is significant. The Commons, to his way of thinking, had an independent existence of its own, standing between the Crown and the people, and it ought to be controlled completely by neither. As will be seen from his relations with Norwich, Smith never varied from a principle which he had laid down in 1792 that it was 'the safest and wisest doctrine, and the most conformable to the constitution of this House as a deliberative assembly, that on all matters of general and national concern, each member should hold himself bound to decide only as the dictates of his own conscience shall direct. . . .'[3] In order for a member to have such freedom he must obviously not be placed in too close dependence on his constituents. Hence Smith's dislike of annual Parliaments. The point of Reform in his mind was only to extend the franchise far enough to ensure an end to corruption, especially to

[1] *Parliamentary History*, XXXIII, 679.
[2] Ibid., pp. 696–7.   [3] Ibid., XXIX, 1248.

95

undue Crown influence, and to place it in the hands of people who could be expected to use it wisely and temperately. Nor, as his attitude toward the payment of members would indicate, and his subsequent stand for a stiff property qualification proves conclusively,[1] did he foresee a radical change in the composition of the House as a result of Reform.

Smith was no democrat. His background had not been of the kind that could be expected to produce one, and his subsequent experience had not been such as to alter entirely his inherited scepticism. With the violent religious bigotry which the English lower classes had of late exhibited on numerous occasions, it is hardly surprising that Smith, as a Dissenter, did not have much faith in the good sense of the common man. Nor did he see any immediate cause for hope. As he had written to Wyvill in 1796:

. . . The extreme torpor of the people . . . makes me despair of any good effects from the best directed efforts on any subject whatever. Were it not for the consolatory "Nil desperandum," I should almost think "Desperandum esset de Republica."[2]

The great majority of Englishmen were, in Smith's mind, aroused to all the wrong issues and to none of the right ones. Under such circumstances, it was impossible to move toward reform any way but slowly and cautiously.

Had his pessimism been completely unleavened, it might have produced the profoundest conservatism, but it was not. Smith was a man of action, not a man of speculation, and his philosophical views must be gleaned from passing references in his speeches and correspondence. But such evidence shows that he was deeply influenced by the doctrine of Necessarianism, advanced by Joseph Priestley and first made part of an academic curriculum by Smith's friend Belsham at Daventry.[3] The basic ideas were simple enough. The universe, moral as well as natural, moved according to laws set in motion by God. These laws were inexorable, but man by the use of his God-given reason could, as the great men of science had clearly demonstrated, understand these laws and conform to them. And man had

---

[1] *Hansard's Parliamentary Debates* (hereafter cited as *Hansard*), XXII, 143.
[2] Wyvill, V, 333.   [3] McLachlan, p. 162.

a positive duty to understand and conform, for by so doing he was advancing the divine plan: Necessarianism was not fatalism.[1] The ideas of the Enlightenment, as interpreted in the Unitarianism of Priestley and Belsham, made Smith basically optimistic. He had a profound belief 'in a progression of improvement' decreed by Providence.[2] He also had the good Necessarian's urge to do all he could to assist Providence. Hence his liberalism. He could believe in a free play of ideas, because he believed that truth would always win in the end. Thus he feared neither Reeves nor the corresponding societies; both played their part in the unshackling of human reason. And thus he fought to keep every channel of information and education open.

Where Smith disagreed with the radicals was in his conception of the timing of the divine plan—and this would soon be a very important disagreement—but for the time being his ideas placed him among the most liberal of the Whig politicians. He was at one with Fox in his assessment of the most important and most pressing issues of the day—peace, Reform, the abolition of all religious tests in civil matters, and the abolition of the Slave Trade.[3]

Not only were Smith's principles correct, he was also able to prove himself a most useful colleague. He was particularly useful in complicated matters which required a careful mastery of detail. In 1795 he led the Whig attack on Pitt's war loan of that year. This loan of eighteen millions had not been offered for public tender, in contravention of a policy which Pitt himself had initiated. Rather it appeared that the minister had made use of it to reward his supporters in the City. On 15 December Smith moved for a Committee of the Whole House to inquire into the matter. This was refused, but a Select Committee was appointed to deal with the question, with Smith as its chairman. The committee held five meetings before

[1] For a detailed consideration of the intellectual background of Unitarian liberalism see R. K. Webb, *Harriet Martineau: A Radical Victorian* (London, 1960), chap. III.

[2] See, for instance, Smith's speech at Norwich in 1816 on Parliamentary reform, *Norfolk Chronicle*, 19 October 1816.

[3] C. J. Fox to William Smith, 15 November 1801, Fox Papers, British Museum (hereafter cited as BM), Add. MSS. 47569, ff. 111–13.

Christmas and eight more after the recess, presenting a fifty-page report of its findings on 9 February. They were most damaging. In the debates on 22 February Smith was able to give a minute account of the negotiations for the loan as well as of previous negotiations of the same persons with the government. He showed that the list of subscribers to the loan corresponded almost exactly with a list of persons who had held a meeting at the Grocers Hall to endorse the bills dealing with Treasonable Practices and Seditious Meetings. He was also able to prove conclusively that the profits to the subscribers had reached the fantastic sum of £2,160,000. And he concluded by moving a string of eighty resolutions, carefully grounded on the evidence, censuring the government. It is such stuff that maintains oppositions, and, though the resolutions were naturally defeated, Smith received his reward in the form of election to the Whig Club shortly thereafter.[1]

It was also early in 1796 that Smith's house began to be mentioned as a meeting place of the Whig *élite*. Samuel Rogers opens his *Recollections* with an account of a dinner at Smith's on 19 March at which Fox, George Tierney, Sir Francis Baring, and James Mackintosh were present. He was beginning to be entertained, as well, in the best circles. Several weeks later Rogers was present at another dinner, this time at Serjeant Heywood's attended by Smith, Fox, Lord Derby, Lord Stanley, and Lord Lauderdale.[2]

Smith moved easily among his new associates. In 1798 he resumed his partnership in the wholesale grocery, taking his father's place at the head of the firm. But his mercantile cares, which might have been a detriment in the aristocratic Whig circles, were worn so easily that hardly anyone but himself ever thought about them. Even his best friends forgot. Wilberforce apologized some years later for being several months late in offering his condolences on a disastrous fire in a distillery in which Smith was a partner, but 'I have not been used to class you in my own mind among men of business . . . '.[3] The greatest effect of Smith's re-entry into busi-

[1] *Parliamentary History*, XXXII and XXXIII, *passim.*, and Lady Stephen's MS., chap. VI, p. 19.

[2] *Recollections* (London, 1859) pp. 1 and 12.

[3] Wilberforce to William Smith, 5 September 1806, Smith Collection (Duke).

ness was to add another three thousand pounds per annum to his income. Doubtless it was useful in helping to sustain the expansion in his way of life necessitated by his new social and political position.

In 1794 the Clapham house was forsaken, and No. 6 Park Street (now 16 Queen Anne's Gate and home of PEP[1]), only five minutes walk from the House, became his residence during the session. Lord Muncaster warned him that it had proved too expensive for its two previous owners, Lords Apsley and Malmesbury.[2] But expense seems to have been no object, and there was no doubt that it was a splendid house. The main apartments were spacious, with fine Adam ceilings and fireplaces, and overlooked Birdcage Walk and St James's Park beyond. There was also a gallery for the display of Smith's growing collection of paintings. Sir Joshua Reynolds's 'Mrs Siddons as the Tragic Muse' occupied the place of honour under the sky-light. And there were a number of other pictures of note. In 1793 he had acquired Rembrandt's 'The Mill' at the duc d'Orleans's London sale. At the sale of Calonne's pictures in 1795 he bought, besides 'Mrs Siddons', Metsu's 'The Sportsman's Visit'. Like the Prince of Wales, he had a special liking for the Dutch masters. He owned two other Rembrandts, 'Portrait of a Rabbi' and 'Rembrandt's Mother'; several Cuyps; Hobbema's 'Water Mill'; and two Ruysdaels. There were also several pictures by Vandyck and several by Rubens; Gainsborough's 'Two Keepers going up a Wooded Lane'; and another Reynolds. In all Smith had about seventy pictures of some merit, enough to make him a noted collector in his own day and one of the most prominent among the small group of noble and aristocratic patrons of art who founded the British Institution in 1805.[3]

Parndon was also building to match Park Street's magnificence. From 1797 to 1803 the original Georgian house was transformed into a large, vaguely Italianate structure, more than double the size of the old house, with its twenty-odd rooms. To modern eyes the architectural transformation can only appear highly questionable,

[1] Political and Economic Planning.

[2] 'Notes dictated by Patty Smith', p. 34, Leigh-Smith Papers.

[3] See Lady Stephen's MS., chap. V, pp. 11–12, and W. T. Whitley *Art in England, 1800–1820* (Cambridge, 1928) and *Artists and Their Friends in England, 1700–1799* (London, 1928), *passim*.

but there is no doubt of the spacious elegance created within. Smith lavished most care on the library which was to house his collection of some two thousand books.[1] His daughter remembered it as

the most agreeable room I ever inhabited. It was long and divided into three compartments, if one may call them so, by arches joining the large projecting book cases on each side, so that there were facilities for a large party in the large middle compartment and for any number of small groups and tete a tetes on the sofas which stood against the walls following all their angles.[2]

It did not lack for company to fill it. At both houses when the family was in residence there was a constant round of dinners and enter-tainments, patronized by a variety of the political, religious, artistic, literary, and scientific friends whom Smith's varied interests drew around him. In order to be a Whig, it was necessary to live like one, and this condition Smith achieved.

The hectic political life continued unabated. In June 1796 Smith once again stood for Sudbury, being returned, as he informed Wyvill, 'with little trouble to me, and with as many circumstances of honour as are usually to be met with in the present impure state of even the most popular Borough elections'.[3] It was his period of darkest pessimism, one shared by his leader. Writing to congratu-late him, Fox remarked that

I think exactly as you do, that we ought to make a stand against acknowledging the justice of the war. [But] from what I hear there is not the smallest chance of peace.[4]

Fox was discouraged, so discouraged that he was soon to withdraw himself from the fray. Smith never would reach this point. The parting of the ways came after the defeat of Grey's motion for Reform on 26 May 1797, in which Smith and Sheridan had acted as tellers for the small minority of ninety-one. This was enough for

---

[1] *A Catalogue of the Genuine Library of a Gentleman . . . which Will be Sold by Mr. Sotheby . . . on Friday, June 21, 1822*, endorsed by Smith 'My own Library, chiefly from Parndon', Leigh-Smith Papers.

[2] Julia Smith, 'Recollections', II, 17, Leigh-Smith Papers.

[3] Wyvill, V, 334.

[4] Quoted in Lady Stephen's MS., chap. VI, p. 14.

Fox who announced that he would end his regular attendance at the House. Most of the Whigs followed him in secession. Not Smith; with Whitbread and George Tierney, he remained to carry on the hopeless fight.

Never was Smith's attendance more regular than during the secession. He was there a fortnight after the debate on Reform to criticize the government policies which had led to the mutinies at Nore and Spithead, as well as its proposed means for preventing such occurrences in future.[1] He was there to oppose the suspension of specie payments which he termed a flagrant robbery of the Bank's depositors. And he was there in 1798 to give his vigorous and violent opposition, which would continue even under the Talents, to the new Income Tax, which, he said, would put 'a spy over every man's property', and would therefore constitute a most violent attack on the liberties of the subject.[2] Fox watched and approved, writing to R. Fitzpatrick:

As to public affairs, I think what W. Smith said in the House of Commons is perfectly true; that if people will not resist this inquisition, they will resist nothing.[3]

Doubtless, it was not inconvenient to have someone in the House to keep before it the Whig line, even if one did not wish to attend oneself.

The Whigs were to continue to have reason for satisfaction with Smith. His attendance at the House continued to be as regular, and his criticism of the government to be as detailed and as biting, right up to the peace of 1801. To this he gave his heartiest support. Following its conclusion, he decided, after consultation with Fox,[4] to give Addington's ministry his qualified support. But his line changed with that of Fox, and for the same reason, the renewal of the war in May 1803. Generally speaking, Smith was willing to put all his trust in the leader of his party, faithfully following all the Whigs'

[1] *Parliamentary History*, XXXIII, 801 and 803.

[2] Ibid., XXXIV, 97.

[3] Russell, *Memorials and Correspondence*, III, 282.

[4] C. J. Fox to William Smith, 15 November 1801, Fox Papers, BM Add. MSS. 47569, ff. 111–13.

tortuous twistings and turnings which preceded their entry into office in 1806. As Fox wrote of the junction with the Grenvilles in March 1804:

. . . I will fairly own that of all my friends, you were one of whose approbation, even if I had gone further than I have gone, I felt myself most secure. You had expressed your wish for a junction, even with Pitt. . . .[1]

Smith trusted Fox and believed in him implicitly. The answer to all problems was to get Fox into power, and he was willing to follow any course which would lead to that happy end. It was to be different when in office the party felt it necessary to sacrifice principles in the interests of power. Then Smith was to take a different line, but in opposition he was everything the party leaders could wish.

His position within the party was being increasingly recognized. In April 1802 he was elected to that very exclusive dining club, for the most part made up of Whig aristocrats and Edinburgh intellectuals, 'The King of Clubs'.[2] For the socially discriminating Whigs, there was probably no higher expression of their confidence and regard. The membership was limited to thirty, including Lords Holland, Cowper, Kinnaird, and King, Lord Henry Petty (soon to be the Marquis of Lansdowne), the Hon William Lamb, the Hon J. W. Ward, James Abercromby, Alexander Baring, Henry Brougham, Thomas Denman, Samuel Rogers, James Scarlett, James Mackintosh, John Whishaw, Samuel Romilly, Francis Horner, the Rev Sydney Smith, Francis Jeffrey, the Rev T. R. Malthus, and Henry Hallam. The members met for dinner about once a month at one of the large London taverns (at first the Crown and Anchor and later the Freemasons), dined well and usually consumed from a half bottle to a bottle of claret apiece, and, doubtless aided by the wine, carried on long and vigorous conversations on whatever happened to strike their fancy. Francis Horner, on a visit to London in 1802, found the conversation very pleasing, consisting 'chiefly of literary reminiscences, anecdotes of authors, criticisms of books etc.' Another

---

[1] C. J. Fox to William Smith, Fox Papers, BM Add. MSS. 47569, ff. 168–9.
[2] 'Register of the King of Clubs, 1798–1823', 10 April 1802, BM Add. MSS. 37337.

Scot, the poet Thomas Campbell, was less complimentary, finding
that 'much as the art and erudition of these men please an auditor
at the first or second visit, the trial of minds becomes at last
fatiguing. . . . The mind, it is true, is electrified and quickened,
and the spirits are finely exhilarated; but one grand fault pervades
the whole institution—their inquiries are desultory, and all improvements to be reaped must be accidental'.[1] It was a powerful,
and sometimes overpowering, combination of high position and
intellect. Smith, however, appears to have been able to hold his own,
faithfully attending the dinners of the club until its demise in 1823.
And even as critical an observer as his own son was forced to admit
that Smith could, when he chose, shine in the best circles. On one
occasion, having accompanied his father on a visit to Lord Holland,
Ben reported to Patty:

They talked a great deal about the Slave Trade and the quarrels with
America and I have never heard my father speak with more ease. I am
not surprised that he has gained the affection of the lady [Holland], if
he always acts there as he did this morning. There was nothing of the
Presbyterian preacher in his manner of speaking and 'point de mau-
vaise honte'.[2]

This sober leader of the Dissenters and darling of Clapham demonstrated a remarkable adaptability and a considerable talent for
getting along in any society he chose to move in.

Not only was Smith received into the charmed circle of Whig
society, he was on occasion coming to be summoned to the most
exalted of the inner party councils. In May 1803, for instance, when
the violent breach with Addington occurred, Smith was called to
the meeting which was to plan the strategy on a motion for the
suspension of hostilities pending negotiations. Fox wrote Grey
suggesting that

Whitbread's house will be best for our meeting, which, however,
should be a small one. I think, besides us three, only Erskine, W.
Smith and Sheridan. I name these because I think Smith is a man who

[1] Quoted in W. P. Courtney, 'The King of Clubs', in Lady Seymour, ed.,
The 'Pope' of Holland House, (London, 1906), pp. 339–40.
[2] Ben Smith to Patty Smith, 29 April 1806, Leigh-Smith Papers.

likes consultations, and who is not unlikely to have made observations on the paper which may have escaped me. Sheridan will probably not come; but I would not let him have it to say he was not asked.[1]

The remark about 'a man who liked consultations' may well, especially with what follows on Sheridan, suggest the rather patronizing assessment that Smith was not a man who liked to be ignored; but even putting this, the worst, construction on to it, it clearly suggests that Fox thought that he was someone who ought not to be ignored. Smith was coming to be a man to be reckoned with—in Whig circles and elsewhere.

[1] Russell, *Memorials and Correspondence*, III, 412.

CHAPTER SEVEN

SMITH AND THE SAINTS

T here was no question on which William Smith felt more
deeply or more passionately than the abolition of the Slave
Trade. For him it was a matter in which qualification was
impossible, in which moderation and patience were out of the
question. As on no other issue, the politician in Smith was subdued,
and the basis of his liberalism showed forth.

His opposition to the Trade came directly from his own deep
religious conviction, from his profound belief in that 'Almighty
Father, "who has made of one blood all nations of men"!' From this
fundamental fact everything else followed easily:

Whatever right over man may be legitimately exercised by the society
to which he belongs; to whatever privation of liberty he may subject
himself, by crime legally proved; though he may forfeit even life
itself; yet as long as he remains a rational, moral, accountable creature, it arises out of the essence of his nature that he cannot be the
proper object of barter and sale, and be indiscriminately transferred
as property from hand to hand—far less than such right can by any
possibility be acquired over his certainly innocent offspring.[1]

God had decreed the greatest possible freedom for men, and to
deprive them of any part of it, unless it could be proven that it was a
just and necessary forfeiture based upon their own actions, was a
most heinous crime. Even worse, it was the grossest impiety.

I say impious: for I hold it to be no less, to erect municipal institutions
in opposition to the eternal law of nature;—to put property, the

---

[1] *A Letter to William Wilberforce*, pp. 11 and 27.

creature of man, in competition with man himself, the creature of God.[1]

Smith was not, it is true, ready to go the whole way by 1807, nor for a long time thereafter: 'I would not emancipate;—by any sudden measure, by any legal provision directly for that purpose, I would not, now or *perhaps* ever, emancipate.'[2] (By this he obviously meant only those slaves at that time in a state of bondage, not, as he had said, their 'innocent offspring'.) His reasoning was founded on what he conceived to be true freedom:

Having from men transformed them into cattle, having stifled every better feeling, I would not mock them with a liberty which we have incapacitated them from enjoying. . . .[3]

With this kind of reasoning, Abolition could not be a real end in itself. Nor was it for Smith or for many of his Evangelical allies. As Wilberforce wrote in 1806, opposing a plan for the importation of Chinese coolies into the Islands:

. . . It would expose the cause of abolition (to you I may add and finally of Emancipation also) to the discredit it would incur from the failure of a fair trial by ourselves (so our opponents would represent it) whether another system could not be substituted in place of working West India Estates by Slaves' labour.[4]

It has become fashionable of late to throw doubt on the motives of those who led the fight for Abolition; some even suggest that the only point of the campaign in their minds was to broaden support for their 'real programme', a general moral reformation of society.[5] This is to do them a very grave injustice. Abolition was, it is true, only a part of the reformation of morals which they aimed to achieve, as was the campaign in England and the introduction of Christianity into India. The point was to make the whole world Christian. The introduction of Christian principles was to solve all problems. But in order to introduce real Christianity into the West Indies, as well as

[1] *A Letter to William Wilberforce*, pp. 29–30.   [2] Ibid., p. 28.   [3] Ibid., p. 28.

[4] Wilberforce to William Smith, 5 September 1806, Smith Collection (Duke).

[5] Brown, pp. 106–15. For a corrective to this point of view, see Standish Meacham, *Henry Thornton of Clapham* (Cambridge, Mass., 1964).

to completely reform the manners and morals of Englishmen, the terrible degradation of slavery, degrading to those who enslaved as well as to those who were enslaved, must be removed. Abolition may have been only a part of the Saints' programme, but it was an important part.

This is not of course to argue that Wilberforce and the Evangelicals were political liberals. This they certainly were not. Political liberalism was completely irrelevant to their scheme of things. It was not political institutions which enslaved men but their own moral degradation. It mattered little what the institutions were so long as man himself was morally and religiously sound on this earth, and thus safe for eternity. This was not Smith's outlook. He too believed in, and supported on all points, the world-wide campaign for moral reform. But he saw it only as a stage in that 'progression of improvement' which Providence intended, as a part of the process of education which was ultimately to prepare all men for the exercise of real freedom and of political power. He made this very clear some years later in a speech on bull-baiting:

Gentlemen apprehended that they rose above vulgar prejudices and were great philosophers because they considered the lower class of people entitled to their own amusements. Such an opinion, so far from being philosophic or philanthropic was founded on an unworthy motive. He thought it arose . . . from a contempt for the lower class of people. It was as much as to say, 'poor creatures, let them alone: they have few amusements, let them enjoy them.' It was similar to the language which, for a long period of time, was common in the colonies —'as long as they [the slaves] work that is all we want, let them seek their own amusements; what signifies it troubling about their morals; we don't care about these, let them take their own way.' . . . Let those who wished the people to be nothing more than hewers of wood, and drawers of water, entertain such sentiments; but if they wished to make them rational beings, let them not educate them with one hand, and with the other turn them loose to sports like these.[1]

But though Smith went far beyond the Evangelicals in his ultimate aims, their immediate objectives were, and were to remain throughout their lifetimes, identical on many issues. Their common zeal in

[1] *Hansard*, n.s. XIV, 649–50.

the great cause of Abolition and in the greater cause of a moral reformation of which it was a part, was sufficient to mask differences on many others. Nor is there any question that among these sober reformers Smith felt more at home than with any other group of men. They were his kind of people, and some, like Henry Thornton, had been childhood friends. It was the son of James Stephen who recorded for posterity 'the heart-stirring laughter of the stout member for Norwich. . . .' Sir James Stephen also wrote the highest eulogium on his character:

He lived as if to show how much of the coarser duties of this busy world may be undertaken by a man of quick sensibility, without impairing the finer sense of the beautiful in nature and in art; and as if to prove how much a man of ardent benevolence may enjoy of this world's happiness, without any steeling of the heart to the wants and calamities of others. . . . If he had gone mourning all his days, he could scarcely have acquired a more tender pity for the miserable, or have laboured more habitually for their relief. It was his ill fortune to provoke the invective of Robert Southey, and the posthumous sneers of Walter Scott[1]—the one resenting a too well merited reproach, the other indulging that hatred of Whigs and Whiggery, which in that great mind, was sometimes stronger than the love of justice. The enmity even of such men he, however, might well endure, who possessed, not merely the attachment and confidence of Charles Fox and his followers, but the almost brotherly love of William Wilberforce, of Granville Sharp and of Thomas Clarkson. Of all their fellow labourers, there was none more devoted to their cause, or whom they more entirely trusted. They, indeed, were all to a man *homoousians*, and he a disciple of Belsham. But they judged that many an erroneous opinion respecting the Redeemer's person would not deprive of his gracious approbation, and ought not to exclude from their affectionate regards, a man in whom they daily saw a transcript, however imperfect, of the Redeemer's mercy and beneficence.[2]

Stephen was wrong in believing that the Saints were ever willing to forget their friend's rejection of the Homoousios (the orthodox trinitarian formula). Far from it, they pursued his soul relentlessly, directly and deviously, and even from the grave. Shortly after the

[1] For Smith's brushes with Southey and Scott, see below pp. 188-9.
[2] *Essays in Ecclesiastical Biography* (London, 1849), II, 322–3.

death of the elder Wilberforce in 1833, his son Robert wrote to Smith:

. . . There was no one for whom I have continually heard my beloved father express a warmer affection than for you. I only wish you could have heard the deep interest with which he spoke of you the very last day that I spent with him, & the earnest desire which he expressed that on that subject which he always felt to be most important you might think as he did. You will excuse my speaking on this subject, but I have been so used to hear my dear father mention his feelings of pain at the difference of opinion between you that at such a time I cannot but speak of it. Would to God my dear Sir that as my father's friend you would allow me to speak to you on this thing freely. Surely the deep conviction of a man like my father, whose understanding as well as his sincerity all men must respect is entitled to no little consideration.

Mrs Wilberforce wrote at the same time and in very similar terms about her husband's feelings, suggesting numerous texts for Smith's consideration.[1] Zachary Macaulay was constantly taxing him on the subject. Failing success with frontal attacks, Macaulay was willing to try other means. He rejoiced in 1816 that Patty Smith, who had a great reputation for her keenness and wit, had made the acquaintance of Hannah More: 'I have a real love and affection for her father and most anxiously desire his own good & that of his children. I am glad she has come within your vortex.'[2] By their own lights, of course, the Saints could not have given a clearer proof of friendship; and there can be no doubt that the friendship was deep and uninterrupted. Contemporaries marvelled at the tolerance of the Saints in maintaining this friendship, but perhaps the tolerance was not all in one direction.

Friendship apart, Smith was most useful in the common cause. And this was very largely because he did differ from Wilberforce and the rest in his religion and in his politics. Smith, like Henry Brougham, was one of those who made a most necessary bridge between

[1] R. I. Wilberforce to William Smith, 19 August 1833, and Mrs Wilberforce to William Smith, 19 August 1833, Smith Collection (Duke).

[2] Zachary Macaulay to Hannah More, 23 July 1816, Huntington Library, San Marino, California, MY 587.

the Saints and the liberal and radical supporters of Abolition. From the nineties onwards this was essential. Most of Smith's correspondents were, like Wilberforce and his friends, ardently interested in the cause of the slaves, but more often than not they were also ardent on issues which the Saints either ignored or on which they took a highly reactionary attitude. Correspondents like John Longley, the Rochester 'well-wisher to the cause of peace, reform, and liberty',[1] and William Rathbone of Liverpool moved easily and naturally from Abolition to Reform and back again. So did J. Yule, of the Royal Physical Society of Edinburgh, who hoped that there was

no impropriety in not forwarding the petition of a Literary Society to Mr. Dundas the City Member as the Physical Society considers its members as Citizens of the World at Large and where can Human Nature find an abler Advocate than yourself?[2]

There was a similar coincidence of interests with M. Leith of Portsay, President of the Universal Liberty Club,[3] and Benjamin Cooper, Secretary of the Society for Commemorating the Glorious Revolution of 1688.[4]

Wilberforce, both from temperament and from strategy, did not wish to be too intimate with such 'Citizens of the World at Large'

[1] John Longley to William Smith, 31 January 1796, Smith Collection (Duke).

[2] J. Yule to William Smith, 25 March 1792, Smith Collection (Duke). See also Yule's letter of 23 August 1792 expressing his 'joy in beholding your name among the truly respectable Friends of the People. That God may give success to your measures is the general prayer of the North'.

[3] M. Leith to William Smith, 27 March 1792, Smith Collection (Duke). The Society had forwarded a petition to Wilberforce; but, as the petition was signed only by the President, according to Scottish custom but against a resolution of the House on this occasion, Wilberforce saw fit to return it. It is significant that he did not do so personally, but referred the matter of communicating with the friends of Universal Liberty to Smith. The Society was not displeased, asking that 'as the Club consists of a body of men who upon admission declare themselves friends to *Civil* and Religious Liberty—the Committee beg leave to request a continuation of your correspondence in other matters which they look upon as of great consequence to the nation, namely, an *equal* representation in Parliament, repeal of the Penal Laws, and trial by jury in civil cases'.

[4] Resolutions of 1791, Smith Collection (Duke).

and 'Friends to Universal Liberty'. Still, what Rathbone remarked of Liverpool—'I scarcely need say that the abolitionists here stand forward also in the Class of Reformers'[1]—held true in many other places. Doubtless, it would have been politically unwise for Wilberforce himself to have entered into too close association with the radicals, but it would have been equally unwise to have ignored their staunch support. Who better to bridge the gap than that very moderate, but very dedicated, friend of both Abolition and Liberty, 'My dear Wm.,' or, if one chose to adopt Lord Stanhope's form of address, 'Worthy Citizen'[2] Smith?

Equally useful, and for the same reasons, were Smith's close connexions with the opposition leadership in Parliament. It was very helpful to have a liaison with a foot in both camps. During the secession, for instance, it would appear to have been Smith who brought out the Whig leadership for the debates on the Slave Trade, Fox writing in 1798 that

I shall certainly be in town for the Slave Trade Monday, but as I go to London merely for that purpose I shall be obliged to you for sending me early intelligence if it is put off.[3]

Smith was clearly a special informant of Fox's on matters connected with the Trade, and quite naturally so.

If Smith was useful while the Whigs were out of power, he was to be doubly useful, when, during the final campaign, they were in power. Early in 1806 he was able to secure the intervention of Lord Moira with the Prince of Wales, eliciting the assurance that the Prince would not stir adversely.[4] He was also a constant source of information on the shifts and turns within the government; it was he, for instance, who supplied the information that Fox, having

[1] William Rathbone to William Smith, 3 February 1793, Smith Collection (Duke).
[2] See Stanhope's amusing letter to Smith of 25 January 1796 in which he tries to convince Smith—and quite obviously himself—that he does not object to his daughter's marrying Thomas Taylor, the Surgeon at Sevenoaks (quoted in Lady Stephen's MS., chap. V, p. 23).
[3] C. J. Fox to William Smith, 24 March 1798, Duff Papers.
[4] Lady Stephen's MS., chap. IX, p. 29.

successfully launched the fight for Abolition on 10 June, would not be able to continue it to its end.[1]

The summer and autumn of 1806 were filled with dangers for the cause of Abolition, dangers almost all of which stemmed from the fact that Fox was a dying man. As Smith wrote to Wilberforce:

If Grenville should now cool as a friend, or Windham grow more violent in his enmity, who is, with half the efficacy, to stimulate the one or restrain the other—in short, who is to occupy his station?[2]

It was indeed a crucial question, for the Talents (so-called because the government was formed of the leaders of several groups, supposedly combining the best talents of all) were deeply divided on this issue, as they were on many others. Besides the very influential Grenvillite William Windham, the Addingtonians were also opposed to the measure. Without strong and dominating leadership, the cause might well be shelved. The problem was to find someone to take Fox's place.

Smith thought that, as much as any other person could be, Grey was the one to assume that position, and in a series of remarkably frank letters he pressed it upon him. As he wrote on 2 July:

When . . . I conjured, and even again conjure you, not to despond, it can only be in reference to the Events which may succeed on such a catastrophe [as Fox's death]. From what you said to me the other night, and from some hints I have heard dropped, I very much fear that in such case You will be so hopeless of stemming the Tide which may set in, as not to exert your utmost Vigour in the attempt:—and therefore, tho' I may once more seem officious and obtrusive, I cannot refrain from urging upon You, not merely the expediency, but the absolute duty of forcing yourself to the level of that too probable occasion;—and, having a sufficient motive, I shall risque both the appearance of flattery, and the chance of offending, rather than omit to say what circumstances appear to me to require. You must one day, possibly 'ere long, quit the Commons;—but tho' this forms some objection to your filling Fox's general Station when he shall be no more, I yet confidently feel that You are the only man in the Kingdom

[1] Wilberforce, *Life*, III, 268.

[2] R. I. and S. Wilberforce, *The Correspondence of William Wilberforce* (London, 1840), II, 91–5.

to whom it will be yielded—and that you may be able to assume it, if You shall so please. But you must make up your Mind to sacrifice popularity more than You have ever hitherto done—You will not suspect me of meaning a sacrifice of honour or principle—but somewhat more of leisure, perhaps even also of business, a good deal probably of Taste and Disposition—and this, permit me to say, You ought to do. The Country will have a right to demand of You this Effort; for without another united struggle much of the ground gained will be lost again; and . . . I repeat that in the present state of the Party, I see none but You who would be accepted as its Leader, and for You to be so, I firmly believe depends chiefly on yourself.

If you have long seen all this, and have resolved to undertake the task, it is now time to act seriously and steadily to the point. You perform, in an exemplary manner, and as I apprehend, to the general satisfaction, the duties of your important office [at the Admiralty]; but You must not let it abstract You either from attendance or from *activity* in parliament. It must not keep You from the public Eye, nor interfere with your habits of debate. You have a right to propose to yourself as your object, the being at the Head both of the Party and the Government. I hope You do so, and will attain it, in spite of the desponding fancies which may arise in your mind.[1]

Events were ultimately to prove Smith right, both as to the character of the new leader and as to the fact that he was the only one whom the party would accept.[2] Crucial at this point, of course, was the fact that Grey was solid on the issue of the Slave Trade, which is why Smith badgered, and continued to badger, him so mercilessly.

Equally important as having proper leadership within the Whig party was, with a better possibility of success than ever before, having a well laid out plan to meet every eventuality. Wilberforce was especially concerned about the dire effects of Abolition on the West Indian social and economic structure, at least in the short run. 'I foresee', he wrote to Smith, 'a perfect hurricane on the other side of the Water, and such a number of hard cases will be stated that nothing would enable us to resist the application that would be

[1] William Smith to Lord Howick, 2 July 1806, Grey Papers, The Prior's Kitchen, Durham (hereafter cited as 'Grey Papers').

[2] On the long-persisting problem of the leadership of the party, see Austin Mitchell, *The Whigs in Opposition, 1815–1830* (Oxford, 1967).

made to Parliament to rescind or at least to suspend the measure. . . .' Nothing, that is, but taking the very highest line of principle from the beginning, which would make any backtracking impossible from 'the disgrace which Parliament would incur in the face of the whole world by reversing on grounds of Interest a measure which it had expressly declared to have adopted on principles of religion, justice and Humanity'. This recognition alone would enable them 'to withstand the torrent we shall have to encounter'. The highest line of principle was a necessary matter of tactics.[1]

Another matter on which Wilberforce thought it would be wise to think, although not yet to speak openly, was some measure to soften the blow to the planters. And he begged Smith's

most serious consideration of this subject and as you have extensive connections you may perhaps be able by having it in your mind to avail yourself of opportunities which may occur of obtaining information or such facts or suggestions as may throw light upon the different parts of the complicated subject.[2]

Smith's broad contacts were not unnoticed or unappreciated. There was one idea particularly, J. T. Barham's already noticed plan for the importation of Chinese coolies to solve the labour problem, on which 'I extremely wish to know your sentiments as well as those of two or three other friends. . . .'[3] Smith was, and was to remain, an important member in every consultation.

All this planning was, of course, based on the premise that Abolition would succeed. There were signs, however, that it might not, at least in any form which would be ultimately successful. There were indications by mid-August, almost a month before Fox's death, that Grenville might prove a serious impediment to the Saints' plans. Then, in an interview which Wilberforce reported to Smith, he had indicated that he was 'strongly bent on abolishing the Slave Trade by means of an increasing Duty on the Importation of Slaves into the Islands. . . .'[4] This was a completely unsuitable

[1] Wilberforce to William Smith, 5 September 1806, Smith Collection (Duke).
[2] Ibid.   [3] Ibid.
[4] Wilberforce to William Smith, 18 August 1806, Smith Collection (Duke).

approach for reasons which Smith summed up succinctly in his reply:

Abolition by duties with any supposable increase is at best gradual, it is liable to all manner of evasion, and every chance of eventual defeat, whilst the great principle, that solid and unsubvertible basis of all our arguments and measures is by such means almost virtually relinquished. . . .[1]

In all this Wilberforce agreed, and he was convinced that if the Abolitionists remained firm Grenville would yield:

I am therefore very anxious that all of us whose opinions are likely to have most weight should consider the subject most maturely, and after making up our own minds, should state the result to Lord G.

And he went on to enumerate those whom he had consulted on the matter, or was going to consult: 'You and Clarkson. . . . I will write to Babington and Gisborne. I have stated the Matter to Stephen and Macaulay. . . .'[2] These, in Wilberforce's mind, were the men of 'most weight' in the cause. Apparently, their influence was sufficient; no more was heard of Grenville's scheme after mid-September.

Meanwhile, Smith was busying himself in all kinds of matters in which he could be useful. He assisted Clarkson, who spent a large part of that summer at Parndon,[3] in the collection of evidence to meet a further eventuality which Grenville had hinted at—another full-scale Parliamentary inquiry. He again approached Lord Moira.[4] And he complied with Wilberforce's request that as 'you are in the habit of seeing Mr. Monroe the American Minister—it would be very well before he leaves England to obtain from him any information that may be useful to us. . . .'[5] Smith also continued to apply pressure on Grey, chiding him on 11 September that

Your attention, my dear Lord, but too willingly directs itself to the

[1] Wilberforce, *Correspondence*, II, 95.
[2] Wilberforce to William Smith, 18 August 1806, Smith Collection (Duke).
[3] Thomas Clarkson to Robert Southey, 21 September 1806, Clarkson Papers, Huntington Library, HM 12, 301.
[4] Wilberforce, *Correspondence*, II, 91.
[5] Wilberforce to William Smith, 18 August 1806, Smith Collection (Duke).

dark side of the prospect, distrustful of the brighter days which I sincerely hope are yet in reserve for you.[1]

Smith's hopes for Grey were, of course, realized. On Fox's death in September, Grey took his place at the Foreign Office, and as leader of the party. But in his own political life Smith suffered a cruel defeat. He was not successful in his fight for re-election at Norwich, which he had represented since 1802, following the dissolution in October. It was probably the bitterest pill he ever had to swallow, for it meant that he was not in on the final stages of the campaign which was to achieve the end for which he had struggled so long, not in the House to give his vote for Abolition. But this did not keep him from the fray completely. Deprived of the opportunity of giving his voice and his vote to the cause, he decided as the next best thing, to give his pen. As he wrote in his *Letter to Wilberforce*:

. . . Surely, after having laboured with you for nearly twenty years, in the endeavour to extirpate this desolating pest, it would . . . scarcely become me to affect total indifference at being prevented from joining in that vote which now seems pressing onward to seal its, I trust, irrevocable doom.—And disabled from raising my voice and giving my suffrage on this occasion, I hope I may be permitted to proffer my mite of assistance in that mode which remains to me.[2]

It was a forceful and well-argued pamphlet, and Smith saw to it that it was circulated to all the leading politicians in the country, to Grenville, Grey, Whitbread and others of similar importance.[3]

Nor did his private pressure on the leaders of the coalition ever cease. Grey, in particular, was treated to a great deal of very frank advice. In February 1807 Smith sent him a copy of his pamphlet:

I cannot deny myself the pleasure of shewing You how we agree on some points at least, and have therefore sent You my little pamphlet— I being neither Secretary of State nor Chancellor of the Exchequer have made much shorter work of the Business than it would have been

---

[1] William Smith to Lord Howick, 11 September 1806, Grey Papers.
[2] *Letter to William Wilberforce*, p. 1.
[3] See the letters of acknowledgement, Smith Collection (Duke).

prudent or decent for You to have done. . . . I have turned down the two or three places I particularly wish You to look at.[1]

There were several things on which Smith might have disagreed with Grey. He violently opposed the Income Tax. He probably also resented that, in power, the Whigs appeared to grow cool on Reform, as is suggested by the fact that he was present at a meeting early in the year between the Whig leaders and several prominent Dissenting ministers where the latter pressed hard for some kind of action on the matter.[2] But his greatest difference of opinion with Grey undoubtedly came over Slave Trade strategy. Grenville and Grey were in office, and wished to stay there. Three of their colleagues, Windham and Lords Sidmouth and Hawkesbury, were still, as they had been throughout, staunchly opposed to Abolition. Naturally, the coalition leaders therefore desired to make the measure as palatable as they could. They would not desert the ultimate end, but they wished to make its implementation as inoffensive as possible. This necessarily involved a certain watering down of principle. To Smith such a watering down was not only personally repugnant, it might lead, for reasons already mentioned, to ultimate failure. Tactics were involved as well as principle.

The problem during the last few months thus became one of keeping the generally well-disposed ministers up to the mark, of reminding them of their moral obligations. Smith set himself to this task. As he wrote Grey on 9 March:

I am sorry I could not see you before I left Town; and the more so, because Wilberforce informs me that You intend to prolong the time in the W. Indies for three Months; for reasons in which he seems to acquiesce, tho' he does not detail them—and therefore, tho' sorry for the delay, I suppose I ought to acquiesce also—but further that the Preamble is to be given up. Why, for God's sake—do, pray, consider well before you concede so much.

What, Smith asked, could possibly be gained by giving up the preamble? True, it damned the Trade in the most detailed and uncompromising terms; but this was quite just, and nothing could be gained by its removal, and a great deal lost:

[1] William Smith to Lord Howick, 24 February 1807, Grey Papers.
[2] Williams, pp. 574–5.

Does anyone expect that the West Indians will afford any cordial cooperation on that account? I cannot so flatter myself. What will be gained with respect to the Slave Merchants? Nothing—nor do You want anything—but, by implication a sort of allowance will be made that their claim for compensation is less objectionable. On the other hand, will it not seem like abandoning our strongest, our inexpugnable ground? Why do we abolish the trade at all, but because we are convinced with the last House of Commons and the two preceding ones, that the Trade is as therein described? and shall we now be afraid to state in the Preamble the ground of the Enactment? Have You not refused to go into further Evidence because the case was sufficiently proved, and will You now hesitate to speak out as before, as if You doubted your former determination? The only reasons for Abolition are the Trade being adverse to Justice and Honesty and to sound Policy. If at last You refuse to declare its contrariety to the former, it may be argued that You in fact rest on the latter ground; and who would willingly chuse the most disputable, however good in itself he might think it? Further, if at any time a clamour should be set up for the restoration of the Trade, what an advantage would this give to the advocacy, if they should be able to make out any partial or temporary deficiency and an apparent expediency in the permission to import an additional supply. To such a Claim the Assertion of the true principle of the Abolition so broadly and explicitly laid down in the present preamble would be a direct and unanswerable reply— but, without it, I really do not see that the whole Question would not be to be re-argued. . . .

This much was an appeal to his reader's reason. But this was not all that Smith did; he also appealed to Grey's honour and to his devotion to a departed leader and friend:

. . . And to You I must put it—do You think Fox would ever have given up the Preamble at all—much more (if the case admits of degrees) after two such majorities? I conjure You, do not yield it. . . .

He went further, stating his own firm and unequivocal position:

. . . I would not descend one degree from our present exalted position—and I am confident to do so would be as little politic as honourable.[1]

[1] William Smith to Lord Howick, 9 March 1807, Grey Papers.

There were few, if any, others among the Abolition leadership who could have appealed to Grey in such a fashion, not only on the grounds of reason, but of devotion and loyalty to the memory of a departed leader whom both had followed. The tone of their correspondence clearly indicates that Grey and Smith were, at this time, on fairly close terms; otherwise Smith could hardly have taken the very frank line which he did, for Grey was not a man who would have borne lightly anything which he considered insulting. This closeness was certainly of some importance in attaining the Saint's final goal. True, they did not get all they wanted, the very detailed preamble being dropped; but they did get an immediate abolition of the Trade and they did get a clear statement that such commerce was repugnant to the basic principles of justice and morality.

At the victory celebration at Wilberforce's house, after the triumphant passage of the bill on its second reading by the huge majority of 283 to 16, the following exchange is recorded:

"Well, Henry," Mr. Wilberforce asked playfully of Mr. Thornton, "what shall we abolish next?" "The Lottery, I think" gravely replied his sterner friend. "Let us make out the names of those sixteen miscreants; I have four of them," said William Smith.[1]

Much has been made of Wilberforce's question and of Thornton's reply to prove that Abolition was in fact not a real objective with the Saints.[2] This, as has been suggested, is going much too far. Doubtless it was only a part of their broader programme for a Christian reformation, but it was certainly a very important part. Still there is some significance in the sequence of Smith's remark. It leaves no doubt of the importance of the measure in his mind. He, at any rate, could think of nothing but the recent triumph and of those who had dared to oppose it.

[1] Wilberforce, *Life*, III, 297–8.
[2] Brown, pp. 107–8.

CHAPTER EIGHT

NORWICH, 1802–1818

With one brief interlude in 1806 to 1807—that crucial interlude which prevented him from casting a vote against the Slave Trade—William Smith represented the city of Norwich in Parliament from 1802 to 1830. With one of the larger electorates in the country,[1] the commercial and manufacturing city of Norwich was a constituency well suited to a man who piqued himself on being a champion of the people and who always gloried in his ties with the mercantile middle classes. Inclinations apart, a popular constituency gave its member a special prestige and an added importance in the unreformed Parliament.

Smith took immense pride in the connexion, asserting that he considered the approbation of the Norwich electorate 'the triumph of his principles'.[2] And there is no doubt that his wife was echoing his sentiments when she declared that the distinction of representing the 'good city of Norwich [is] an honor I court for you more than that of any title whatever'.[3]

Because he took such pride in his connexion with the city, Smith took great pains to explain his political position in Norwich. Particularly in the years 1802 to 1818, when he was involved in contested elections, there is no better place to follow the development of his political ideas. The Norwich connexion is interesting for other reasons. In Norwich, Smith was involved in conflicts of

---

[1] The franchise was vested in all freemen, resident and non-resident, and as Norwich was a county in its own right, in the forty-shilling freeholders. In 1802, 2878 voted; in 1807, 2351; in 1812, 2785; and in 1818, 3483.

[2] *The Norfolk Chronicle*, 2 July 1802.

[3] Frances Smith to William Smith, 1 October 1812, Leigh-Smith Papers.

principle and policy of a sort that were to dominate his later political career. For one thing, the conflict between Church and Dissent was at the very foundation of Norwich politics. Equally significant was the fact that among his own staunchest supporters Smith first encountered representatives of a new generation of Unitarians, politically more radical and aggressive than his generation, whose ideas of immediate objectives and of tactics were frequently to clash with his own. (Indeed, there was a certain identity of personnel, the Taylor family particularly providing leadership of the new Unitarianism in the nation as well as in Norwich.) For several reasons, then, Smith's association with Norwich is worthy of attention.

Smith's pride in Norwich was justified—indeed, more justified than he himself was willing to admit—for, paradoxical though it may seem at first, while they were certainly impure, Norwich politics were at this period, at any rate, basically uncorrupt. It is impossible to deny the superficial truth of the observation made by the editor of the *Norwich Mercury* in 1818 on the 'open, enormous, profligate, detestable system of corruption that had been for years established in the various municipal and general elections of this city . . .'.[1] Yet though every known means of corruption was liberally employed, the elections of these years seem to prove conclusively that the end result was not, in fact, corrupting. Undoubtedly, as one observer remarked, the voters expected 'the trifling compliment they have been accustomed to receive at Elections after they have voted',[2] and they expected lavish entertainment besides. Candidates, Smith included, and their wealthy supporters, almost always spent enormous sums on elections:[3] which was one very

[1] *The Norwich Mercury*, 20 June 1818.

[2] An 'Operative', *To the Freemen of Norwich on Purity and Freedom of Elections*, a broadside of 1826, Colman Library, Norwich.

[3] In 1820, an uncontested election, the Smith family alone spent at least one thousand pounds. Smith himself was in financial difficulties, but his son Ben contributed nine hundred (Sam Smith to Fanny Nightingale, 17 November, 1823, Verney Papers). And W. E. Nightingale wrote from Naples that 'news is just arrived that Carters, Wilberforces, Nicholsons etc. etc. are all vying and cannot subscribe fast enough to pay the expenses of the return . . . and I send off by the same post my congratulations and a petition to have my name put on the list for £100' (W.E.N. to Ben Smith, 12 April 1802, Bonham-Carter Papers).

good reason why they constantly bemoaned the corruption of the electors. But the fact is that all this expenditure did not have a great effect in determining votes. Partly, this can be explained by the fact that the two parties in the city seem to have been roughly equal in financial resources, but in large part it was simply that the electors were willing to ignore monetary advantage. In any case, it was not money, nor even more legitimate forms of influence, which were the most important determinants in the outcome of Norwich elections. Whatever may have been the rule in the rest of the country, Namierite generalizations do not hold for Norwich: in Norwich issues and principles were crucial factors in politics.

Politics in Norwich operated on two levels. One level was that of the great mass of the electorate. The other that of the middle-class merchants, manufacturers, and professional men, with a sprinkling of country gentlemen, who financed and largely made up the two parties in the city. The issues which stirred the two levels were not always identical.

Trade, however, was a concern of both, which made national policies important issues in Norwich politics. There may once have been some justice in 'Melchisedech Timbertoe's' sarcastic salute to the

> happy Town in whose blest plains
> Meek-Eyed Faction ever reigns;
> Careless of Britain's Weal or Woe
> Whilst thy Looms with Yarn o'erflow . . .[1]

But the time when Norwich could afford to be unmoved by the affairs of the nation had long since passed. By 1802 her looms were not only not overflowing, they had been largely stopped for ten years; and one had to look far from Norwich to find the reason.

Norwich had grown rich on the worsted industry, and its prosperity was still overwhelmingly dependent on that industry. Once there had been a large internal market for her product, but during the eighteenth century, with the growing competition of cheaper cotton goods, the city had become increasingly dependent upon the export trade. By the last quarter of the century almost all of the

[1] *An Irregular Ode for the Fourth of May*, 1802, Colman Library.

Norwich worsteds flowed to foreign markets—chiefly to Europe, to a much smaller degree to China and India through the East India Company, and to America.[1] Anything, therefore, which damaged the export trade damaged Norwich.

The wars of the French Revolution and Napoleon could have been nothing but a disaster for the city, for Britain was almost constantly at war with the city's most important continental depot, Holland, and for long periods with the whole continent. The Norwich stuffs exported dwindled to a mere trickle, bringing as an inevitable result, as Smith put it in 1802, 'the decay of its manufactures almost to annihilation—and scarcity among the poor, nearly to want of subsistence, notwithstanding an unexampled and most oppressive increase of rates and contributions for their support'.[2] After 1802 the situation gradually improved, with the introduction of the manufacture of new cotton and silk goods; but there was always the background of the long and bitter depression, and always the fluctuation of the market which raised the dread of a new one.[3] Save for 1818, when the city was in the middle of a brief post-war boom, there were always the distressed to appeal to, for those who wished to do so.

There was another issue which played a critical part in determining the political complexion of Norwich—religion. By 1829 the total number of Dissenters, not including Methodists, was estimated at about 6,000 in a population of some 60,000,[4] and there was a not inconsiderable Catholic population as well.[5] Norwich possessed, in addition to a depressed population, one in which there was a large minority which had other reasons for feeling disaffected from the existing system.

[1] See B. D. Hayes's excellent general study, 'Politics in Norfolk, 1750–1832', Ph.D. dissertation, Cambridge University, 1957, pp. 58–9.

[2] Smith's address to the electors, *The Poll for Members of Parliament* (Stevenson and Matchett; Norwich, 1802), x–xii.   [3] Hayes, p. 61.

[4] J. Chambers, *A General History of the County of Norfolk* (Norwich, 1829), II, 1269.

[5] I can find no estimate of their numbers, but there were at least two Catholic chapels, and, on 7 August 1813, the *Chronicle* reported that on the preceding Sunday about fifty persons had been confirmed in the chapel in St Swithins and a larger number in that of St John's Maddermarket.

There was, as will be seen, only one Parliamentary election during this period in which religion was clearly the central issue. That was in 1807, and the crushing defeat suffered by the candidate who attempted to exploit religious bigotry kept the religious issue out of popular politics thereafter. But religion had long been, and was to remain, the key issue for the upper- and middle-class leaders of the two parties in the city, which went by the names of their colours, the Tory Orange and Purples (significantly enough, the names of the two orders of Orangemen[1]) and the Whig-Radical Blue and Whites. There was little difference in the social composition of the party leaderships.[2] But while the Orange and Purples were Churchmen to a man, the Blue and White leaders were mostly Dissenters, and, with the notable exception of the great Quaker banking family, the Gurneys, mainly Unitarians.

Following the familiar pattern, the parties had divided over the issue of Repeal in the late eighties. The predecessors of the Orange and Purple party strongly opposed Repeal and rejoiced on its final crushing defeat in 1790 that

> . . . the sons of Schism
> Were most completely ditch'd.[3]

In Norwich, as elsewhere, this division of opinion was followed by one over the French Revolution and the issue of Parliamentary reform. The favourable reaction of the Dissenting party to both undoubtedly exacerbated party conflict still further, strengthening the religious prejudices of its opponents with political ones. A combination of the two led the Orange and Purples to take their legally correct, but completely unprecedented, action of insisting on the enforcement of the Corporation Act in the Common Council elections of 1801. The effect of this step on the elections is unclear,[4] but it was the last time it was tried.

[1] Hereward Senior, *Orangeism in Ireland and Britain, 1795–1836* (London, 1966), p. 78.

[2] See Hayes, pp. 72–4 and 261.   [3] Quoted in ibid., p. 235n.

[4] The election of Common Councillors in the Mancroft ward took place on a Monday. It was requested that the Corporation Act be read and announced that the election of anyone who had not qualified would be challenged. This was followed by the return of the Orange and Purple candidates by large

Thereafter, there was no attempt to impose a religious test for office in the Corporation, and Dissenters prospered exceedingly. There were many in both the Common Council and the Court of Aldermen. Indeed, between 1802 and 1819 at least three Dissenters, and perhaps more, occupied the highest office in the city.[1] The Corporation Act had ceased to function in Norwich.

Neither side, however, either forgave or forgot. However much the Orange and Purples might eschew the religious question in elections, it remained true that their candidates—John Patteson, Charles Harvey, and Jonathan Peel—were always ranged against the Dissenters and the Catholics when their claims arose in Parliament. And the Blue and Whites, for their part, continued unabated their demands for the 'repeal of all penal statutes in matters of religion'.[2]

Religion was an issue in the first election that Smith fought in Norwich. The Blue and White answer to the provocation given by the Orange and Purples' insistence on the Corporation Act the previous year was to put forward the leading Dissenting politician as their candidate in 1802. Smith's Tory opponents were William Windham, Pitt's Secretary for War, and Canning's great friend, John Hookham Frere. And as Windham and Frere pointedly remarked in one of their election addresses:

That this is a political contest, in which important principles of Church and State are at issue on either side, is too obvious to be dis-

---

majorities. But whether the result would have been different without the insistence on the Test, it is impossible to say. The election for the Wymer ward followed on Wednesday, and a similar request for the reading of the Act was made. The Recorder, Charles Harvey, advised the Blue and Whites of the necessity of compliance with the law. His warning was unnecessary, for, though the Blue and Whites protested their willingness to put up unqualified candidates and to take the matter to the courts, as it happened all their candidates were qualified; and they won (*Mercury* and *Chronicle*, 28 March 1802).

[1] Edward Rigby in 1805, Sir John Harrison Yallop in 1815, and Nathaniel Bolingbroke in 1819, all Unitarians (B. Cozens-Hardy and E. A. Kent, *The Mayors of Norwich, 1403–1835* [Norwich, 1938]).

[2] A toast at the 1813 Independent Whig Club dinner, *Mercury*, 16 October 1813.

puted. Could any doubt have existed, it must by this time have been completely done away . . . by the choice made by the Party of the Gentlemen who is brought down to head them. . . . What the principles are of the Party alluded to it is unnecessary to point out; it remains to be seen, whether they are the principles of the City of Norwich.[1]

The results of the election were to be a partial answer to the parting question. But there was another issue, the question of war or peace, which was of prime importance to every Norwich elector and which overshadowed all other issues in this contest. The alternatives could hardly have been more clearly presented. Windham, the head of the war party in the Commons and a bitter critic of the recently concluded Peace of Amiens, stood against Smith, the consistent opponent of the war and a staunch defender of the Peace. And it was almost certainly Smith's stand on this national question which gave him the election. His opponent had every advantage of local influence and connexion. Windham had represented the city since 1790 and he came from an old and much-respected Norfolk family. Nor does he appear to have suffered from any lack of funds. The number of London voters brought down is an easy gauge of the financial heat of any contest, the expense involved in transporting, maintaining, and entertaining them being tremendous. Considering that Smith had the advantage of an efficient and directly interested London representative as well as a wholesale grocery,[2] the 119 votes for Windham and Frere was not a bad showing as opposed to the 165 for Smith and his running mate Robert Fellowes, a local country gentleman. But Norwich itself spoke decisively against the war party, and for peace. Fellowes received 1097 Norwich votes, Smith

[1] *Chronicle*, 2 July 1802.

[2] As usual, Mrs Smith managed matters in London, combating rumours that her husband had withdrawn from the contest, hounding the supplier of transportation, who she was sure had been seduced by Windham's supporters, and overseeing the entertainment of the electors. The grocery was the headquarters of the campaign, and a very useful one. On one day Mrs Smith was able to report that 'five men had gone over from Windham to us because there was no wine at their House, nor anything to eat that they liked' (Frances Smith to William Smith, n.d. 1802, Leigh-Smith Papers).

1045, Windham 832, and Frere 819, with the weavers and wool-combers as 151:100 for peace.[1]

Yet, though the Norwich electors responded to issues, they did not always respond to the same kind of issues. They could be highly unpredictable—and, in Smith's view, irresponsible—as they demonstrated in 1806. Commenting on that election some years later, the editor of the *Mercury* remarked:

Mr. Patteson's first return was a sudden burst of popular feeling and popular regard, in which few of the former *heads* of the party were supreme, or indeed directing agents. His great majority was, we repeat, obtained from the feelings of the people.[2]

Admittedly, the editor had always been a loyal supporter of John Patteson, but there is every reason to believe that he was right, that this election was a clear expression of popular feeling.

It took place on 3 November, and until barely a week before that date there had been no candidate opposing Smith and Fellowes, and no signs of one appearing; but by 29 October Smith was writing to Grey that he was

in the midst of an Opposition the more dangerous because wholly unexpected, and what will be the event I cannot tell; as, exclusive of the spirit of party, we have an abominable clamour raised about a paving bill, which does us much injury and has indeed served as the foundation of the business.[3]

The paving bill was one of the usual sort, setting up a special commission to oversee the improvement of 'the watching, lighting, and paving of the city'. It had not started as a party measure, originating under an Orange and Purple Mayor in 1800, but strongly supported by such Blue and White stalwarts as John Gurney and Edward Rigby.[4] It had, however, run into strong opposition from the smaller householders, and not until 1806 was a bill introduced into Parliament. Then, Fellowes strongly supported it, Smith maintained a strict impartiality, and Patteson (as M.P. for Minehead)

[1] *The Poll* (Stevenson and Matchett, 1802), p. 70; Hayes, p. 60n.

[2] *Mercury*, 6 June 1818.

[3] William Smith to Lord Howick, 29 October 1806, Grey Papers.

[4] The *Iris*, 5 February 1803, in this its first issue, dedicated itself to the twin aims of supporting the Blue and Whites and the paving bill.

firmly opposed it on the grounds that the city was in no financial condition to undertake the increased burden.

The latter was undoubtedly the most popular stand, and the issue was cleverly exploited. On 21 October the Orange and Purple club, which called itself the Castle Corporation, organized a large public meeting at which it was resolved that

the populous and manufacturing city of Norwich is entitled to be represented by gentlemen conversant with its trade and interest, in social intercourse with its inhabitants, identified with its prosperity, and liberal to its various charitable institutions.[1]

On 23 October Patteson was nominated as the Orange and Purple candidate; and despite Smith's efforts to broaden the debates, the issue remained that of a citizen representative.[2] Patteson was a large Norwich brewer, the commander of the local Volunteers, an Alderman of the city. These were the arguments that were stressed, and on the day of the election Patteson was chaired in his scarlet gown and robe of justice.[3] What he thought of national issues, he refused to say—and a great many appear not to have cared.

The result was an overwhelming victory for the Orange and Purples. Despite the fact that Patteson had publicly withdrawn from the contest on the 26th and remained so for several days, and despite Smith's having brought up 204 London voters to his fifty-nine, on the first day Patteson stood well at the head of the poll, with 1575 to Fellowes's 1238 and Smith's 1198.[4] Smith wished to

[1] *Mercury*, 25 October 1806.

[2] As Patteson said in his speech of acceptance: '. . . The gentlemen who now represented the city were in all that regards fortune, condition and capability, most eligible. He did not, therefore, throw down the gauntlet of opposition, but he was selected to assert the general wish of seeing Norwich represented by one of its Citizens. From what he had seen in the last four years, he had learned that other cities were actuated by similar views. London, Bristol and Liverpool, with many others he could enumerate, were all represented by inhabitants; in the metropolis indeed it was a *sine qua non*, that the candidate should be a member of the corporation. Nor could any one have that extensive opportunity of serving the city, by any other means, whatever might be his wishes' (*The Poll* [Stevenson and Matchett, 1806], viii).

[3] *Chronicle*, 8 November 1806.

[4] Ibid., and Chambers, II, 1014.

concede in his colleague's favour; but his supporters, irritated with Fellowes's growing conservatism, desired exactly the opposite result, and demanded that the poll be continued. On the following day the Blue and Whites voted plumpers for Smith. Their efforts were foiled by the Orange and Purples who gave their second votes to Fellowes, a staunch Anglican—whatever their election stand, the leaders of the party had not forgotten the broader issues which had first led them to oppose the Dissenters' greatest champion.

The mass of the electorate—at least, a large majority of them—appear to have forgotten broader issues altogether, however.[1] To Smith, with the Whigs at last in power and the project which was perhaps nearest to his heart, the abolition of the Slave Trade, nearing a successful conclusion, this indifference to national issues was profoundly shocking. His deep disillusionment is clear in his parting letter to the electorate:

Disappointed, as I must be, in falling short of what I have publicly stated as one of the dearest objects of my ambition, I am spared the severer mortification of apprehending that by my own conduct, either public or private, I have in any degree forfeited the esteem of those highly valued persons, by whom I was first invited to represent you. It is also some satisfaction to reflect, that the conflict, in which I was then successful, was one to which the abilities and consequence of that most respectable opponent [Windham] with whom I have no longer the misfortune to be at variance,[2] and the general effect to be produced, gave an important character.—On the present occasion I have felt the contention to be comparatively trifling. A popular complaint, well founded to a certain extent, but swelled by artful representation beyond its just magnitude, but unfairly directed—a sudden clamour for a resident Citizen.—Such things may excite a temporary cry of irresistible violence, but Defeat, in these cases, is not attended with Disgrace, nor is any solid or permanent advantage secured by Victory.[3]

[1] *The Poll* (Bacon, 1806), p. 95. In the city itself Patteson received 1250 votes to Fellows's 882 and Smith's 896. Patteson received the largest total vote, 1733, of any achieved during the period, except for the very exceptional election of 1818.

[2] Windham, with the other Grenvillites, was now in coalition with the Whigs and a member of the ministry of All the Talents.

[3] *Chronicle*, 8 November 1806.

Smith was contemptuous of the issue on which he had been turned out, and deeply disappointed in those who had turned him out. Events such as this—the fact that temporary cries of 'irresistible violence' *could* arise in large popular constituencies—help to explain Smith's later caution and pessimism in approaching liberal reforming efforts.

The Norwich electorate was to conduct itself much better, from Smith's point of view, in 1807. In the 1807 election Robert Fellowes was dropped by the Blue and Whites because he had refused to join in a vote of censure against the Portland ministry in the first few weeks of its existence. The reason he gave was reluctance to condemn the new ministry untried, an unimpeachable reason in terms of traditional political conceptions.[1] But traditional arguments left his former supporters unmoved; and, this being the case, Fellowes decided to attempt an exploitation of religious bigotry. He had previously hedged on the issue of Catholic commissions which had caused the downfall of the Talents:[2] 'The King dismissed his late Ministers, from the genuine dictates of conscience (whether right or wrong it does not become me to enquire).'[3] Now he decided to wage his campaign on the issue of 'No Popery' and the support of 'Church and King'. It is significant that Patteson, the single Orange and Purple candidate, refused to have anything to do with Fellowes,[4] and even more significant is the latter's resounding defeat. In the two previous elections he had run ahead of Smith, receiving 1532

[1] *The Poll* (Stevenson and Matchett, 1807), p. 5.

[2] The coalition government had proposed to abolish the Test Act as it affected the senior ranks in the army. Though this would have benefited all non-conformists, the main aim was to pacify the Irish. George III refused to agree, dismissed his ministers, and asked Portland to form a new government.

[3] Ibid., p. 5.

[4] 'Several attempts, both before and during the election, were made by the friends of Mr. Fellowes to unite that gentleman's interest with that of Mr. Patteson, who from the first declined, and throughout very honourably discountenanced, a junction with any other candidate. Indeed, the printed boards with the words "Church and King—Patteson and Fellowes", which were carried before Mr. Fellowes's chair, decorated with orange and purple, were afterwards withdrawn' (Ibid., p. 8). This despite the fact that in the previous election the Orange and Purple leaders had been so anxious to defeat Smith that they had given their second votes to Fellowes without prompting.

votes to Smith's 1439 in 1802 and 1370 to Smith's 1333 in 1806, but in this election he stood third and lowest on the poll, with 546 votes to Smith's 1156 and Patteson's 1474.[1] Religious intolerance in any form was manifestly unpopular with the Norwich electorate; and, while the Orange and Purple leaders were to remain predominantly High Church Tories, after this election the religious issue was avoided like the plague.[2]

The two remaining elections during the period tell little of issues. Had the sitting members had their way there would have been no contest in 1812, both Smith and Patteson having expressed the hope in 1807 that that election would end political controversy in the city.[3] But at the last moment, decidedly against Patteson's better judgement, a second Orange and Purple candidate was put forward, Charles Harvey, Recorder of the city and a member of the party's leading family. The result more than justified the assumption on which the 1807 truce had been based—that neither party, under ordinary circumstances, could elect two members. Smith received 1544 votes to Harvey's 1349 and Patteson's 1221. But Smith's large lead could easily have been the product of bad feeling in the opposing ranks; 160 of Harvey's supporters and fifty-three of Patteson's voted for him.[4]

The 1818 election, though it tells little of principle, tells much of

[1] Fellowes had been almost completely deserted by the Blue and White electors. There were only seventeen who combined votes for Smith and Fellowes. Five hundred and ten Orange and Purple electors voted for Fellowes as well as for Patteson; but, had they so desired, all could have done so with impunity and at extra profit (*ibid.*, p. 72).

[2] In 1812 Charles Harvey told the electors after the poll that 'there is no man who detests religious intolerance more than myself. I had rather have received no education at all, than have received such an education as should have implanted in my mind any principles that can justly be called intolerant. Therefore, whenever the question of Catholic Claims comes before Parliament, I shall vote for it being taken into consideration'. This was met with 'loud and continued applauses from the whole assembly' (*The Poll* [Stevenson and Matchett, 1812], pp. 11–12). Harvey subsequently voted against Catholic Emancipation; but, as he did not stand again in 1818, his vote never became an issue.

[3] *Chronicle* and *Mercury*, 9 May 1807.

[4] *The Poll* (Stevenson and Matchett, 1812), p. 85.

corruption in Norwich, and its effect—or, rather, lack of effect. The Gurneys were engaged in a concerted effort to elect one of their own family to Parliament. They started their campaign in the municipal elections which preceded the general election. Corrupt practices never reached a higher peak in Norwich. According to one opponent, as much as fifty pounds was paid for a single vote for members of the Common Council in the Wymer ward, whose control would determine the control of the city.[1] But the result only barely justified the effort, the Gurney's Blue and White candidates receiving only 361, 357, and 355 votes to the opposing Orange and Purple candidates' 345, 340, and 322.[2]

No chances were taken with the general election. In addition to using the usual means of bribing, cooping, and intoxicating the electors on an unprecedented scale, several hundred new freeholders were created to ensure success.[3] Success they had, Smith receiving 2089 votes and R. H. Gurney 2032; but despite all their efforts, the Orange and Purple vote of 1475 (1333 plumpers) for Edward Harbord remained higher than it had been in any election since 1802, save for Patteson's great victory in 1806.[4] It was the new freeholders and the 228 voters they had brought down from London that gave the Blue and Whites their victory. The great majority of the electors seem to have voted as conscience, or habit, dictated, taking whatever monetary reward came their way only as an added benefit.

Issues appear to have played little part in this election. Peace and prosperity had removed the major factor in popular politics, and neither party supported the existing government of Lord Liverpool. Smith appealed to the electorate on his long record; Gurney endorsed that record; and Harbord, who had no record, also refused to make any statement of his political principles.

There was an issue which might have attracted voters to the

---

[1] *A Letter from J. F. G. Atkinson, Esq. to J. J. Gurney, Esq.*, a broadside of 1819, Colman Library. The *Chronicle*, 14 March 1818, put the prices paid for votes at £15 to £40.

[2] *Chronicle*, 14 March 1818.   [3] *Mercury*, 20 June 1818.

[4] In 1802 their two candidates received 1356 and 1328; in 1807, 1474; and in 1812, 1349 and 1221. Patteson got 1733 votes in 1806.

Blue and Whites, but it seems unlikely that it did. The issue was Parliamentary reform. There had, however, been no mass demonstration of popular support for the Reforming agitation which preceded the election. It appears that, while the more humble Norwich electors generally voted on issues, the issues on which they voted did not induce them to adopt any broad principles of politics, nor, as far as the Blue and White voters were concerned, produce any desire to alter the existing political system of the country. The great issue for them was always war and its effects.[1] War brought depression and misery. Government was responsible for the war and the way in which it was conducted and financed. The obvious conclusion was to vote against the government's supporters. But beyond making this very simple assessment of the situation the great mass of Blue and White voters do not seem to have gone. Had the Orange and Purple party been willing to make religion more of an issue the situation might have been different; but, as they were not, popular politics in Norwich tended to resolve themselves around bad times, and the fear of bad times. The liberal vote was the vote of the disaffected, but during this period disaffection did not breed any broad lower-class political programme.

There was plenty of radical agitation in Norwich, but it came from above, not from below. The disaffection of the populace allowed it to function, but it did not create it. Norwich radicalism was solidly middle-class.

One of the reasons for the strong radical element in the Norwich middle classes has already been alluded to—religion. Norwich radicalism was led by Dissenters, mostly Unitarians. Wealthy and well-educated, successful business and professional men, they deeply resented the stigma imposed by the Test Acts. And their very considerable success in the politics of the city only made that stigma more irritating. As good disciples of Priestley and Belsham, they

---

[1] This was true even in 1812, when Smith had long been giving his general support to the war in Europe. Apart from the issue of corruption, it was Smith's record of votes against the Orders in Council and the other measures which 'cursed the country with an American War', against the Excise, and against the Leather Tax, both war taxes, which were stressed in the handbills distributed by the Blue and Whites (*Plain Questions*, Norwich Public Library).

firmly believed that the shackles on religious freedom, with all others on liberty, would disappear in the inevitable march of progress. And like all good Necessarians, they were anxious to speed that march along its way.

Given the religious basis of Norwich radicalism, however, there were other issues aplenty to feed and develop it. One does not have to search far to find what agitated these middle-class Dissenters; the Common Halls,[1] which they called and dominated, tell the story. The impeachment of Lord Melville in 1805 and the investigation of the Duke of York's affairs in 1809 brought disclosures of corruption in government which roused them to a fury. In 1814 and 1815 they demanded that the Corn Laws should not be revised in the interest of the landowners. In 1815 and 1816 they called loudly for the abolition of Income Tax. And in 1816 they demanded the greatest possible retrenchment in public expenditure and the abolition of all sinecures. These were the issues which aroused them; and their solution, put forth in Common Halls in 1809 and 1816, was the radical reform of Parliament.

The wars of the French Revolution, which they disapproved on principle, had wrecked their trade. War had also, while decreasing their ability to pay them, tremendously increased the burden of taxes and rates which fell upon their shoulders. And the same government which had taken away their prosperity and which dunned them for ever greater sums, only added to their burdens by what appeared to them its terrible corruption. The 1815 Corn Law, raising the price of food and hence of wages or poor rates—it mattered little which—was the last straw. It shattered beyond repair their confidence in a system dominated by a land-owning oligarchy which seemed to them determined to wreck the commerce which had made England great, and whose only concern was to batten upon her misery. The system must be radically changed, and the people brought in to sweep it clean.

It must be emphasized again that in Norwich during this period

[1] The Common Hall was a meeting of the inhabitants of the city, usually called by the Mayor upon the requisition of several or more freemen. It was a favourite device of the radicals to demonstrate their confidence in the support of public opinion.

'the people' did not respond. Popular radicalism was to come in the late twenties, but from 1802 to 1818 it was middle-class Dissenting radicalism which dominated the liberal politics of the city.[1] This did not make it any less radical. In 1816 the penny subscription Reform societies and the handbills calling for annual Parliaments strongly suggest the depth of Norwich middle-class radicalism. The Norwich party wanted radical Reform and there is nothing to indicate that any Reform would have been too radical—and everything to suggest the contrary. Nor did Norwich radicalism pale with the violence of 1817 and 1819.[2] These middle-class Dissenters had reached the end of their tether, and they intended to strain, with all the force they could muster, until it snapped.

On fundamental issues there was a broad general agreement between Smith and the Norwich party which had sought him as its candidate. Norwich radicals would have heartily endorsed the three basic objectives which Smith had outlined to Fox in 1801—'Parliamentary Reform in some shape or other, Abolition of all Religious Tests as to Civil Matters, and Abolition of the Slave Trade'.[3] But within this broad general agreement there was room for an important difference of opinion on extent and on means. Such a difference occurred, often and sharply.

Professor Roberts has classified Smith as being in the extreme liberal section of the Whig party,[4] and doubtless, in Whig terms, he was 'left'. Certainly, with regard to the key issue of Parliamentary reform Smith was much more enthusiastic than either the bulk of the party or its leadership. But though he was a warm personal

[1] As Hayes, p. 318 points out, the thirty-nine signatories of the 1816 requisition for a Common Hall on the issue of radical Reform had two things in common: all, save one Roman Catholic, were Dissenters; and they were solidly middle-class, not one coming from below the shopkeeper-small entrepreneur class. And, while the requisition list had more names upon it than usual, it contained all the familiar ones—Taylor, Martineau, Rigby, Alderson, Bolingbroke, Gurney, and others—which had appeared regularly on requisition lists since 1805.

[2] Ibid. and ff.

[3] C. J. Fox to William Smith, 15 November 1801, Fox Papers, B.M. Add. MSS. 47,569, ff. 111–13.

[4] Michael Roberts, *The Whig Party, 1807–1812* (London, 1939), p. 190.

friend of Samuel Whitbread, the leader of the extreme Whigs, and worked closely with him on questions of Parliamentary and religious reform, Smith differed from Whitbread in important respects. He did not share Whitbread's unshakeable pacificism, for one thing. And, as will be seen, on certain issues with regard to the conduct of the war, Smith was to take a much more favourable attitude toward government policy not only than Whitbread, but than much more conservative elements in the party. Smith was a very independent Whig, and difficult to classify. Smith's Norwich supporters, on the other hand, were consistent supporters of the extreme Whig line— indeed, more than that, of the Burdettite radical line.

No more bitter and virulent attack was ever made on Smith than that by a disillusioned Norwich supporter in 1809.[1] Under the Talents, Smith, with the majority of his party, had swung to a kind of grudging acceptance of the war. Smith's reason was probably personal loyalty more than anything else. He idolized Charles James Fox, and, for him, anyone who could resist Fox's blandishments had to be incorrigible: Napoleon had done so, with the result that Fox's efforts to end the war which had broken out again in 1803 came to nothing. Thereafter Smith gave the war his general support. It was not a shift of position that he ever explained entirely satisfactorily, but having made it, he was willing to go much further in his support of the war than most of his party.

This was profoundly shocking to his erstwhile supporter, who launched his diatribe with a long attack on this act of apostasy. Smith had, he said, 'at a public dinner in Norwich . . . most warmly applauded the ministers in their exertions relative to the unfortunate expedition to Spain'. He had, by his silence, discouraged a petition for peace: 'Had there been from you any wish or only a hint, that we should have petitioned, I am bold to say, ten thousand names would have graced the parchment. . . .'[2] But, worst of all, was Smith's

---

[1] 'A Freeman of the City', *A Letter Addressed to Wm. Smith, Esq., M.P. for Norwich Shewing that His Political Conduct Has Rendered Him No Longer Deserving the Support of His Constituents* (Norwich, 1809) (hereafter cited as 'A Freeman'), Norwich Public Library.

[2] This must have been in 1809; for in the previous year Smith had stated his opposition to all such petitions in the most definite terms (*Mercury* 13 February 1808).

attitude toward the attack on Copenhagen and the seizure of neutral Denmark's fleet in 1807. 'The Ministers approved the act, and in my hearing you said, if they could persuade you it was right, you should not condemn them.'

There was a time when even Pitt himself could not have led you astray: there was a time when you, the friend of the people, the friend of reform, the enthusiastic admirer of Gallic liberty struggling with and overcoming royal despotism, would not have sanctioned such proceedings. There was a time when neither Hardy nor Stone, neither O'Connor nor Tom Paine would have applauded such bloody deeds, and I think there was a time when you would have agreed with them on this as well as other subjects.

The Whig party in Parliament, too, was almost unanimous in reprobating the Copenhagen expedition, because of its impolicy and, even more, as an immoral act.[1] Not so Smith; as he wrote to William Roscoe, a fellow Unitarian and a close ally in the campaign against the Slave Trade, who was also one of the most bitter critics of the war:

I am now probably about to surprise you. You have seen or may see, my name in the minority on the division for the Copenhagen papers—but notwithstanding everything, even the excellent reasoning of your own book, I must acknowledge to you that I should not have been ready to have condemned Ministers for that measure. My hesitation on the subject has been from the commencement:—allowing in its full extent the violent and unjust character of the Transaction on the face of it, I do not think it incapable of defence, even without positive proof of collusion of Denmark. Had Ministers obtained such proof, I should have thought them doubly worthy of high praise—for skill in obtaining it, and for vigour in action. In its absence, tho' I cannot afford so unrestrained an approbation, yet in the marks which exist of a disposition, to say the least of it, unfriendly and jealous towards this Country, and in the nature and extent of the danger averted, I think I see such a case made out, as that if the Danes had permitted their Navy to fall into B's hands, and the Russians should have added their force, our Government would have incurred a censure nearly universal for want of foresight and decision.

[1] See Roberts, pp. 111–16.

It might well be that the Danes had ample reason for their distrust of Britain, 'but the question is not respecting the justice of their previous displeasure, but its existence'. He explained that the only reason that he had joined in the call for papers was that he 'most earnestly wished for a public justification of the step, to the uttermost point'.

It concerns me much to be obliged to differ from so many of the most valued of my friends on so many important subjects, in which the highest principles are so deeply involved—those principles however I do not consider myself *as at all* abandoning:—thinking that the other party [France] by their conduct towards us have forfeited their right to the full and rigid application of them.[1]

Unlike Whitbread and Roscoe, Smith did not believe that there was no danger and nothing to fight for; and he could not, therefore, join in their constant demands for peace. On this general issue he was broadly in agreement with most of the rest of his party, although not with Norwich. But, as the Copenhagen affair showed, even with his party he demonstrated a healthy independence. He valued the Whigs to whom 'not withstanding this accidental difference I am firmly attached and regard as the best depository of good principles of Civil and Religious Liberty'.[2] But he insisted on judging each issue on its own merits, and on acting accordingly. His was not the kind of mentality that made a good party man, nor the kind which made relations with a radical constituency like Norwich easy.

Smith's differences with his constituents over the war were largely masked in the long run by the constant carping and cavilling in which the opposition was able to indulge over its conduct. Doubtless, there was much to criticize; and on some issues Smith felt strongly—as, for instance, on the Orders in Council and the American war.[3] On the general issue of the war, therefore, both

[1] William Smith to William Roscoe, 5 February 1809, Roscoe Papers, Liverpool Public Library.

[2] Ibid.

[3] 'Mr. Wm. Smith said, that upon the subject of impressment, Mr. Monroe had personally expressed to him his sense of the importance of the question. He would ask, what would Great Britain say, if any foreign power maintained

Smith's own conscience and his constituents could take a good deal of comfort in his conduct. But over the issue of Parliamentary reform, the other great question that divided them, the clash was more open. Both were agreed in desiring some kind of Reform, but here their agreement ended. The Norwich radicals wanted the most extensive Reform possible, and they did not care how they got it. Smith wanted only a moderate Reform, and he was very much concerned as to how it was attained.

As has been seen, Smith's approach to Parliamentary reform had never been that of the more extreme radicals. In 1795 he had pressed a moderate programme on 'The Friends of the People'. He had opposed universal suffrage and he had been very cool toward annual Parliaments. Then, and in the Reform debates of 1797, he had pressed for a uniform householder franchise as the best reform possible. Such a reform, Smith believed, would allow the Commons to fulfil its proper function under the Constitution. And that function, as Smith saw it, was very different from the radical conception of it. The Commons was intended, Smith had said, as a barrier interposed between the Crown and the people; it was meant to be a bulwark to protect the people against executive oppression. But the Commons was not, therefore, to be simply a reflection of the popular will. It ought to exercise an independent judgement of its own. The Crown's influence had grown so great that the majority of members no longer possessed the necessary independence to fulfil their proper function. Therefore, the Crown's influence must be reduced by Parliamentary reform. But, precisely because the main point of Reform was to restore the rightful independence of the Commons, Smith did not envisage giving it a new master.[1] Smith believed in the traditional balanced constitution.

Such had been Smith's views in the nineties. They remained the same when he first stood for Norwich in 1802. He came, as he told the electors, 'declaring myself, as I have uniformly done, in public

---

a *right* to search *her* ships for subjects? and surely a Government that could submit to such a right was not fit to exist as such!' (*Chronicle*, 27 February 1813).

[1] See above, pp. 93-6.

and in private, a decided Friend on Principle to the Constitution of this Country in its present form of Government, by King, Lords, and Commons, (though an enemy to those abuses and that corruption by which it has been deformed and endangered)'.[1] And his views were never to change. Reform was to be a corrective. For the foreseeable future, at any rate, the aim was to restore a proper balance, not to reform the whole Constitution, root and branch. This being his view, Smith could not fail to react strongly against the Reform movement which had its birth in 1809; for the radicals, to attain Reform, turned on the basic institutions of the country.

It was Colonel Wardle's charges that the Duke of York had been a direct party to the sale of military commissions by his mistress, Mary Anne Clarke, that gave the radicals their chance, and they seized it. Popular constituencies all over the country held public meetings, applauding Sir Francis Burdett and the others who had voted for the direct censure of the Duke, and coupling their applause with an endorsement of the Burdettites' demand for Parliamentary reform[2]—and no constituency was more vociferous than Norwich.

Smith had anticipated this sentiment among his supporters. Indeed he met it head on in his speech of 10 March 1809 concluding the debates:

He had always been and still continued a firm and zealous advocate for a Reform in Parliament, and would be ashamed to leave the adversaries of that important measure in full possession of one of their strongest and most favourite arguments—that those who owed their seats to popular elections would always be afraid to stem the tide of popular opinion, tho' they should be convinced of its opposition to justice. He believed that on the present occasion the most severe sentence would be the most popular. . . .

But he did not believe that a direct censure was justified, and he would vote against it—whatever his constituents might think.[3] His reward was a direct snub from the Norwich meeting, which passed resolutions warmly approving those who had voted with

[1] *The Poll* (Stevenson and Matchett, 1802), x-xiii.
[2] Roberts, p. 199ff.
[3] *Chronicle*, 18 March 1809.

Wardle and Burdett, and deploring the corrupt motives of those who had not. Smith faced his constituents unrepentant, 'not being conscious of having formed his opinion under any improper, much less any corrupt bias, but merely from a careful, and, he believed, an impartial attention to the case, he neither had been, nor should he ever be afraid or ashamed on any occasion to avow it. . . .'[1]

He was not ready to condemn the Duke on what he considered insufficient grounds, and he was certainly not ready to condemn him only so that Parliamentary reform might prosper on the disrepute of the monarchy. Many of his constituents, however, were ready to do so, and Smith was publicly taxed with being a panderer to Royalty and a friend of corruption.[2] His disillusioned supporter expressed great surprise that Smith's name should appear as 'one of the *Stewards* at the Dinner in London where the advocates for *Parliamentary Reform* are to assemble'. But Smith duly appeared at the Crown and Anchor Meeting on 1 May to tell it, to the accompaniment of loud hissing and booing, that success was very far away. He

wished to call the attention of the meeting to the nature of the opposition they had to experience, which consisted not only of the Treasury, of great families and borough-holders, but also in that of corrupt voters. The meeting must not imagine that all voters were disposed to act upon the same independent principles as those of Westminster. But it was not from corruption only they had to expect opposition. They would also encounter it from prejudices. There were many in the country who thought very differently from the meeting, and yet could not be charged with corruption. These men had been nurtured in all the delusions of the old school, every proceeding of a popular nature filled them with alarm, and there was nothing they so much dreaded as the word Reform. . . . In this state of things . . . you must oppose your threefold enemies with means suited to the character of each class. To corruption, oppose integrity and vigilance—to prejudice, moderation and calm reasoning—to apathy, zeal and activity;—but above all, be fortified with patience to withstand disappointment, and with perseverance to maintain the struggle.[3]

[1] *Mercury*, 15 April 1809.
[2] 'A Freeman'.
[3] *Chronicle*, 6 May 1809, and Roberts, p. 247.

Smith's may well have been good advice, but it was not what the meeting wanted to hear. Alderman Waithman delivered a sharp attack on Smith for attempting to dampen the ardour of the meeting; here, he said, was a typical example of 'The Friends of the People' and of Whiggery, always ready to pay lip service to Reform but never ready to move decisively to bring it into effect.[1]

It was the kind of situation in which Smith would increasingly find himself. He had been the only Whig of standing and respectability who attended the meeting—even Whitbread had not been there—yet temperament and principle would not allow him to agree with the radicals, and honesty would not allow him to conceal their differences. He called for patience and moderation—they possessed neither. Again and again, he appeared to align himself with the radical cause, only to be forced to differ.

He was bound to differ in 1810, when Burdett decided to attack Parliament itself. Burdett had challenged the right of the House of Commons to imprison for contempt, and, as a result, had been himself committed to the Tower. Smith had opposed this action by the House, but he never questioned its right to take it, and when the Middlesex electors did so, he demanded that their petition should not be accepted. It might be true that the House no longer enjoyed the respect of the people—and rightly so. 'Yet it should still exert all its due privileges.' The House could be, and ought to be, a bulwark defending the people's liberties and its privileges used to that end. Intelligent Reform would solve the dilemma, but in the meantime 'respectability was not to be sacrificed for consistency, and, in the case before them, he must vote against the popular feeling of the day'.[2]

Smith had been deeply shocked by the whole affair, and his approbation of Burdett's part in it would appear to have been confined solely to the latter's decision not to take part in the popular demonstrations that accompanied his release.[3] His party in Norwich thought differently. At the annual dinner held in July to celebrate the anniversary of Smith's election, toasts were drunk to 'Sir

[1] *Chronicle*, 6 May 1809, and Roberts, p. 247.
[2] *Chronicle*, 12 May 1810.
[3] F. Burdett to William Smith, 29 June 1810, Bonham-Carter Papers.

Francis Burdett (with three times three, and continued and enthusiastic plaudits)' and 'May the Laws of the Land ever be paramount to the undefined Privileges of Parliament'.[1]

Smith would never waver in his assertion of the rights of Parliament, nor of his own right of independent judgement. And he never let slip an occasion to state his position. In 1811 the great Coke of Norfolk (afterwards the first Earl of Leicester) attacked Smith for his alleged approval of an agreement between the Ministry and the London brewers to continue the distillation of sugar to the exclusion of barley; and Coke warned Norfolk farmers never to trust anyone who had a connexion with the West Indies. Smith replied in a letter to the *Chronicle*, denying that he had signified approval of the agreement, but tartly remarking that 'although the eager pursuit of their separate emolument in this case may in each separate class be *allowable*, it is not, in any of them *laudable*; no more in the Landholder or Barley Grower of Norfolk than in the Slave-holder and Sugar Grower of Jamaica. . . .' At this time of crisis, he said, the main consideration must be the preservation of the whole Empire and the maintenance of all its resources to that end—and, when he made up his mind on this particular matter, it would be on this basis, and none other.[2] He was no less firm with the 1815 Common Hall, called to pass resolutions against the Income Tax. On this issue Smith was at one with his Norwich supporters, but he had taken exception to some remarks which had been made about the binding nature of a constituency's instructions to its member. And he told the meeting in no uncertain terms that

in matters of general national concern, he felt no further bound than to receive their instructions with deference and respect, and carefully weigh and consider them; but if after the best attention he could give, he still found himself unconvinced, then his duty to the Country, and even to his constituents, obliged him to follow the dictates of his own judgement.[3]

Smith's insistence on a member's duty to rise above sectional interests was modern enough. But there were elements in his thinking which were not. As has been seen, Smith genuinely believed—

[1] *Chronicle*, 7 July 1810. [2] Ibid., 2 March 1811. [3] Ibid., 21 January 1815.

for the foreseeable future, at any rate—in the concept of the balanced constitution. He stated this belief in Norwich again and again, in a variety of ways. In 1812, for example, he told the Norwich electors:

Governments will be good, generally speaking, in proportion as they are watched. . . . It is the business of Parliament to watch the motions of the Executive Government, but if they are not incorrupt, if they succumb to the same temptations, your interests must inevitably suffer. The Constitution has wisely provided that *you* should be the watchers over *them*. . . .[1]

The electorate must have some check over Parliament, as Parliament must have some check over the executive; but no more in the former case than in the latter was this to mean the right to complete control. Proper Reform—which, it must be remembered, stopped for Smith short of universal suffrage—would ensure men of high principles and independence in Parliament; and, as an extra safeguard, Smith always advocated a stiff property qualification for M.P.s.[2] In such representatives—in men not unlike himself—the country would, and ought to have, the fullest confidence.

Smith never advocated democracy, nor did he have much hope that he would live to see even the limited Reform which he desired. Though broadly optimistic about the future, Smith was deeply pessimistic about the present.

The source of his pessimism is not far to seek: Smith had a deep distrust of the majority of his fellow-countrymen—which is not to say a dislike. His relations with the mass electorate in Norwich are enlightening in this regard. To the generality of his constituents, Smith behaved like the benevolent headmaster of an unruly school. In 1809 he told the Tory mob which was shouting down the anti-Corruption meeting that

every cool and rational person will view all such clamorous attempts, as the strongest possible concession of weakness in argument. For in this way a single individual, and he the most unworthy and insignificant of human beings, may succeed in throwing a whole assembly

---

[1] *The Poll* (Stevenson and Matchett, 1812), pp. 8–10.
[2] *Hansard*, XXII, 143.

into confusion—and gain the merit too of as great success as if a set of *equally loud animals* were brought to the door.

This salty appeal to good sense and fair play was received with laughter, applauses, and capitulation.[1] He had similar success with the radical mob which attempted to silence the sole opponent of Reform at the 1816 Common Hall. Both Nathaniel Bolingbroke and Edward Taylor, the leading radical politicians in Norwich, appealed in vain to 'the populace, who in a deep and solid phalanx filled the great aisle of the Hall in front of the hustings'. (St Andrew's Hall holds several thousand.) Smith then came forward, and 'the storm being instantly hushed', delivered a short and effective lecture on freedom of speech.[2] Smith was always lecturing the electors. In 1806 he had chided them for their fickleness. And in 1812, as well as on countless other occasions, he directed himself to the 'lower classes, who highly respectable as those of this city were, how much soever they were benefited by knowledge which was now open to all, and however improved in their habits of combining causes and effects, might still profit by a piece of advice', followed by a long chastisement of their corruption.[3]

Quite obviously, Smith loved the rough and tumble of Norwich politics. And he was as fond of the people of Norwich as they seem to have been of him. But equally obviously, though he certainly believed his lower-class constituents educable, he had no very high opinion of the stage which the process of education had attained. And, if his beloved Norwich left much to be desired, Smith's view of the rest of the country was even more gloomy.

Smith's Norwich supporters continued to assess the situation differently, however. Never were the Norwich radicals more enthusiastic or more uncompromising than at the great Reform meeting of 1816. But Smith remained of the same opinion as he had been in 1809, and in a long speech he reiterated and elaborated the points which he had made at the Crown and Anchor meeting. He had, he said, always been an advocate of Parliamentary reform 'as far as the people could proceed with it'. But he saw little hope at

[1] *Chronicle,* 15 April 1809.
[2] Ibid., 19 October 1816.
[3] *The Poll* (Stevenson and Matchett, 1812), pp. 8–10.

this time for any Reform measure. It would be a long struggle, with many obstacles to overcome. The first was Parliament itself, still strongly opposed. Nor would its attitude soon be changed by an active public opinion; for 'another antagonist was to be found in an unmoved and uninterested public'. It need not be expected, he warned, that this meeting would be followed by many others; indeed, 'if he had not known previous instances in which the citizens of Norwich stood forward with the view of leading the public mind, and in which their endeavours were not wholly disappointed, he should have been induced at once to say that the present meeting was premature'. For there was another enemy still very much in the ascendant:

You have against your course the whole body of corrupt electors in the kingdom: and in vain will Parliament be reformed, in vain will it be attempted to make choice for its members of men faithful and zealous in the discharge of their duties, unless the electors themselves be honest and incorrupt.

Here Smith looked not only at the possibility of Reform, but speculated on its impact. Reform at this time was not only impossible, it might be undesirable; its sole effect might well be only to add more corrupt electors to an already corrupt system. Attitudes as well as institutions must be changed, and, of the two, attitudes were perhaps more important in his mind.

In concluding, Smith affirmed once again his belief in the ultimate necessity of Reform: 'If the wisdom of man did not actively employ itself in correcting what was bad, and fortifying what was good, no form of society or of national policy could go on, as Providence intended it should, in a progression of improvement. . . .' He ended by emphasizing once again the essentially conservative motives which prompted his desire for Reform. It remained his opinion of the British Constitution that 'taking it for all in all, it was the best calculated of any that ever existed, for securing, during a series of years, the prosperity and happiness of an Empire. . . . It was because he thought it so good that he wished to see it more perfect; that it might be as permanent, as it was excellent'.[1]

[1] *Chronicle*, 19 October 1816.

Perhaps Smith believed—he almost certainly did—that in time the 'progression of improvement' which Providence intended would raise mankind to a point where all could participate in government. But that time was very far in the future. For the time being, one could only hope for a little—and expect nothing.

Smith's pessimism, and his resulting caution in approaching liberal reforms, coupled with a lingering attachment to traditional institutions and conceptions, made him far removed from the new radicalism espoused by his Norwich supporters. Their ultimate objectives might be identical, but their immediate objectives and their ideas of the desirable rate of change were often very far apart.

Why, then, did Norwich so long remain loyal to Smith? The *Chronicle*, no ardent supporter, gave part of the explanation in its comment on his re-election in 1812:

It was the triumph of good sense, of private and political integrity. . . . Whatever differences of opinion may exist among speculative men on points of religion and policy, all honest men agree in offering homage to singleness of heart, to strength of understanding, to simplicity of manners, gentleness of disposition, and uprightness of conduct. These virtues told upon the day of election to the equal honour of the Constituents and the Candidate—they fixed the doubtful in his favour, and disarmed even the rabble of half their hostility, and all their intemperance. Without the slightest intention to derogate from the merits of either of the gentlemen who opposed him—and such intention we cannot be expected to entertain—it must be acknowledged that a general sentiment prevailed, that the city of Norwich would suffer, perhaps something in its character—certainly something in its interests, if Mr. Smith were not returned one of its Representatives to Parliament. . . .[1]

Smith showed himself at his best in Norwich, and his best was appreciated.

But a more practical and immediate concern undoubtedly motivated the radical politicians who chose Smith as their candidate election after election. First and foremost they were Dissenters, and William Smith had become the foremost advocate of the Dissenting cause.

[1] *Chronicle*, 17 March 1812.

147

CHAPTER NINE

LORD SIDMOUTH'S BILL

For the greater part of the time that William Smith represented Norwich, he was also the acknowledged leader of the Dissenting cause in the country. Smith was unanimously elected Chairman of the Dissenting Deputies at their general meeting in January 1805, and he retained that position for twenty-seven years, longer than any other Chairman in their history.

Smith's great influence in Dissent goes a long way toward explaining not only the continuing allegiance of Norwich, but also the respect which he enjoyed among the Whigs and the Saints, both of whom courted Dissenting support. But, more important, it was as the leader of Dissent that Smith had his greatest impact on history. The fact that his place among the early Parliamentary reformers, within the small group that led the fight for the abolition of the Slave Trade, and in the Whig party, has never been sufficiently recognized, is certainly one justification for a study of his career. But there can be no doubt that his most important contribution to the cause of human freedom, the cause which gives connexion and meaning to all his political activities, was in the extension of religious liberty. In this endeavour, Smith stands out clearly and unquestionably as a major figure in his own right. It was Smith who directed the negotiations for the broadening of the Toleration Act in 1812. It was Smith who drew up and guided through Parliament the Unitarian toleration act of 1813. And it was Smith, as Chairman of the United Committee, who presided over the successful campaign to repeal the greatest badges of Dissenting inferiority, the Test and Corporation Acts, in 1828. These were Smith's major achievements, and they will be the main concern of the balance of this book.

Until now, Smith had been considered largely as a public figure in opposition. He was to remain so, but he was also to become a constructive politician. Previously, he has been seen mainly in the public arena, in Parliament and in Norwich. Now he will be followed to quieter places, to the closets of ministers and prelates, to the small committees which shaped the policy of Dissent. In places such as these, Smith made his greatest achievements. His previous career was by no means unimportant in his new activities. Experience had shaped a firm political philosophy; he had learned much of men and of affairs; and he had attained a political standing and made political contacts which were to be invaluable in his new role. We shall now see what use he made of his experience in advancing the interests of his fellow-Dissenters.

The Dissenting Deputies, and Smith as their most distinguished representative, had not been inactive since the nineties. Both at home and in the colonies they had continued to be the vigilant and effective guardians of religious liberty. At home, they had successfully contested numerous cases of refusal by Anglican clergymen to bury Dissenters. They had established the right of Dissenters to the free use of toll roads in going and coming from Sunday worship. They had also secured liberalization of the Militia and Indemnity acts in favour of Dissenters. And they had successfully prevented attempts to tax Dissenting meeting houses and trusts.[1] Outside England, the Deputies had succeeded in thwarting persistent attempts by the Jamaica colonists between 1802 and 1812 to abridge the Toleration Act in that island.[2] Relations between the Deputies' Committee and government continued to be highly satisfactory, and particularly in their troubles with Jamaica, Smith and the Committee secured ready co-operation from the ministers.[3] The first decade of the nineteenth century was one of solid, if undramatic, achievement for the Deputies. But the calm was to be shattered. The Deputies were to face the greatest crisis in their history—and they were not to face it very effectively.

In view of all that has been said of the contribution of the Deputies

[1] *Sketch*, pp. 64–83, and Minutes, *passim*.
[2] *Sketch*, pp. 61–84, and Minutes, *passim*.
[3] See Earl Bathurst to William Smith, n.d., Smith Collection (Duke).

under the leadership of William Smith to the cause of religious liberty, it is startling to find them apparently almost inert in face of the most dangerous challenge to religious liberty since the reign of Queen Anne. It is even more startling to find them charged with aiding and abetting attempts to restrict religious liberty. Yet the facts are that William Smith and the Deputies' Committee did remarkably little to oppose the introduction of Lord Sidmouth's bill to restrict the registration of Dissenting ministers in 1811 and that they were widely believed to have given Sidmouth encouragement in bringing the bill forward. These strange circumstances have never been satisfactorily explained, and they need explanation.

A few introductory remarks will make the explanation of this extremely complicated question clearer. It will be remembered that Sidmouth's was not the first contemplated abridgement of the Toleration acts (of 1689 and 1779). Pitt had considered severe restrictions in 1800. His motivation had probably been a fear of all popular movements mixed with a repugnance to what were considered the excesses of evangelical revival. Fear and repugnance continued and to them was added the anxiety of High Tory Anglicans that because of the obvious success of the revival there would soon be, as Sidmouth was to say in introducing his bill in 1811, an established church and a sectarian people.

It was against this background that Sidmouth first mooted the question in Parliament in 1809. What once again concentrated attention on the Toleration acts was probably the need for an increasingly extensive mobilization of manpower as the Napoleonic wars continued. The acts provided for the exemption of ministers from burdensome offices and military service—or, at any rate, provided for the exemption of a certain category of ministers. And on 25 May 1808 Smith had summoned the Committee 'in consequence of the Local Militia Bill before Parliament and to take into consideration how far Dissenters engaged in the ministry may be affected by the operations of the bill as it now stands and as to what clauses of exemption it may be necessary or advisable to get introduced therein'.[1] What action, if any, was taken does not appear. It seems

[1] Minutes, 25 May 1808.

150

likely, in view of their later attitude, that the Committee did not think it 'advisable' to attempt any extension of exemptions. At any rate, the act left, as had always been the case, only ministers of 'settled congregations' exempted from service.

When Sidmouth first broached the matter in Parliament in June 1809, it was to exemptions that he especially directed himself. He said he believed that many were seeking registration as Dissenting ministers simply to secure exemption from service, and he called for a return of the registrations of ministers under the Toleration acts since 1780, amended by the House to 1760.

Sidmouth was not speaking for himself alone, and—a crucial point for understanding the Deputies' policy—others had already taken it upon themselves to reinterpret the Toleration acts, not only before Sidmouth introduced his bill, but before he even raised the question in Parliament. Two months before Sidmouth's initial remarks in June 1809, the Aylesbury Quarter Sessions had refused to *register* one William Carr on the grounds that he was not the minister of a settled congregation.[1] As will be seen, the argument of the Aylesbury magistrates was to be sustained by the most eminent legal opinion and ultimately by a ruling of King's Bench. Previously, the Dissenters had considered the automatic registration of anyone who presented himself a *right* under the Toleration acts. This was not the case. In other words, two years before Sidmouth introduced any legislation, the Aylesbury magistrates, soon to be followed by others, had already reinterpreted the Toleration acts in a very practical fashion. Sidmouth's bill therefore could be seen not so much as a reinterpretation of the acts as a clarification of them.

In June 1810 Sidmouth announced that as a result of the returns, he felt justified in undertaking remedial legislation the next year. His stated concern, however, had changed radically. He was no longer primarily agitated about exemptions, but, as he was to say again in the following year, with the kind of people who, in large numbers, were becoming Dissenting ministers—'cobblers, tailors, pig-drovers, and chimney-sweepers', among others of low estate and no education.

From a concern with the abuse of the law, Sidmouth had changed

[1] Ibid., 24 March 1809.

151

to a concern with the quality of the Dissenting ministry and proposed to tighten up the Toleration acts to improve the situation. This was a very important shift indeed. Many Dissenters were willing to admit that there had been abuses of the law, but none were willing to admit restriction of the traditional freedom of preaching under the Toleration acts. Dissent had already been roused to the issue. At the end of June 1809, shortly after Sidmouth had first noticed the question, there had been a meeting between representatives of the Deputies and the Dissenting Ministers, and this meeting had resolved to solicit the opinions of as wide a number of country Dissenters as possible. The result of these consultations had been a general concurrence 'in reprobating any design to explain or alter the law so as to abridge the freedom in religious matters then enjoyed by Dissenters'. (It must be borne in mind that, in fact, as has already been seen, that freedom was at this very time in the process of being explained, altered, and abridged.) The only point on which there was some disagreement among Dissenters was 'as to the description of persons who, it was thought, might reasonably expect from the legislature the advantage [i.e. exemptions] of Dissenting ministers'.[1] But this, it must be stressed, was an entirely different question. It had, it is true, been Sidmouth's stated reason for raising the issue in the first place, but it was hardly the main aim of the bill he finally introduced in May 1811. That bill was clearly intended not so much to regulate exemptions for preachers as to limit severely the opportunity of becoming a preacher in the first place.[2]

The bill would have altered drastically what had been, until recently at any rate, the accepted interpretation of the Toleration Act and of its modification in the act of 1779 which relieved Dissenting ministers of the necessity of subscribing to the doctrinal Articles. The major provision of the bill was that which required all ministers of congregations, others who officiated as ministers (e.g. Methodist local preachers), and probationers, to present testimonials to their character and ability to the justices in Quarter Sessions,

[1] *Sketch*, p. 85.
[2] A summary of the main events in the controversy and of the Parliamentary debates will be found in ibid., pp. 83–4 and 91–3.

as a preliminary to registration. Especially important was the description of those who were to provide the testimonials. In the case of ministers, they were to be provided by six 'substantial and reputable householders'. In the case of probationers, by six ministers.[1] Obviously, the former description was the crucial one. What constituted a 'substantial and reputable householder'? Only the magistrates could decide. The effect of the bill, therefore, would have been to place a very important element in the freedom of Dissenting worship completely at the discretion of the magistrates: the Toleration acts as they applied to Dissenting ministers would have been eviscerated.

Sidmouth may well have thought that his bill would mainly affect the Methodists. But, if he did, he was only illustrating a profound ignorance about Dissenting affairs which was, and was long to remain, common among English statesmen.[2] It had long since become impossible to draw any hard and fast distinctions between Methodism and 'old' Dissent. For, as has been suggested earlier, almost from the beginning the Methodist revival had become merged in a broader evangelical revival which affected all the older Dissenting sects save for the Presbyterians, and even the Church itself. For one thing, large numbers who started out as Methodists had from the beginning crossed denominational lines and assumed older names, and this process was still going on. Calvinist Methodists easily became Independents and Particular Baptists.[3] The General (or Arminian) Baptists split in the 1770s as a consequence of the revival. The New Connection swung into the evangelical camp, while the old General Baptists followed a course very similar to the Presbyterians and were becoming closely associated with them in the new Unitarianism.[4] Nor were all those who still bore

---

[1] The full text of the bill appears in *The Monthly Repository*, VI (1811), 332–6.

[2] For example, see below, p. 224, n. 3.

[3] In Lewes in Sussex, which was to play an important role in Dissenting anti-Catholic petitioning in 1825 (see below, pp. 224–6), Calvinistic Methodist congregations spawned a Particular Baptist congregation in 1785 and an Independent congregation in 1816 (T. W. Horsfield, *History of Lewes* [Lewes, 1824–27], p. 302ff.).

[4] The best general surveys of the course of the revival are still to be found in the old work by H. W. Clark, and the still older book by H. S. Skeats and

the name Methodist, even apart from the always distinct Calvinistic Methodists, still associated with the main body of Wesleyan Methodists. The autocracy of the Conference alienated many Methodists, and there was a continuing process of secession. Several groups seceded during the period when the controversy over the Toleration acts was going on. Probably the most important of these—at any rate for suggesting what Sidmouth and others were reacting against —were the Primitive Methodists, or 'ranters' as they were significantly nicknamed by their enemies, and long commonly known. The emotional frenzy of their camp meetings was shocking to the Conference, which banned such extravagances in 1808, and it would undoubtedly have been even more shocking to those of Sidmouth's views. Methods very similar, however, were used by those who bore traditional Dissenting names—and they were used by the same sort of people. Cobblers, tailors and the rest preached not only to Methodists, but to those in the older denominations, and such people would have been fairly common, particularly in the Baptist ministry. In attempting to curb the ranters, Sidmouth could not have failed to strike at the vital interests of 'old' Dissent.

What was especially frightening to men of Sidmouth's way of thinking was the fact that the new methods were working with startling success. This was clearly suggested by the returns he had requested in 1809,[1] and the rapid growth of Dissent which they indicated has been confirmed by modern scholarship. The possibility of an established church and a sectarian people was more than a mere wild figment of Sidmouth's imagination. And he, and those whom he represented, were terrified by the prospect. Once again the forces which supported the establishment in Church and State began to move, and Lord Sidmouth became their spokesman.[2]

C. S. Miall, *History of Free Churches of England* (London, 1891). A more sophisticated, though necessarily limited, account is given in Bolam *et al.*

[1] Reproduced in Manning, pp. 130–1.

[2] Of critical importance both on the negotiations between Sidmouth and local magistrates before he took action and on the growth of Dissent during this period is an unpublished M.Litt. thesis by M. B. Whittaker, 'The Revival of Dissent, 1800–1835', Cambridge, 1958. As will be seen, I take strong

When Sidmouth introduced his bill it not surprisingly met with a firm and united opposition both from those who had traditionally borne the name 'Dissenter' and from the Methodists. The Deputies and the Dissenting ministers passed strong resolutions against it. So did the Wesleyan Methodists. And a new group, soon to become the Protestant Society for the Protection of Religious Liberty, was founded to meet the challenge of the bill. The Protestant Society had Unitarians, and even liberal Anglicans, among its founders, but from the beginning its main support came from evangelical Dissenters, Independents and Baptists, and from those who now began consciously to identify themselves with the Dissenting cause (though some, at any rate, had looked to the Deputies for assistance well before this time), Calvinistic Methodists in both England and Wales, and seceders from Wesleyan Methodism. As will be seen, there was a widespread feeling among evangelicals that the Deputies had not been very ardent in supporting their interests. This was the main reason for the founding of the Protestant Society, and there is no doubt that it was much more aggressive than the Deputies in its policy towards Sidmouth's bill. The Protestant Society and the Wesleyan Methodists, independent of the Deputies and without much assistance from them, organized a highly effective mass petition campaign, which produced almost 700 petitions in less than a week. According to Lord Holland:

For some days no places were to be had on the stage coaches and diligences of the Kingdom; all were occupied with petitions to parliament against the measure. . . . The peers could hardly get to the doors, the avenues were so crowded with men of grave deportment and puritanical aspect; when there, they had almost equal difficulty in gaining their seats, for loads of parchment encumbered and obstructed their way to them. . . .[1]

This forceful response was sufficient to secure a governmental disavowal of the measure and its defeat in the Lords.

---

exception to some of his conclusions which have been given currency by Ursula Henriques, but much of great significance remains. One hopes these results will some day be published.

[1] *Further Memoirs of the Whig Party* (London, 1905), p. 101.

Dissent had won a great victory, but in the process its traditional leaders suffered a serious blow to their prestige. It is an undoubted fact that the Deputies had not been very forceful, and they took almost no part in the marshalling of Dissenting strength which was responsible for defeating the bill. Moreover, they were suspected of worse than apathy. William Smith individually and the Dissenting Deputies as a body were subjected to the most damaging charges with regard to their attitude and policy toward the bill. At its second reading on 21 May Sidmouth stated that 'he had understood, from the communications he had had with several respectable Dissenters, that they were desirous that some such measure as this should be adopted, or at least they approved of it. He was much astonished, after this, at seeing [the Deputies'] Resolutions advertised on the subject, with the name of a member of Parliament to them, with whom he had also had communications'.[1] And among Sidmouth's papers his biographer found a memorandum asserting: 'Mr. Smith repeatedly told me that the bill was so reasonable in its principle, and so just and moderate in its provisions, that he could not oppose it.'[2] Spencer Perceval, in a letter to Smith in 1812, after they had had a long interview on the situation of the Dissenting ministers, was also under the impression that Smith had approved of the bill.[3] Lord Stanhope openly taxed Smith with having approved it in letters published in the *Morning Chronicle* the same year.[4] As was suggested above, the charges were even credited within Dissent itself, the Protestant Society averring in a circular letter at the end of 1812 that Sidmouth had been 'emboldened by the unresisting acquiescence, or encouraged by the private approbation of those who were considered as the guardians of the rights of conscience'.[5]

These were serious charges, but neither Smith nor the Deputies' Committee ever made a direct public denial of their truth. The

[1] Quoted in *Sketch*, p. 107.

[2] G. Pellew, *The Life and Correspondence of the Right Hon. Henry Addington, First Viscount Sidmouth* (London, 1847), III, 65n.

[3] Spencer Perceval to William Smith, 10 April 1812, Liverpool Papers, B.M. Add. MSS 38,247, f. 185.

[4] *Monthly Repository*, VII (1812), 461–2.

[5] Ibid., p. 761.

closest they came was in an address by the Deputies, published under Smith's signature, directed to English Dissenters generally in 1811, in which it was stated that they did not 'believe that any Dissenters encouraged his lordship to imagine, that such infringements on their accustomed possessions could ever meet with the approbation of their body'.[1] A mild statement, especially as the charges were entirely unfounded.

Though Smith and the Deputies' Committee maintained an aloof silence with regard to Sidmouth's allegations, Thomas Belsham did not. In a published letter to Sidmouth immediately after the defeat of the bill, Belsham declared that it would have been impossible for the Deputies' Committee to have given their approval since they had not even seen an abstract of the bill prior to its introduction. And, Belsham said, Lord Sidmouth was very much mistaken if he believed that they had ever approved of any measure of the sort.[2] Belsham was undoubtedly well acquainted with the facts of the matter. He was an old and intimate friend of Smith and his minister at the Essex Street Chapel. He was also in close touch with Sidmouth, both personally and through their mutual confidant, Benjamin Hobhouse. Belsham's public denial of Sidmouth's allegations must, therefore, have great weight.

Another of Smith's close associates, John Gurney, the Deputy Chairman of the Dissenting Deputies, also denied Sidmouth's contention in the most emphatic terms. Writing to Belsham after the publication of the *Letter to Lord Sidmouth*, Gurney stated:

A sub-committee of the Deputies had one conference and one only with Lord Sidmouth and there neither was nor could be any misapprehension between Lord Sidmouth and the gentlemen who composed that sub-committee. They dissuaded Lord Sidmouth, as strongly as they could from bringing in his bill and certainly expressed nothing like approbation of it but very much the contrary. . . .

Lord Sidmouth undoubtedly alluded to other individuals with whom he had communications.[3]

---

[1] *Sketch*, p. 120.

[2] Thomas Belsham, *A Letter to Lord Sidmouth* (London, 1811), pp. 34–6.

[3] John Gurney to Thomas Belsham, 26 June 1811, Dr Williams's Library, 12.58, no. 23.

Gurney is borne out by the Minutes. There was only one meeting between Sidmouth and a sub-committee of the Deputies (though Smith had had a private meeting with him previously). The meeting took place on 10 May 1810, a year before the bill was introduced, and at that meeting the sub-committee had stated its objections in detail and attempted to dissuade Sidmouth from introducing any legislation.[1]

Smith had headed the sub-committee which called on Sidmouth and had acted as its chief spokesman. He is, therefore, on record as having opposed Sidmouth's intentions. Nor would his statements in Parliament have given Sidmouth any reason for assuming his support. Indeed, at almost the same time that Sidmouth was first announcing his intention of introducing legislation (in June 1810), Smith was the seconder of a resolution by Whitbread to abolish *all* restrictions and disabilities for religious belief.[2] In other words, Smith wished to render the Toleration acts themselves obsolete, let alone any interpretations such as Sidmouth proposed.

The only possibility that remains of Sidmouth's charges being true is that Smith made private assurances which contradicted his public stand. But, as R. B. Aspland remarked: 'Prudent and unduly cautious he was sometimes thought to be, but no man doubted his inflexible integrity.'[3] Character apart, it would have been an inexplicable act of folly for Smith to have promised privately what he was certain to have to renounce publicly. The only evidence by a direct party to the negotiations that Smith did give assurances of support is Sidmouth's, and Sidmouth was notoriously untrustworthy on this matter. He told Wilberforce, who called on him in April 1811 to attempt to argue him out of his proposed course, that he had the firm support of the Dissenters and the Methodists, a belief that no remonstrance from his visitor could shake. He afterwards told a delegation of Methodists that he had the support of Wilberforce![4] Sidmouth was totally incapable of recognizing oppo-

[1] Minutes, 25 May 1810.

[2] *Monthly Repository*, V (1810), 314.

[3] R. B. Aspland, *Memoir of the Reverend Robert Aspland* (London, 1850), p. 263.

[4] Wilberforce, *Life*, III, 509–12.

sition when he encountered it. His charges against Smith cannot be taken seriously.

Yet, though it was reasonably easy to exonerate Smith and the Deputies' Committee of having encouraged Sidmouth, it is very difficult to establish a case for their having done sufficient to discourage him. There is only one reference in the Minutes to Sidmouth's proposed legislation between May 1810 and May 1811, when the bill was introduced. On 29 March 1811 the Committee resolved that

in case Lord Sidmouth should bring forward any motion in Parliament applicable to the Dissenting interest that the sub-committee already appointed be empowered to wait upon Lord Erskine or any other Member of either house of Parliament thereon as they may think fit or see necessary.[1]

The resolution suggests that the Committee thought there was a possibility Sidmouth might not introduce his promised bill. But, in the event he did, the Committee does not, at this time, seem to have decided on total opposition. The initiative was left to Sidmouth, and the Committee was leaving the way open for manoeuvre.

This was not because the members of the Committee did not know generally what Sidmouth had in mind. The main outlines of his measure had been made known to them in 1810 and remained unaltered in 1811: (1) the requirement of testimonials; (2) imposing some regulation of itinerant preaching; and (3) preventing lay preachers from claiming exemption from military service and parochial office.[2] All this information the Committee had, yet it did little or nothing to prepare for the impending crisis. Why?

In a letter to Belsham, John Gurney stoutly defended the policy of the Committee previous to the introduction of Sidmouth's bill. Those who criticized it, he said, gave no credit 'for caution or prudence'.[3] Gurney referred particularly not to Sidmouth's efforts to restrict the registration of Dissenting ministers, but to the actual restrictions imposed by the Quarter Sessions in several counties.

[1] Minutes, 29 March 1811.

[2] Ibid., 25 May 1810.

[3] John Gurney to Thomas Belsham, 28 June 1811, Dr Williams's Library, 12.58, no. 24.

The actions of the Quarter Sessions had been possible because of certain ambiguities in the existing laws. The wording of the Toleration Act differed from that of the act of 1779. Clause 7 of the Toleration Act simply *empowered* the magistrates to register ministers, while 19 Geo 3 *required* them to do so. But, while in this respect the 1779 act was more favourable to Dissenters, in another respect it was not. According to the Toleration Act, 'no person in holy orders, or pretending to holy orders, *nor* any preacher or teacher of any congregation of Dissenting Protestants' who went through the proper procedures should be subject to penalties. The act of 1779, however, was worded, 'in holy orders, *being* a preacher or teacher of any congregation of Dissenting Protestants'.[1] Thus it could be argued, as the Buckinghamshire justices argued in the Carr case, that it was necessary to be the minister of a congregation at the time of the application in order to qualify for the protection afforded by the acts. From 1809 onwards, several Quarter Sessions chose to follow the example of the Bucks magistrates and so argue, thus excluding probationers and occasional or itinerant preachers from any protection. At the same time, justices in several counties began to enforce the long-disused Conventicle Act of 1670, which provided heavy fines for anyone preaching at, or attending, services other than those of the Established Church.[2] Combined, these actions of the magistrates created the possibility of a highly dangerous situation for Dissent.

The Committee of the Deputies met the challenge with the utmost deliberation and caution. The Committee dealt only with cases of refusal to register, doubtless because these were the only cases in which they had any legal grounds. The refusal to register Carr was followed by long but fruitless negotiations between Smith on the one hand, and the Lord Lieutenant, the Marquis of Buckingham, and the Chairman of the Quarter Sessions, on the other.[3] The

---

[1] *Sketch*, pp. 203 and 214.

[2] Prosecution would not, of course, have been possible against preachers and congregations properly registered according to the provisions of the Toleration Act. But a long period of apparent security had produced considerable laxity, and many had not even made an attempt to conform to the law (Ibid., p. 156).

[3] Minutes, 29 April 1809.

Committee's decision on a second batch of refusals in January 1810 was that it would not be 'prudent to agitate the question of magistrates refusing persons to qualify just at the present moment'.[1] The third case came in January 1811. The Bucks magistrates had refused to register 'Mr. Peter Tyler the regular Minister, but not the ordained Pastor, of the Baptist Church at Haddenham. . . .' The Chairman of the Quarter Sessions had stated: 'We will register no man unless he be regularly settled over a Congregation, and we will have a Certificate signed by several of the Congregation attesting that he is their Pastor and also a person in Court to prove the Signature of such Certificate'.[2] This refusal, the Committee decided to challenge. On 26 April it sent instructions that 'Mr. Tyler attend the next Quarter Sessions . . . and, in case of being again refused, . . . inform the Magistrates that application will be made to the Court of King's Bench for a Mandamus'.[3] The threat apparently proved sufficient. The Quarter Sessions registered Tyler. It is significant, however, that the case on which the Committee chose to take its stand fell clearly within the provisions of the act of 1779 (since Tyler was the regular minister of a congregation). The magistrates' discretion in *all* cases was not being challenged in this instance.

In his *Letter to Lord Sidmouth*, Belsham made reference to the refusals by Quarter Sessions to register. Gurney's justification of the policy pursued by the Deputies' Committee toward these refusals is highly significant. 'The apparent inactivity of the Deputies' upon the subject you mention has', he said, 'not been the result of inattention but of much consideration'. According to Gurney, most persons who applied to qualify as Dissenting ministers did so under the act of 1779. When the variance between that act and the Toleration Act first became apparent, the Committee had taken eminent legal opinions on the matter, including those of the Attorney General, Sir Vicary Gibbs, and Mr. Serjeant Heywood. The results gave them 'no encouragement to stir the question'.

We discussed the subject several times and on the whole thought it better to lie still for the present waiting a more favorable opportunity

---

[1] Ibid., 26 January 1810.   [2] Ibid., 25 January 1811.   [3] Ibid., 26 April 1811.

—for an administration which would at once concede the point to us if it should be determined against us by the Court of King's Bench. When such an administration should be in power we proposed litigating the question. Till then we thought we would injure the Dissenters materially by exposing the defect in the law which has not been generally known and the Dissenters are in most places enjoying the benefit of an enlarged and liberal construction.

The difficulty of our position is considerable because we cannot publish the motives of our conduct without defeating our object.[1]

Gurney's letter makes clear the reason for the seemingly strange inactivity of the Deputies not only toward the challenge given by the magistrates, but toward the very similar challenge by Sidmouth. Smith and the Committee were desperately anxious to avoid any full-scale confrontation on the interpretation of the Toleration acts until such time as their Whig friends should be in power. And when it is remembered that the coming of the Whigs to power was thought to be imminent throughout the crisis period, from 1810 when George III became hopelessly mad until 1812 when the Prince Regent finally definitively threw his Whig friends over for Spencer Perceval,[2] their policy of inactivity becomes more understandable.

Given this general aim, the Committee's first hope with regard to Sidmouth's proposed legislation would undoubtedly have been that he could be dissuaded from bringing in any bill at all. This was by no means an impossibility. Though neither Smith nor the Committee as a body appear to have done anything to discourage Sidmouth after May 1810, they had powerful allies working for their cause. Wilberforce, then at the height of his influence, stated his opposition not only to Sidmouth but to the Prime Minister.[3] The government, for its part, was never enthusiastic about Sidmouth's intentions, and though Perceval and Lord Liverpool were reassured by Sidmouth's unshakeable certainty of the support of all parties concerned, they drew back in horror at the first signs of opposition.[4] Smith would almost certainly have known of Wilberforce's activities

[1] John Gurney to Thomas Belsham, 28 June 1811, Dr Williams's Library, 12.58, no. 24.

[2] Roberts, p. 2.

[3] Wilberforce, *Life*, III, 509–12.

[4] Pellew, III, 61–2.

and probably, through him, of the government's coolness to Sidmouth's proposals. Smith's position and the Committee's had already been made as clear as possible, and if Wilberforce's representations were without effect, there would have been little reason to hope that any would have been more effective.

In the event of Sidmouth's bringing in a bill, it is very probable that the Committee's intention was to negotiate. This is strongly suggested in the Committee resolution of 29 March 1811,[1] and there are other similar indications. It must be borne in mind that the Committee knew nothing of the 'substantial and reputable householder' clause. Indeed their understanding of Sidmouth's intentions on the whole question of testimonials was very different from those indicated in the bill. The impression gained at the interview with Sidmouth in the previous year had been that he was desirous of

requiring some species of testimonial to the moral character, and qualifications (insisting but little on the latter) of those who should demand licences as Dissenting teachers under the Toleration Act;— such testimonials to be given by persons of their own sect or persuasion and not to be subjected to any discretion of the magistrate.[2]

Had the testimonials been as innocuous as Sidmouth seems to have suggested they would be—and as the Committee certainly understood him to suggest—there would have been considerable reason for accepting them. And as Smith's correspondence with Perceval quoted in the next chapter would indicate, it is likely Smith would have accepted them—under such conditions. The difficulty was that in the bill itself the testimonials were far from innocuous, for the reason that they did precisely what the Committee understood they would not do—vested discretion in the magistrates. As Belsham remarked in expressing his regret that the Committee had not been shown the bill before its introduction, 'in the shape which it appeared, [the bill] could not but create universal alarm'.[3] But in understanding the Committee's policy before the bill was introduced, what is important is not the measure Sidmouth actually introduced, but the one they thought he would introduce. If the bill had lived

[1] See above, p. 159.
[2] Minutes, 25 May 1810.
[3] Belsham, *Letter*, p. 36.

up to their expectations, there would have been some justification for not rejecting it out of hand.

But even after all the details were known the impression persisted that something might have been done with the bill. After its rejection Belsham pointed out to the Rev Robert Aspland that it would have protected 'many who are at present unprotected, and it makes registration imperative upon the magistrate, which many now consider as discretional'.[1] John Gurney agreed in seeing advantages in the bill: 'If Lord S. had been right in his construction of the Toleration Act his bill would have enlarged Toleration.'[2]

In a sense, Belsham and Gurney were right. The bill would have given protection to probationers and occasional and itinerant preachers, and it did specifically *require* the magistrates to register applicants. The difficulty was, of course, that what was given with one hand was taken away with the other: the 'substantial and reputable householder' clauses rendered these improvements nugatory. Belsham, however, felt that Sidmouth could have been persuaded to remove the objectionable clauses. He told Aspland that 'I happen to know that, antecedently to any the least suspicion of the opposition to the Bill, [Lord Sidmouth] was ready to have introduced many material changes. . . . There was scarcely any alteration which could be suggested to which he was unwilling to accede, so desirous was he of making his Bill acceptable to the Dissenters . . . '.[3] Gurney likewise believed that Sidmouth's intentions were good, and he suggests Smith did. 'I agree with you', he wrote to Belsham, 'that the Deputies were wrong in charging Lord S. with a "*design*" to abridge Toleration. Had I been present I would have opposed that word. Mr. Smith did so in vain'. Gurney went on to say that he only wished Sidmouth had 'begun with repealing the Conventicle Act—that is a great practical grievance and we must try to get rid of it'.[4]

[1] Thomas Belsham to Robert Aspland, 25 June 1811, Aspland, p. 268.

[2] John Gurney to Thomas Belsham, 28 June 1811, Dr Williams's Library, 12.58, no. 25.

[3] Thomas Belsham to Robert Aspland, 25 June 1811, Aspland, p. 268.

[4] John Gurney to Thomas Belsham, 28 June 1811, Dr Williams's Library, 12.58, no. 25.

Such faith in Sidmouth's good intentions would seem to have been unjustified, especially in view of his remarks in introducing the bill, in which he said that one of the things he most feared was having an established church and a sectarian people. But that remark was made with regard to the necessity of building more churches, onto which subject he eventually strayed—by exactly what logical process is unclear. The fact of the matter is that Sidmouth was—in his public utterances, at any rate—as unclear about his intentions in introducing the bill as he was wrongly certain of general support. In 1809 he suggested that he was mainly concerned about the abuse of the exemptions from military service and parochial office. In 1810 and 1811, however, he seemed to feel that the main purpose of his legislation would be to raise the standards of the Dissenting ministry. At all times, he was lavish in his assurances of his worthy motives and of his solicitude for the Dissenters. After his private interview with Smith, preceding that with the Deputies' sub-committee, Sidmouth had written: 'On the subject of our last conversation, I will at present only express my earnest wish that if any measures should be adopted, they will be such as the great body of Dissenters will [find] reasonable and approve.'[1] He was equally genial and reassuring with the sub-committee: 'He expressed many very liberal opinions on the general subject, and declared that far from harbouring any hostile intentions towards the Dissenters, he had entertained hopes of their concurrence in his views; and tho' he might be mistaken or ill informed, he meant not to alter any thing but what if a Dissenter himself he should be even desirous of supporting.'[2] And the same golden haze of affability enveloped his negotiations with the other parties to the controversy.

An explanation of Sidmouth's true motives is a task for his biographer, not Smith's. And Sidmouth's latest biographer quotes the contemporary appraisal of Sydney Smith:

We are convinced Lord Sidmouth is a very amiable and well-intentioned man: his error is not the error of his heart, but of his time *above which few men ever rise*. It is the error of some four or five hundred thousand English gentlemen, of decent education and worthy character

[1] Quoted in Lady Stephen's MS., chap. XI, p. 13.
[2] Minutes, 25 May 1810.

who conscientiously believe that they are punishing and continuing incapacities for the good of the State; while they are, in fact,
(though without knowing it), only gratifying that insolence, hatred
and revenge which all human beings are unfortunately so ready to feel
against those who will not conform to their sentiments.[1]

Sydney Smith was certainly right that Sidmouth only reflected a
very wide sentiment—and one which had been put into practice,
which was what made the situation particularly dangerous for
Dissent. And accurately reflecting that sentiment, it is certain that
Sidmouth would never have conceded all that the Dissenters wished.

Belsham was the only Dissenter to defend Sidmouth publicly—
and all that Belsham did was to state his belief in Sidmouth's good
intentions. A careful reading of Belsham's *Letter* and of his private
correspondence with Sidmouth amply justifies Dean Pellew's
observation that Belsham took the position that 'whilst the Dissenters were willing to accept any relaxation of the existing law in
their favour that might be contemplated in Lord Sidmouth's bill,
they would not in return submit to the slightest restriction whatever in the provisions of the Toleration Act . . .'.[2]

There is other evidence of Belsham's firm opposition to the
whole thrust of Sidmouth's bill. There is no foundation for suggestions like B. L. Manning's (who undoubtedly had Belsham mainly
in mind) that

there seem to have been elements in Dissent itself which were not
entirely averse from some check on the new activities. Some of the
older, more sober, more scholarly ministers (and perhaps some of the
less orthodox) had no wish to be confused with the itinerant hot-
gospellers of the Evangelical revival.[3]

It is undoubtedly true, and Belsham made it abundantly clear on
this and later occasions, that he had a deep aversion to 'Methodist'
practices. But this does not mean that he desired such activities

[1] Philip Ziegler, *Addington* (New York, 1965), p. 298. Mr Ziegler, however, only quotes Sydney Smith as the 'most urbane expression' of a 'dis-
proportionately violent' reaction. His discussion of the question is not the
most satisfying part of his book.

[2] Pellew, III, 57n.

[3] Manning, p. 132.

to be curbed by law. He made his position quite plain in a letter to his (and Smith's) close friend Benjamin Hobhouse in 1809. Hobhouse had held office in the Addington (Sidmouth) administration, and Belsham urged him to use his influence to persuade his chief not to consider tampering with the Toleration acts:

Whoever thinks himself qualified to teach and to preach, whether he be learned or unlearned, let him by all means hold forth to those who are willing to hear him, without being exposed to the penalties of persecuting laws, or being dependent upon the discretion of bishops to grant or to withhold a license. This is the grand principle of Toleration, and in defense of it the Dissenters of all denominations, Trinitarians, Arians, Unitarians, Calvinists, Arminians, Presbyterians, Independents, and Baptists, and the vast and growing body of Methodists, would all unite as one man; and to infringe it would, in my humble opinion, be the excess of imprudence and impolicy, and would tend to bring back the times and troubles of Laud, if not Bonner.[1]

If Manning's surmises were correct, though he specifically excludes them, it might seem reasonable to fix similar suspicions, for similar reasons, on the Deputies. It is significant, however, that the only existing justification of their policies from one of their own members comes from John Gurney, a Baptist[2]—of all the old Dissenting sects, the one which would have suffered most from the restrictions Sidmouth had in mind. There is no reason to believe that there was any difference of opinion among Dissenters on the matter. Besides Belsham's attitude, another probable source of confusion (one which, as has been seen, clouded the issue from the beginning) is that there was a difference of opinion on the matter of exemption from burdensome offices. Some probably felt that it was wisest to accept the law as it stood, others that it was necessary to press for further relief. But this was a different question.

What both questions illustrate is a difference within Dissent, not on principles but on strategy. That the Dissenters could have

[1] Williams, pp. 587–8.
[2] Gurney came from an old Baptist family in Bedfordshire. He later became an Anglican, but his brother William Brodie Gurney, who was to be on the Deputies' Committee in the twenties, remained an active and prominent Baptist (see the articles on both in the *D.N.B.*).

gained all they wanted by negotiation is unthinkable, even taking into account the powerful backing of Wilberforce and the coolness of the government toward the bill. Nor did Smith and the Committee of the Deputies, at any rate, ever expect to gain so much. Their policy is an admission that they did not. Had they felt certain of securing the interpretation of the Toleration acts they desired, there would have been no point in waiting for a Whig administration. Smith and his colleagues followed the policy they did, a policy which for the time being could only have resulted in imperfect toleration, because they rejected the alternative.

The alternative, as Gurney suggested, was to institute court proceedings to clarify the interpretation of the acts and then, should the results be unfavourable, to go to Parliament and demand their own interpretation. This would necessarily have involved a full-scale public agitation of the question and a forceful petitioning campaign. Just such a mode of proceeding appealed to the Protestant Society, and it was one which filled the traditional leaders of Dissent with alarm. Belsham wrote to Aspland, who was a member of the Society's Committee, that he dreaded 'lest the energies of your Committee should be retaliated upon us another day by the clamour of—The Church in danger!'[1]

Belsham told Aspland that he wished the direction of the opposition to the bill had been left entirely in the hands of the Committee of the Deputies and the Dissenting Ministers. But what would they have done if the direction had been left in their hands? What they did do is plain enough. Upon the bill's introduction both the Deputies and the Ministers met and petitioned against it. But the rousing of public opposition to the measure was left almost entirely to the Methodists and the Protestant Society. Beyond having a thousand copies of the bill printed, and making these available to the Protestant Society for distribution, the Committee of the Deputies played no part in the public agitation against the measure.[2] The traditional leaders of Dissent were desperately afraid of any public controversy.

Belsham's attitude (and it was certainly Smith's as well) may, with the benefit of hindsight, seem ridiculously alarmist—and be

[1] Thomas Belsham to Robert Aspland, 25 June 1811, Aspland, p. 268.
[2] Minutes, 15 May 1811; *Sketch*, p. 103.

discounted as a real explanation on this account. But one must bear in mind their previous experience. Both had seen another great public agitation born in hope, and they had seen where it ended. Smith had trod the smoking ruins of Birmingham, and it was to Belsham at Hackney that Priestley had fled. The experience of the nineties had not been a happy one; and, as Smith demonstrated in Norwich, they did not see much evidence that public opinion had subsequently become much more enlightened. On the other hand, they had seen that quiet negotiation with the great and the powerful, while it would not gain everything, would gain a good deal. To them, the conclusion was obvious. They made every effort to mobilize quiet pressure behind the scenes—through Hobhouse and Wilberforce,[1] for example—but they avoided public agitation like the plague.

'Prudence and caution' were terms with which Smith's critics taxed him. He prided himself on just these qualities. And what he meant by 'prudence and caution' was the avoidance of controversy (combined with an extreme solicitude for the feelings of powerful politicians, as he showed in Sidmouth's case) and confining himself to private negotiations and Parliamentary manoeuvre.

His policy did not get the Deputies very far in 1811. It raised very understandable doubts and fears among their constituents, and, in the Protestant Society, it gave rise to new leaders who were to be a constant challenge to the Deputies' leadership of Dissent in the critical years ahead. The policy was, in short, a disaster. What had been accomplished in 1811 had been accomplished by others, and though accomplishing nothing, the Deputies had managed to damage their prestige severely.

[1] Just how central a role Wilberforce played in the negotiations, and how closely he worked with the Dissenters, is shown by a letter from Samuel Whitbread, another staunch ally, to Belsham early in the following year: 'Since my arrival in town I have heard that Mr. Perceval has declined making any concession to the Protestant Society: and as my conduct must in some degree be guided by what he has determined to do in that respect, I shall be much obliged by your giving me the fullest information in your power as to the views, intentions, and probable success with the Minister, of Mr. Wilberforce and his friends. . . .' (14 January 1812, Dr Williams's Library, 12.58, no. 57).

CHAPTER TEN

RELIGIOUS LIBERTY EXPANDED, 1812

The year 1812 was a more fortunate one than 1811, for Dissenters as a body, and certainly for the Deputies and those who guided their policies. The government of Lord Liverpool conceded what was, in large part, the Dissenters' own interpretation of the Toleration acts. Furthermore, the Conventicle Act and the Five Mile Act, which prohibited nonconformist preachers from coming within five miles of a corporate town or city (unenforced since the seventeenth century but still unrepealed), were abolished outright. For the first time since 1718, when the Occasional Conformity Act and the Schism Act had been repealed, restrictive legislation was wiped from the statute books.

William Smith was the leading representative of his fellow Dissenters in the negotiations to secure all of these very important improvements in the law. He continued to be extremely wary and cautious in his advocacy of the Dissenting cause throughout the negotiations. But in these negotiations, unlike those of the previous year, wariness and caution were essential.

The status of the greatest domestic issue of the day, the Catholic question, and the inescapable relationship of Dissenting demands to that question, dictated discretion to the Dissenters. It was extremely difficult in principle to separate the Catholic and the Dissenting causes. Catholics and Dissenters shared many of the same grievances (which is not, of course, to suggest that Dissenters actually suffered to the same extent). Their freedom of worship, at least in theory, and sometimes in practice, was restricted by law. More important, they shared common political disabilities. The Test and Corporation Acts barred all nonconformists, whether Catholic or Protestant,

170

from all municipal offices and from all military, executive, and administrative offices under the Crown. Only in their right to sit in Parliament were Dissenters legally in a superior position to Catholics.

Catholic Emancipation, the removal of Catholic political disabilities, had been a burning issue since the Union of Great Britain and Ireland in 1800. Pitt had wished to couple Emancipation with Union, and had resigned when George III refused to consider it. In 1807, the King had ousted the ministry of All the Talents rather than accede to their proposal that the senior ranks in the army be opened to Catholics. And since that time the maintenance of a balance favourable to the 'Protestant', or anti-Catholic, position had been the major consideration in the formation of every government. Perceval and Liverpool, who succeeded as Prime Minister after Perceval's assassination, were both firm 'Protestants'. And, critical for the Dissenters, it was largely their concern over maintaining the 'Protestant' position which had caused their coolness to Sidmouth's proposals.

On 20 May 1811 Liverpool had written to Sidmouth:

The Dissenters, as a body, have brought forward no claims, and have engaged in no political controversy with the establishments of the country for the last fifteen years. We have hitherto felt the advantage of this conduct in all our contests with the Catholics; and I own I am apprehensive that, if the measure in question [Sidmouth's bill] is to be persevered in, we may unite the Catholics and all other Dissenters in the same cause.[1]

When Liverpool wrote, the activities of the Methodists and the Protestant Society were already in full swing, the petitions were raining in, and it had become fully apparent what a hornet's nest Sidmouth had stirred up.

Of particular concern to the ministers was the fact that the Dissenters had been aroused simultaneously with the revival of the Catholic claims in Parliament. At the end of May 1811 Henry Grattan moved for a Committee on the Catholic grievances. An exchange between Smith and Perceval on 31 May illustrates both the anxiety of the ministry and its cause. Smith expanded on a question put by a previous speaker:

[1] Pellew, III, 62.

It had been asked, if this measure was extended to the Roman Catholics of Ireland, would it not be expected that it should go to the different sectaries in England also? He did not know what was expected, but he could say that in his opinion it ought to extend to all. The right of sitting in that House was all the privilege they [the Dissenters] enjoyed more than the Catholics; and during the years he had been a member, he could not have held a situation of the most trifling kind under the crown, without transgressing the law of the land, for which he must be punished were it not for the annual Indemnity Bill. All the evils of which we had to complain arose from the absurd notions of toleration and indulgence. He abhorred such terms. He knew of nothing but religious liberty, which was the right inherent in every man to worship God in his own mode. For this he contended, and he thought the Catholics were entitled to it as well as every other sect of Christians, as a matter of right.

Perceval was on his feet at once: 'The hon. gent. . . . had revived the claim of right . . . which had not been heard of tonight till introduced by [him]. . . . That toleration might be claimed as a right he did not mean to dispute; but that there would be any right to political power in consequence was a proposition he should contend against to the utmost'.[1] The argument of the Dissenters—the argument of religious liberty—was also that of the Catholics, and it was almost impossible to recognize the claims of one group without also recognizing those of the other. Perceval, and Liverpool after him, were therefore determined to recognize the claims of neither.

This was the situation which confronted those who wished well to the cause of Dissent. If the Dissenters expected anything from the ministers, the Catholic question had to be handled delicately. The fears of Perceval and Liverpool that the two causes would become one dictated considerable non-political concessions to the Dissenters. But, if their fears seemed to be becoming a reality, concession might well be abandoned as useless. These were the limitations under which Smith worked, and he was acutely aware of them.

Almost immediately after the defeat of Sidmouth's bill, Smith set about tempering the enthusiasm of the Dissenters' friends. As has

[1] *Hansard*, XX, 418.

been seen, in June of the previous year Whitbread had presented a petition, drawn up by Wyvill and signed by about 1700 persons, calling for the removal of all disabilities for religious belief. He had moved a resolution to this effect, and Smith had seconded it.[1] It had certainly been only a gesture, doubtless aimed at Sidmouth who had recently announced his intention to propose a bill the next year: the lateness of the session made serious consideration of the resolution impossible. But now, in May 1811, Whitbread intended to introduce another resolution. On 1 June (the day after Smith's exchange with Perceval), however, he wrote Wyvill that after consulting various people, and particularly calling upon the 'able and dispassionate assistance of our friend Mr. Wm. Smith', he had decided against any action. He enclosed a letter received from Smith that morning. 'It so fully expresses my opinion, and in language so succinct and precise, that I refer you to it for an exposition of my opinion rather than attempt to express it more fully myself.' Unfortunately Smith's letter has apparently been lost or destroyed; so one can only surmise what his arguments were. Whitbread goes on to say, however, that he had come to the painful conclusion that

the gratification of the advocate must not be put in competition with the welfare of the cause itself: and I am quite convinced that if I were to gratify myself by the agitation of the question *now*, I should soon have the mortification of finding that I had put back the [clock?] I wish to advance.[2]

The great danger of the motion from Smith's point of view would certainly have been that it went much too far, particularly in that it would naturally have included Catholics as well as Dissenters in its benefits. To have diverted Dissent into such a campaign would have been to gain nothing, and perhaps to lose everything. This was a danger which Smith and the Deputies were determined to avoid. Smith's arguments convinced Wyvill, who replied to Whitbread that he completely concurred and would inform 'Mr. Smith how sincerely I approve the decision to which you have jointly acceded;

[1] See above, p. 158.
[2] Whitbread to Wyvill, 1 June 1811, Whitbread Collection, Bedfordshire County Record Office (hereafter cited as 'Whitbread Collection'), L. 4310.

and how much my hope of final success is confirmed by his confidential co-operation with you, and by the whole tenor of his letter and yours'.[1]

Smith had something much more limited, but much more attainable, in mind. And it was something which this grandiose scheme would certainly not have advanced. John Gurney had expressed to Belsham immediately after the defeat of Sidmouth's bill his concern about the Conventicle Act and his conviction that action must be taken to repeal it.[2] On 31 January the Committee of the Deputies resolved

that the Chairman be requested in the name of the Deputies to take such measures as shall appear to him to be expedient to obtain the repeal of the 17th Car. 2nd c. 2 (commonly called the five mile act) and the 22nd Car. 2nd c. 2 (commonly called the conventicle act).[3]

Two of the more obnoxious acts under which Dissenting ministers might be prosecuted were to be abolished.

Nor did the Committee stop with this objective. The thorny problem of the interpretation of the Toleration acts was to be tackled as well. On 8 February Smith obtained an interview with Perceval,[4] which he discussed in a long letter to him on 16 February.[5] Smith had, he said, understood Perceval to have expressed an opinion

generally in favour both of the principle and the provisions of Lord Sidmouth's bill, but differing with him as to the expediency of bringing it forward "till the Toleration Act . . . having received a more limited exposition [by the courts], the parties who would thereby be affected should apply to be relieved from the inconveniences they might feel or apprehend—when the legislature might consider the conditions of such relief;—some of which might, perhaps not improbably or improperly, be of the nature proposed by his Lordship".

It is significant that Smith did not see fit to question Perceval's

[1] Wyvill to Whitbread, 3 June 1811, Whitbread Collection, L. 4311.

[2] See above, p. 164.

[3] Minutes, 31 January 1812.

[4] Perceval to William Smith, 8 February 1812, Verney Papers.

[5] William Smith to Perceval, 16 February 1812, Liverpool Papers, B.M. Add. MSS 38,247, f. 84.

approach to Sidmouth's bill as a measure aimed at protecting the Dissenters. It is also significant that in Perceval's reply, where he suggests that Smith had been favourable to the measure, he singles out testimonials as the major point upon which he agreed with Sidmouth. These, he thought, would have tended to raise the standards of the Dissenting ministry.[1] This strongly indicates that Smith might have agreed to the testimonials so long as some relief had been involved; that is to say so long as the magistrates had been deprived of their discretion in registration.

Sidmouth's measure was now in the past, however, and Smith was out to make the most of the existing situation. The factors which had brought about an attempt at what 'we call the new interpretation' of the Toleration Act had, in his mind, been two. First were 'the claims of exemption from parochial offices, but more especially from military service, set up by persons, who, as was reasonably believed, for that purpose only, demanded and obtained licenses as Dissenting preachers. . . .' He thus admitted one of Sidmouth's major contentions. But he denied that any re-interpretation of the law had been made necessary by these abuses. The law was clear in providing exemptions only for ministers of settled congregations.

The remedy therefore was obvious and easy—but the Magistrates in many cases instead of applying this plain and unobjectionable cure of refusing *the claim to* the exemption, preferred the obnoxious, and as we contend, illegal, course of refusing the License—thereby quitting that ministerial function imposed on them by the Law, for the more pleasant and dignified exercise of Discretion and Authority—but which, as an Usurpation, has been uniformly complained of and resisted.

In short, Smith contended, all the fuss had been over nothing, and all the onus lay on the magistrates who had misapplied the law.

He then went on to what he considered the other major factor in the recent controversy.

The second, and as we suppose, the most extensive cause, of which the Dissenters are equally innocent, will probably be found in the apprehension respecting the rapid increase of the Methodists. This Body,

[1] Perceval to William Smith, 10 April 1812, Liverpool Papers, B.M. Add. MSS. 38,247, f. 185.

engaged as they think in the best possible of all causes, are unquestionably very powerful from their number and their zeal—perhaps also in some degree from their organization. The doctrines they teach, if not exactly those of the Articles, are at least so near them, that few can distinguish the difference—and the Church has been told by many of her best and most attached sons, that if the regular clergy wish to put down the Methodists, it must be done by a more skillful and Laborious use of their own weapons. Persecution in any form or *degree*, may degrade the character of the Establishment, or may raise a flame dangerous to the peace, or even safety, of the Country: but, if Methodists be a Nuisance, will not abate it.

These were strong words, and doubtless so intended. Smith was not above playing on useful fears, even though he had opposed the agitations of the Methodists and the Protestant Society which were mainly responsible for creating those fears.

He next proceeded to more general considerations, arguing that, even assuming that the purposes of the re-interpretation were legitimate and valuable, the mode being pursued was both adverse to the usual rules of law and highly impolitic.

We affirm that in point of fact the Toleration Act has undeniably for more than a century, received the "large and liberal interpretation" with almost undeviating uniformity—and that this is the true one. Is it consonant to legal usage and to legal maxims—re the "stare decisis" and "super antiquas vias,"—to endeavour,—after such a lapse of years, to unsettle such a uniformity?—to set up new and *restrictive* constructions of a statute of *concessions*; which are to be supported (if at all) by verbal criticisms, and suppositions (new ones too) respecting the intentions of the Legislature at the time, contrary to what appears from the practice to have been accepted as their sense, at that time, and almost ever since? . . . And all this for some theoretic improvement? Lord Wellesley observed the other night, as an acknowledged truth, that "restrictions were in themselves evils and put the onus probandi of the overbalancing good on the imposer"—that they are not apparently harsh or very burthensome, is no sufficient justification. Trifles may be aggregated till they become an intolerable load. And at any rate the principle is to be resisted by those who may eventually suffer, to an extent unforseen and indefinite.

He apologized for occupying so much of Perceval's valuable time, but I avow my object to be to lead you to consider whether it may not be more advisable rather to discountenance than to encourage these novel (as I take the liberty to call them) constructions of the acts in question—which *I have heard have been rather recommended by some authority to various magistrates as fit to be acted on.* At any rate you will not accuse me of want of frankness in thus opening so considerable a part of my case, nor of hostility in pointing out, though incidentally and respectfully to yourself, what I bona fide regard as the easiest and best means of avoiding a contest, which, as I firmly believe, will certainly involve you in much trouble, and may not terminate to your advantage.

Smith may not have created the position from which he argued, but, having been provided with it, he pressed it hard.

The Deputies, however, carefully continued to avoid any unnecessary provocation. On 28 February the Committee met to consider 'the propriety of joining in [a] petition to the House of Commons for a repeal of the several penal laws by which dissenters from the Church of England are so materially affected'. This petition had been signed by 'many members of the Establishment, Catholics, and Protestant Dissenters in various parts of the country'. It was another of Wyvill's efforts and would obviously expose the Dissenters to the same dangers as Whitbread's proposed motion of the previous year would have done had it been persisted in. The matter was handled delicately but firmly. A special meeting of the Deputies was summoned to consider the 'propriety and expediency' of the petition being submitted for signature among their various congregations. The petition was read, upon which there was an immediate adjournment.[1] The Deputies could not bring themselves to reject it, but policy dictated that they not support it. Policy won.

By mid-April the Deputies' negotiations, and perhaps their caution, showed signs of bearing fruit. On 10 April Perceval expressed his willingness to proceed with some kind of remedial legislation. In a private letter to Smith he stated his view that if Lord Sidmouth's bill 'had been accepted by the Dissenters in the spirit in which it was intended, it would probably have averted much, if not all, of the inconveniences which Dissenters have since

---

[1] Minutes, 28 February and 13 March 1812.

experienced'. He still thought that 'testimonials would be of advantage, but it is a point on which, as I conceive, the Dissenters are more interested, and better qualified to judge, than a member of the Established Church; and as they seem to prefer being without it, I shall give up my opinion to theirs'.[1] The means of relief which Perceval proposed were, as he informed the Deputies, to go 'to the extent at least of rendering *legal the former practice*. . . .'[2] That is, he was willing to go back to something like the practice of automatic registration of Dissenting ministers which had prevailed before 1809. The details remained to be worked out.

There was one further delay caused by the fact that Perceval wished to take no action before a decision pending in King's Bench on the meaning of the wording of the Toleration acts. On 6 May the court handed down its interpretation.[3] The Deputies then acted almost at once, meeting the next day and resolving to take immediate steps. Whitbread had also announced his intention of introducing legislation; and on 11 May Smith, who had been in constant communication with him on the subject, wrote to apprise him of the latest developments:

Since our last conversation there has been an unusually large meeting of our Deputies; where, in consequence of what passed in K. B. on Wednesday they came to a resolution desiring me to take up the business in Parliament on the footing to which P. had previously given his assent, and appointed a committee to have an interview with him on the subject. This took place on Saturday when P. acknowledged that he thought the opinions of the Constitution as declared by Lord E[llenborough] . . . afforded sufficient ground for going immediately to Parliament and that he was not desirous of putting himself forward

[1] Perceval to William Smith, Liverpool Papers, 10 April 1812, B.M. Add. MSS. 38,247, f. 185.

[2] Perceval to William Smith (for the Deputies), 10 April 1812, copy, Whitbread Collection, L. 4341.

[3] The case had to do with the Gloucestershire magistrates having refused to register an applicant on the ground that he was not the minister of a congregation. It hinged on the crucial clause of the 1779 act beginning 'pretending to holy orders'. Lord Ellenborough ruled (though the rule was quashed) that it was not necessary to be a minister of a congregation to come under the meaning of the clause (*Monthly Repository*, VII [1812], 388–90).

as the person to grant the boon, but would support any other gentleman, *you* or me, by whom the question should be moved. One of our
Deputies then informed him that our meeting having of course a wish
that their own chairman should move this question, had desired me
to undertake it. . . . We then went into conversation on the subject
with a view to understand one another precisely, as to the specific
measure, on which we must have further communication. . . .[1]

It is indicative of Smith's influence and place in the negotiations,
that Perceval so readily agreed that he was the proper man to
undertake the legislation, and that Whitbread seems to have concurred in this opinion.

A brief, but highly dramatic, halt was brought to the negotiations
on the very afternoon that this letter was written. Smith had
suggested to Whitbread that they meet for further conversation in
the lobby of the House at five. Hardly had he arrived when a shot
rang out and a small figure lurched toward him, falling at his feet.
For an awful moment he thought that it was Wilberforce who had
fallen to the assassin's bullet, but when he stooped to raise the
wounded man he found that he had been wrong—it was Spencer
Perceval, the victim of the insane Bellingham. They carried Perceval
to the Secretary's room, and Smith held him for half an hour while
he was probed for the bullet. But all efforts were in vain.

As Smith walked back to Park Street, with blood still on his
hands and one of the dead man's gloves in his pocket,[2] he may well
have wondered what effect this tragedy would have on the hopeful
turn which the negotiations of the past months had so recently
taken. But there was no need to worry; Liverpool, who succeeded
Perceval, was equally anxious to conciliate the Dissenters.

It must have been shortly after this that Liverpool, under the
impression that Smith was to introduce the proposed legislation,
issued an invitation for a general conference with himself and Smith
of all parties concerned, which was turned down by the Protestant
Society and the Methodists.[3] It was probably this incident, doubtless

[1] William Smith to Whitbread, 11 May 1812, Whitbread Collection, L.
2541.

[2] The whole incident is described in Patty Smith's Diary for 1812, pp. 27–
8, Duff Papers.

[3] *Monthly Repository*, VII (1812), 475.

to be explained by an understandable reluctance on the part of the Protestant Society and the Methodists to allow others to reap all the glory of a situation which their forceful measures had done so much to create, which deprived Smith of the honour of introducing the measure and led to the government's decision to introduce legislation itself. But it did not end Smith's activities in the negotiations, nor, strangely enough, did it end active and apparently cordial co-operation between the three organizations. Almost immediately the Methodists requested an interview to discuss strategy and proposals.[1] And there was another interview between representatives of all three organizations just previous to the introduction of the final measure.[2]

A sub-committee of the Deputies, headed by Smith, obtained an interview with Liverpool on 23 June at which they requested not only a return to the previous practice of registration, but their originally stated object, a repeal of the Five Mile Act and Conventicle Act as well. Liverpool, to whom these extended proposals clearly had not been previously broached, requested time to confer with the rest of the government, promising to inform Smith of the results.[3] Smith was able to lay the reply before the Committee on 26 June. It was Liverpool's opinion that

under the present circumstances of the session of Parliament, the most satisfactory course which can be adopted for all parties respecting the relief intended to be afforded to the different classes of Protestant Dissenters appears to be that the bill proposed by Lord Liverpool the substance of which was communicated to the several gentlemen who assembled at Lord Liverpool's house on Tuesday the 23rd instant should be immediately brought into Parliament and there will be no objection to insert a clause in it for the repeal of the Five Mile Act.

With respect to the repeal of the Conventicle Act, it would require more consideration than could probably be given to it by Parliament at the present moment, especially as it is connected with the Toleration Act, some of the provisions of which it might be necessary to retain. It is therefore proposed that a clause should be inserted in the

[1] Minutes, 29 May 1812.
[2] Ibid., 26 June 1812.
[3] Ibid., 23 June 1812.

Act intended to be brought in to suspend or stay any proceedings under this act till two or three months after the next session of Parliament.[1]

The government bill relieving the Dissenting ministers had been based largely on a draft submitted by the Methodists; the Deputies' Committee had drawn one up but had not presented it for consideration. Obviously, the Methodist draft of the bill had included no provisions for a repeal of the Five Mile and Conventicle Acts and the government had not contemplated repeal. This large concession was a result of the Deputies' activities.

The basis of the relief act was now worked out in its general outlines. But Smith continued to negotiate, seeking interviews and making suggestions right up to the eve of its introduction. One thing which he proposed was an inclusion in the act of a clause granting toleration to the Unitarians. This, Liverpool thought, would complicate the passage of the measure, and he begged Smith not to consider it.[2] After further consultation on the matter with the Prime Minister and the Archbishop of Canterbury, Smith readily agreed to drop it for the moment. But he had not yet done with the Prime Minister. On 19 July, while the bill was in the process of its final passage, he again wrote to Liverpool, this time on the matter of a restriction of the previous exemptions for ministers:

There yet remains one point which, tho' but a small one, is a restriction of an old right, *as far as the present Bill is concerned,* and therefore I must request one more interview when I trust I shall be able in a very short time to convince your Lordship of the propriety of this small concession. I shall do myself the honor to call within an hour, and shall hope to find your Lordship at Liberty for a few minutes.[3]

The new restriction which he wished to eliminate was that limiting exemptions to only those ministers who pursued no other profession than that of schoolmaster (a restriction which would affect the ministers of many poorer congregations, particularly among the

[1] Ibid., 26 June 1812.

[2] Liverpool to William Smith, 11 July 1812, Liverpool Papers, B.M. Add. MSS. 38,328, f. 27b.

[3] William Smith to Liverpool, 19 July 1812, Liverpool Papers, B.M. Add. MSS. 38,570, f. 104.

Methodists and Baptists). This had first been proposed by Perceval in April and had been resisted by the Deputies at that time.[1] Without success, however. Nor was Smith's interview with Liverpool any more successful in attaining its deletion. The restriction was included in the final bill, and despite a last attempt by Smith to amend it out of existence on the third reading, it became part of the new act.[2] But Smith was constantly probing and testing, constantly attempting to widen and extend the coverage of the bill, to slip in some new liberal clause. On occasion he went too far, as with Unitarian toleration, and had to draw back. Sometimes, however, he was successful, as with the suggestion of repealing the Five Mile and Conventicle Acts. But, whether successful or not, it is evident that Smith wrang every possible ounce of benefit out of the government measure. His methods were clever, sometimes devious, but effective.

The measure was, in fact, even more of a success than Liverpool had indicated to the Committee it would be. Clause I repealed outright the Conventicle Act as well as the Five Mile Act. Clause II provided, as had previously been the case, that all places of worship must be registered. There was, however, a considerable liberalization in Clauses IV and V, which provided that any person preaching or teaching in a place duly registered was automatically qualified for the benefits of the Toleration Act, unless specifically required by the justices to register with them. Clause VII required the justices to administer the necessary oaths on application, and Clause VIII that they should provide a certificate attesting to the oaths having been taken. These provisions were pure gain—the right of anyone to preach had been established. On the matter of exemptions, as has been seen, success was more qualified. On the one hand, Clause IX no longer limited them to ministers of 'settled' congregations; itinerant preachers could thus qualify. But, on the other hand, a new limitation was imposed by the provision that a minister who pursued any profession other than that of schoolmaster was excluded from receiving exemptions. Another irritating provision was that in Clause II which, though repealing the Conventicle Act, still placed

[1] Resolution of the Deputies, 24 April 1812, Liverpool Papers, B.M. Add. MSS. 38,247, f. 194.
[2] *Monthly Repository*, VII (1812), 588.

a limit on the number of persons meeting for prayer or religious exercises in unregistered premises. The number was, it is true, enlarged from five to twenty, but any restriction was resented.[1] Yet although these continuing restrictions clouded, they could not completely obscure, what was undoubtedly a great victory. For the first time in almost a century penal laws had been wiped from the Statute Books. It was a great victory.

The question is whether enough had been asked, whether with different methods more could have been achieved? And it was a question asked at the time. Just before the act was introduced the Lords had considered another bill, introduced by Lord Stanhope, which, in effect, proposed to solve the problem by making a clean sweep of all the penal statutes in matters of religion, save those which imposed political restrictions; the question of Repeal and Catholic Emancipation would have been left untouched by his measure.[2] The bill's aim, as stated in a protest by several Whig lords on its rejection, was to do away with 'partial and conditional exemption' and to establish, not toleration, but 'religious liberty'.[3] In the course of his speech on the second reading of the bill Stanhope launched into an hysterical attack on Smith, which, when boiled down, amounted to the fact that the latter was willing to acquiesce in what was only imperfect toleration.[4] The result was an exchange of letters in the *Morning Chronicle*. In defending himself Smith repeated Stanhope's charge and asked:

. . . What must be thought of a disputant who imputes to his antagonist "a proposal for the continuance of unbounded absurdities, contemptible principles, and infinite oppression," *because* he endeavours, in the way which approves itself to his judgment as most effectual, to destroy and abolish as many of those absurdities, follies and oppressions, as his power and Opportunities enable him to cope with? The truth is, that Lord S. has been *saying* a great deal, and I have been endeavouring to *do* as much as I could. I quarrel not with him for his saying; on the contrary, I very generally agree with the principles and proposed enactments of his Bill; but I knew it could not pass, and said so to many who were fascinated with

[1] The full text of the act appears in ibid., pp. 577–83.
[2] The full text appears in ibid., pp. 391–2.
[3] Ibid., pp. 455–6.   [4] Ibid., pp. 452–5.

its theoretic beauty. . . . I object to the word toleration, and the doctrine implied in it, as much as he can do, for the same reason too, and have long since declared that opinion in Parliament as explicitly as himself; but I will not refuse to accept a real and attainable good, because there is something yet better which I cannot yet obtain. . . .[1]

This was all there was to say, and despite the fact that Stanhope rejoined with a specific charge that Smith had acquiesced in Sidmouth's bill, he said no more.

In commenting on the controversy, the radical Unitarian *Monthly Repository* expressed the opinion that 'both parties, we are convinced, wish equally well to religious liberty, but they may differ in the paths each chose to obtain it'.[2] This was indeed the key to the whole controversy, and it was a controversy which extended well beyond the individual participants themselves. Smith and the Deputies' Committee favoured a policy of slow, piecemeal reform, attacking each problem as it arose, and thus gradually extending the structure of religious freedom. They were pragmatic politicians, judging men and events and attempting to turn them to their own advantage. What was lacking in their policy was a willingness to look beyond the closed political system. It was this which led to their major blunder with regard to Sidmouth's bill. There can be no doubt that it had been their intention to extract every possible benefit out of that measure as they did later in the negotiations over the government bill of 1812. But even at their best, Smith and the Committee could never have achieved by negotiation and Parliamentary manoeuvre what the Protestant Society and the Methodists achieved by forceful public agitation. This was the other policy.

The whole point of the Protestant Society's nation-wide organization (as distinct from that of the Deputies, which was directly representative only of London), including Calvinistic Methodists and Wesleyan seceders as well as traditional Dissenters, was to allow a broader and more forceful display of public opinion. And the *Monthly Repository*, whose editor, Aspland, was on the Committee of the Society, rightly saw that such a policy was implicit in Stanhope's approach:

We are inclined to prefer [to Smith's] the mode pursued by Lord

[1] *Monthly Repository*, VII (1812), pp. 459–60.   [2] Ibid., p. 473.

184

Stanhope, which comprehends and unites all bodies dissenting from the church, and all in the church, who are affected equally with Dissenters by its ridiculous enactments. . . . If instead of aiming each sect for itself, all will join in the general principle, desiring nothing for itself which it would not grant to others, religious liberty will, we believe, be obtained, after a few struggles, to the general joy of all parties, in which we include a very great majority of the established church.[1]

The proper method, according to this view, was to take a firm stand on principle and to force the acceptance of that principle on Parliament by utilizing the power of public opinion.

Here was the basic conflict. Far from believing that the Dissenters could muster enough support to force through a broad programme, Smith believed that public agitation on their part was very likely to wreck any chances of reform at all. For him, the only possibility for advance lay through manoeuvre within the existing political system, not by going outside it. Reform must therefore, of necessity, be gradual and piecemeal, dependent on the existing political situation and the extent to which the politicians could be persuaded to agree.

There can be little doubt that in 1812 Smith's approach was the right one. Public agitation had been extremely effective as a purely defensive measure in 1811. But in 1812 the Dissenters were still faced with a very practical problem which required an immediate solution. Such a solution depended on the assistance of the government, and, despite their fears, it is very clear that neither Perceval nor Liverpool had collapsed completely upon the flexing of the Dissenters' muscles in 1811. Nor would they have done so had it continued. Catholic Emancipation was uppermost in their minds, and, while they were willing to make concessions to keep the Dissenters out of the Catholic camp, the very object of those concessions limited their extent. Nothing could be conceded which would weaken the 'Protestant' position on the great issue of the day. It was clear throughout that in order to get what it desperately needed, Dissent would have to play the government's game. Smith played it with maximum benefit for the Dissenters.

[1] *Monthly Repository*, VII (1812), pp. 473–4.

Even the Protestant Society was forced to recognize the facts of the situation. At its annual meeting in May 1812 John Wilks, the Secretary and principal leader of the Society, said that 'the committee desired to obtain relief by the repeal of all statutes interfering with the freedom of religious worship. . . .' But he indicated that the Society's Committee would be satisfied with a good deal less.[1] As it turned out it had to be. Agitation was a weapon whose use was limited, a fact which was recognized by everyone who was in any position to use it.

But the appeal of a broad, forceful programme was by no means dead. The Protestant Society largely dropped such a programme after 1811; its first great agitation was also its last. But the hue and cry was taken up by others. In 1813 the Deputies passed a resolution calling for 'breaking every bond and abolishing every shackle' in matters of religion. Some have ascribed this to the impetus given by the formation of the Protestant Society.[2] But the resolution was moved by J. T. Rutt, a Unitarian and the biographer of Joseph Priestley. A new radicalism was at work within the Deputies themselves, which would have profound consequences for them and for their Chairman.

[1] *Monthly Repository*, VII (1812), p. 398.
[2] Manning, p. 47.

CHAPTER ELEVEN

THE EMERGENCE OF UNITARIANISM

T he demands of Smith's role as the chief representative of Dissenting interests by no means precluded his participation in a wide variety of other activities. His public life and his personal life remained as full as ever.

The most consuming of his additional political interests was, as always, the affairs of the slaves. His friendship with Wilberforce grew ever more firm as the years passed, the latter remarking in his diary of 1823: 'What a lesson does he give to evangelical Christians! I am never with him without thinking of talis cum sis, utinam noster esses, not with a party feeling, but from Christian love.'[1] They might disagree on basic religious principles, but the friendship was none the less deep for that. And their co-operation in common objects was never closer.

Professor New has pointed out that from 1807 to 1830 it was not one great leader but a great team that held the anti-Slave Trade and anti-Slavery forces together. Policies emanated from conferences rather than from Wilberforce—or, later, Buxton—alone. In identifying the team responsible for these policies, Professor New notes that of the twelve conferences mentioned in Wilberforce's diary between 1810 and 1818, James Stephen attended nine, Brougham nine, Zachary Macaulay eight, William Smith five, Lord Lansdowne five, and others in lesser number.[2] And in all probability no major decision was made before the five mentioned by name were consulted, whether they had been present at the conference or not.

---

[1] Quoted in Brown, p. 482.

[2] C. W. New, *The Life of Henry Brougham to 1830* (Oxford, 1961), pp. 120 and 125.

Certainly Wilberforce continued to seek the advice of Smith and others privately and individually before taking any important steps[1] —as, indeed, he had done before 1807.

Scottish problems also took up much of Smith's time. From 1803 to 1818 he was one of the three Royal Commissioners appointed to supervise the building of roads and bridges in the Highlands. Until his death he was Vice-Chairman of the British Fisheries, an organization founded to promote the Scottish fishing industry.[2] These activities required at least three tours of Scotland of several months each, in the summers between 1809 and 1818. His efforts were generally widely acclaimed. In 1809 Edinburgh voted him the freedom of the city as 'a friend to the improvements and prosperity of Scotland'.[3] But there was one dissident voice. It was at the same time, in the same city, that he had an encounter with Walter Scott which gave rise to some rather unspecified charges that Smith had been injurious and insulting in his remarks on the Highlanders, charges made by Scott in a letter to Southey in 1817.[4] Scott, however, seems to have been alone in his bad opinion, and, considering that these charges were made in the middle of a controversy between Smith and Southey, Sir James Stephen is probably right in attributing them to Scott's general dislike of 'Whigs and Whiggery'.[5]

To the 'Whigs and Whiggery' Smith retained a firm allegiance. He never ceased to look upon the party as the true repository of the most liberal principles and as an essential organ for the education of public opinion. However pessimistic he was about the possibilities of any broad programme of reform, however cautious and limited his objectives in the give and take of practical negotiations, Smith never ceased to take the most liberal stand in Parliament. He was as ardent as he had ever been in the cause of complete religious liberty. He never lost an opportunity to give his support to the cause of Parliamentary reform. And he was bitterly critical of the

[1] Wilberforce to Whitbread, 20 June 1814, Whitbread Collection, L. 4161.

[2] *William Smith, Formerly Member for the City of Norwich*, p. 6.

[3] *Norfolk Chronicle*, 23 December 1809.

[4] J. G. Lockhart, *Memoirs of the Life of Sir Walter Scott* (London, 1837), IV, 71.

[5] See above, p. 108.

government's repressive policies in the latter years of the decade. It was during the course of a debate in 1817 that he attacked the poet laureate Southey for some recent articles in the *Quarterly Review*, charging him with being a 'renegade' for so completely turning his back on his radical youth. These remarks gave rise to a heated public controversy, Southey defending himself in a pamphlet and Lord Byron entering the lists on Smith's behalf.[1] It was not only in Dissenting circles that Smith was a controversial figure.

Smith's private interests continue to show an astonishing breadth. His appointment book for 1817–18[2] indicates that he maintained his very active participation in the affairs of the British Institution and the British (later the National) Gallery. To his devotion to art was added a keen interest in science. In 1806 he was elected a Fellow of the Royal Society, and in 1811 of the Linnaean Society. Sir Joseph Banks and Dr (later Sir) J. E. Smith were frequent visitors at Park Street and Parndon.[3] He corresponded with Sir James Sinclair on agricultural science. He intervened with the government in the interest of the mathematician Charles Babbage and his computer. He gave aid and assistance to J. T. Rutt in the compilation of Priestley's works.[4] And he gave his patronage as well to Samuel Parkes, the first five volumes of whose *Chemical Cathecism* were dedicated to him.[5] Smith was also a Fellow of the Society of Antiquaries. The number of charities in whose management he took an active part is too great to bear enumeration. Time cannot have lain heavily on his hands.

There was one cloud on the horizon. His uncle Benjamin's death in 1803 had left him richer by some sixty thousand pounds, at a conservative estimate. But thereafter his financial affairs steadily worsened. In 1806 he lost heavily in a fire which destroyed a distillery at Millbank in which he had recently become a partner. In

[1] Robert Southey, *A Letter to William Smith, Esq., M.P.* (London, 1817); E. H. Coleridge, ed., *The Works of Lord Byron* (London and New York, 1901), IV, 481–2.

[2] Leigh-Smith Papers.

[3] Patty Smith's diary for 1812–13, Leigh-Smith Papers.

[4] Rutt, dedication to vol. XXV.

[5] For this information, as well as for most of the rest on Smith's scientific interests, I am indebted to Dr Mary French of Queen Mary College, London.

1813 his very lucrative partnership with Joseph Travers was dissolved in an exceedingly acrimonious dispute, the firm's customers being deluged with the bitter recriminations of the two parties.[1] Smith, so restrained in political disputes, became a very different personality when his business ability was called into question. Unfortunately, there was all too good reason to question it. The main point of contention was Travers's disapproval of the activities of Smith's son Adams who had recently been taken into the business.[2] It would appear that Travers was more than justified in his reservations. After the dissolution of the old firm Smith formed a new one with Adams and his cousins Kemble. By 1819 a combination of Adams's mismanagement and that, or worse, on the part of the Kembles had brought the firm to the verge of bankruptcy. It was saved by Smith's eldest son Ben, who had made a fortune in the distillery where his father had lost so heavily. But Parndon and Park Street had to go, and when the firm was finally liquidated in 1823 Smith was left with only a modest income.

Smith, however, was blissfully unaware of the impending disaster until it struck. The rounds of parties in town and country continued. He dined regularly at Lansdowne House, at Holland House, and at 'The King of Clubs'. Three of his daughters were wealthily, if not always happily, married, Ann to Samuel Nicholson, Fanny to W. E. Nightingale, and Joanna to John Carter (later Bonham-Carter). His sons were properly launched. Ben went from Trinity to the distillery; Samuel from Trinity to the Bar; Octavius to the distillery; Adams to his unfortunate career in the business; and Frederick, the youngest, to a commission in the Indian army. Everything seemed to be going more than smoothly, providing a suitable background to a crowded public life.

Of all the accomplishments in that public life, there can be no doubt of Smith's most important achievement during this period. This was the passage of the Unitarian toleration act, popularly known as 'Mr. William Smith's bill'. It was his own, and to him goes all the credit.

He approached the question with all his considerable political

[1] Travers Papers.
[2] A memorandum by Smith, n.d., photostat, Travers Papers.

astuteness. At first, as we have seen, he had wished to slip Unitarian toleration through in the act of 1812, and had approached Liverpool to this end.[1] At the same time he had sought an interview with the Archbishop of Canterbury

to acquaint him of my decision and to receive from him such communications as he should think fit to make. The result of a very open and friendly conversation on the subject with his Grace was a clear conviction in my own mind that I needed not to be uneasy about any opposition to be expected from him—but he explicitly declared his disinclination to pledge himself to any particular point, till he had taken the sentiments of his Brethren, whom on such matters it was his wish to consult, and said that as the Spring was pretty far advanced, and several of the Bishops had left London . . . he would be glad to have the business postponed to the next year. . . .[2]

This, together with Liverpool's opposition, was enough to clinch the matter. Smith was a patient negotiator, and he had laid his foundations firmly. Opposition had been scotched before it had arisen.

Early in the next session he once again approached the Archbishop, who was of the same general disposition. This time, however, he had some specific suggestions to make:

He . . . told me that supposing my object was only to remove every obstruction to sane argument and discussion, he was willing to consent to the repeal of all the Statutes inflicting penalties or Disabilities for impugning or denying the Doctrine of the Trinity either by writing or advised speaking: but that he supposed I did not any more than himself, intend to open the door to all manner of prophaneness and impiety in *the mode of treating* subjects of so solemn a description; therefore, that the Crime of Blasphemy should still be left open to the animadversion of the Common Law; I, and I have no doubt His Grace also, understanding by the term "Blasphemy," of course, not that constructive and inferential imputation of the Crime which might be fastened on every doctrine relative to the Divine Nature differing in any aspect or degree from that of the Established Church, (an

---

[1] See above, p. 181.

[2] William Smith to Jeremy Bentham, 9 January 1818, Bentham Papers, B.M. Add. MSS. 33,545, f. 258.

191

interpretation wholly subversive of the very liberty and relief intended to be granted), but that which is its common and, I imagine also its legal import—the use of language and epithets in themselves reproachful, reviling and abusive, levelled immediately at the Majesty and Character of the Supreme Being. On this footing I most readily agreed to place the question; persuaded that however plausible an argument may be raised for the abstract right of using in any controversy, such terms as disputants may think most applicable to the subject, yet that such latitude is not here necessary or even advantageous to the legitimate object of all controversy—the successful investigation of Truth, and, therefore, that respect to the National Worship, Tenderness to the Opinions, or even prejudices, of serious and sincere Religionists, and, above all, the venerable nature of the subjects in question, completely justify, if they do not absolutely demand, the prohibition of such language, as useless, indiscreet, and mischievous.[1]

Having secured his flank, Smith next approached the government. Armed with the acquiescence of the Church, his task here was not difficult. The government was more than willing that he should proceed, 'and only desired that in the progress of the Bill I would not by unnecessary discussion incur the risk of inciting a spirit of alarm and opposition which then appeared to lie dormant, but pursue my object as quietly as circumstances should permit'. This was a request that hardly need have been made. Smith cheerfully agreed to this 'reasonable proposition'. He then had another interview with the Archbishop and the Chancellor of the Exchequer, when, together, they moulded the bill into the final shape in which it passed the House of Commons.[2] Throughout the negotiations Smith had taken the greatest pains to keep all parties fully informed of every step he intended to take, and of every proposal which he was going to advance, supplying the Archbishop with copies of the heads of the bill and of its full text as soon as they were available.[3] Nothing that could be done to smooth its passage was left undone.

Unexpected opposition was encountered in the Lords. Eldon, the

[1] William Smith to Jeremy Bentham, 9 January 1818, Bentham Papers, B.M. Add. MSS. 33,545, f. 258.

[2] Ibid.

[3] See Canterbury to William Smith, 12 May and 21 June 1813, Verney Papers.

Lord Chancellor, and Ellenborough, the Lord Chief Justice, objected to the sweeping repeal of the several Blasphemy acts involved, insisting that only the sections specifically affecting the Unitarians should be abrogated. As the session was nearing its close this might well have been disastrous. But the Archbishop assured Smith of his continued support, and Eldon and Ellenborough were equally co-operative, agreeing to do everything to expedite the bill's passage so long as their objections were met. The first bill was accordingly negatived by the Commons and a new one immediately introduced and passed. The Lords acted with equal expedition, pressing through its third reading on the last day of the session.

The act was far from perfect. In the haste of rushing it through, clauses of the Blasphemy acts affecting Ireland went unnoticed and were thus left unrepealed.[1] Those clauses knowingly left in existence and the continuance of blasphemy as a crime under the Common Law also led to difficulty. As will be seen presently, there was one more attempt, albeit an unsuccessful one, to prosecute a Unitarian.

These limitations on the effectiveness of his bill Smith had not foreseen. But there were others which he did foresee. Some have suggested that he was fully 'prepared to accept an Act which (he hoped) would protect respectable Unitarians, while leaving the wilder Deists outside'.[2] Literally, of course, this is quite true. But this does not mean that Smith himself agreed with the continuance of such restrictions. He was in favour of a continuance of some limit on unlicensed profanity. But he opposed any limitation of what could legitimately be considered freedom of discussion. In the twenties he was to give his constant support to Joseph Hume's bills for free discussion, as well as to defend Richard Carlile, editor of *The Republican*, and Robert Taylor, the deistic clergyman, in those specific cases in which there was an attempt to impose limitations.[3] Nor was

[1] William Smith to J. Hone, 3 February 1814, Peel Papers, B.M. Add. MSS. 40,235, f. 92. So far as I can determine, these clauses have never been formally repealed. However, by the Dissenting Chapel Act of 1844 Irish Unitarians received all the practical protection necessary—the protection of their chapel properties (see E. M. Wilbur, *A History of Unitarianism* [Cambridge, Mass., 1952], pp. 318 and 360–2.)

[2] Henriques, p. 210.

[3] See *Hansard*, n.s. IX, 1398 and n.s. XI, 1079.

he willing, in principle, to justify the extent of his bill even in 1813. In replying to a charge that he had not gone far enough he observed:

It . . . remains . . . a common law offence to make a general attack, even argumentatively, on Christianity, as the Religion of the Country, or on the general authority of the Holy Scriptures; whether wisely, is another question—but it is one in which Protestant Dissenters, *as such*, have no particular concern. For myself, as a Christian, I have no hesitation in acknowledging, that for my religion I desire no such protection; let Truth stand or fall as she is able to support herself, nor seek assistance from means equally applicable to the defense of falsehood.

His only justification was that from the beginning he had set himself only a limited object and that, if he had not confined himself to that, nothing whatever would have been attained: 'It was my earnest wish not to excite but to allay all hostile feeling, especially in those whose opinions were of the greatest weight. . . .'[1]

He had achieved largely what he had set out to do. As he said, 'in the merely religious view of the subject, it completes the Toleration of every denomination of Christians; all of whom, by whatever name they are called, may now preach their respective tenets without let or hindrance, "none, legally, daring to make them afraid"'.[2] This was generally true. Except in Ireland, Unitarianism was now legal in the United Kingdom. The name could be used with impunity, which was probably the bill's most important practical effect.[3]

There is no better single example of Smith's approach to the problem of reform than this one. As has been emphasized before, he did not believe that the state either of Parliamentary, or of public, opinion allowed of the broad and sweeping reform which was his ultimate objective. In order to educate both, he believed in the constant discussion of all issues, and in the constant presentation of the most liberal programme. He believed in talking, and did a great

[1] *Norfolk Chronicle*, 24 July 1813.

[2] Ibid.

[3] See R. M. Montgomery, 'A Note on the Acts of Parliament dealing with denial of the Trinity', *Transactions of the Unitarian Historical Society*, VI (1935–8), 209–12.

deal of it. It was probably about this time that the little verse quoted in the *Dictionary of National Biography* made its appearance:

> At length, when the candles burn low in their sockets,
> Up gets William Smith with his hands in his pockets,
> On a course of morality fearlessly enters,
> With all the opinions of all the Dissenters.[1]

But it was necessary to act as well as to talk. No opportunity must be lost to take a chip from the great block of restrictive legislation whose complete destruction was the final objective. While opinion was being educated to accept a liberal system, a process of erosion could be attaining it. This was a task which called for a clever and wily politician. Smith could be both.

Ironically, Smith's triumph of tact and diplomacy in the Unitarian toleration act was to create an added necessity for both qualities. For, to the extent that it aided in the emergence of a separate and distinct Unitarian sect, it added significantly to the tensions within the Dissenting body, and thus to the problems of those who were attempting to lead that body. The clearest example of the effect of the act is seen in the trust suits which began almost immediately; when Unitarians shed their protective colouration and asserted a 'Unitarian' title to trusts founded by trinitarians, there were bound to be difficulties. But there can be no doubt that the act only speeded up an existing tendency toward controversy. Unitarianism was already growing into a separate, and very aggressive, sect, with no assistance from Smith—at least in its sectarian aim— and against his wishes. The aggressiveness of Unitarianism was in part, at any rate, a response to the aggressiveness of evangelical trinitarians. For the latter had lost none of their fire and having, in a sense, brought Christ back into religion, they were not about to see Him turned out again. Differences of opinion inevitably grew sharper as enthusiasms clashed. It is to the tendency toward controversy that attention must now be turned.

Unitarianism, as describing a distinct and separate movement within Dissent, as a 'party' appellation, is a term that cannot be used

[1] W. E. Nightingale refers to this verse in a letter to Ben Smith, 2 April 1820, Bonham-Carter Papers.

with accuracy before the foundation of the Unitarian Society in 1791. Not until then did it cease to be an intellectual movement particularly in Presbyterianism and among individual members at least of the other Dissenting bodies, and begin to emerge as a sect. For, however much some of its founders may have later argued against it, this was to be the necessary result of the Society's actions. In the preamble to its rules it was stated that

the fundamental principles of the Society are, that there is but ONE GOD, the SOLE former, Supporter, and Governor of the universe, the ONLY proper object of religious worship; and that there is one Mediator between God and men, the MAN Christ Jesus, who was commissioned by God to instruct men in their duty, and to reveal the doctrine of a future life.

The beneficial influence of these truths upon the moral conduct of men will be in proportion to the confidence with which they are received into the mind, and the attention with which they are regarded. Consequently, all foreign opinions which men have attached to this primitive system of Christian doctrine, and which tend to divert their thought from these fundamental principles, are in a large degree injurious to the cause of religion and virtue. While, therefore, many well-meaning persons are propagating with zeal opinions which members of this Society judge to be unscriptural and idolatrous, they think it their duty to oppose the further progress of such pernicious errors. . . .

This was strong language, and was meant to be. As Belsham, the author of the preamble, notes, 'the object of the Society was by no means to collect a great number of subscribers, but chiefly to form an association of those who thought it right to lay aside all ambiguity of language', and the stiff wording of the preamble, especially the use of the word 'idolatrous', was aimed as much against the Arians as against the orthodox.[1] What the Society's founders wished to do was to bring the Unitarians out into the open, despite the fact that many sympathizers would be excluded. This is exactly what they did. Six of the roughly fifteen London ministers of unorthodox views could not subscribe to such a strenuous statement and doubt-

[1] Thomas Belsham, *Memoirs of the Late Reverend Theophilus Lindsey* (London, 1873), pp. 196–9.

less many more throughout the country had similar scruples.[1] But the Unitarian cause had been fairly launched. Tentativeness was no longer easy, though Richard Price joined the Society despite the fact that he did not subscribe to all of its views.

The Unitarian Society was, however, distinctly limited in its objective, and hence in its appeal. It was solely an organization for propaganda. It never had more than about 150 subscribers (as Belsham pointed out, numbers were not its primary object), and its activities were confined to the publication of learned and complex theological works. Obviously, its appeal could only be to the highly educated, which meant, in practice, that its efforts were aimed, at the lowest, at the upper middle classes. It seemed self-evident to those who dominated the society that Unitarianism would progress as education and rationality progressed; but, on the other hand, it would progress only so fast. Unitarianism and education went hand in hand; the one could not exist without the other. Hence, they argued, the lower classes were not yet open to their endeavours.

Other Unitarians, however, took a very different view. William Vidler founded a Unitarian Evangelical Society in London in 1804. This was followed in 1806 by the Unitarian Fund, organized by Vidler, Aspland, David Eaton and a half a dozen others to undertake missionary work throughout the country. The Fund announced in its preamble that

it has long been a subject of complaint among Unitarians, and a topic of reproach to their adversaries, that so few active measures have been taken to diffuse among the lower classes of people the doctrines of Rational Religion. A knowledge of this . . . has prevailed upon a number of individuals, zealously concerned for the spread of scriptural Christianity and the promotion of the happiness of the Poor, to institute a Society for the encouragement of Popular Preaching on Unitarian principles.[2]

The example of the evangelicals was consciously followed, with the employment of lay preachers, not necessarily 'possessing the advantage of regular education'. Quite naturally this produced a strong

[1] Aspland, pp. 185–6. In fact, five of the six Arian congregations in London ultimately became Unitarian.
[2] Quoted in ibid., p. 282.

negative reaction among many of the older and more learned ministers.[1] Among them, Belsham was prominent. In his *Letter to Sidmouth*, Belsham had made clear his aversion to 'Methodist' practices and to those who followed them, particularly in his reference to 'honest John', who

after having *tried his gifts* till he is tired . . . will return in peace to his bodkin or his awl, perhaps convinced that he has mistaken his vocation, or more probably denouncing the vengeance of Heaven upon the ungodly crew who refuse to listen to the admonitions of so divine a teacher.[2]

Such remarks upset Aspland, but Belsham replied that, while 'my expressions against illiterate preachers are strong . . . my argument required it. I wished to state and prove that even the miserable fanatics who could obtain no testimonials to their character and talents ought not to be exposed to the penal laws.'[3] But though he opposed legal proscription, Belsham's attitude is plain enough. Aspland's was very different, which is probably why he was so active in founding the Protestant Society, feeling in one sense a closer affinity with his evangelical than with some of his Unitarian brethren.

Certainly the founders of the Fund were unrepentant in the face of criticisms like those of Belsham:

It is to be regretted that the Society [the reference here is to the Unitarian Evangelical Society] is regarded by some of our Unitarian brethren with a dubious sort of feeling, bordering on suspicion and dislike. They think we shall degrade the Unitarian cause, and put ourselves on a level with the Methodists . . . [but] the Methodists are praiseworthy for their zeal—their zeal as displayed in the fervour of their devotions, and their activity in popular preaching.[4]

There was no reason, they felt, why the Unitarians could not compete with the Methodists on equal terms; for theirs was the true and simple doctrine of the gospel. So they thought, and so they acted.

Such evangelical zeal on the part of the Unitarians was bound to

[1] Belsham, *Memoirs of Lindsey*, p. 204.
[2] *Letter*, p. 19.
[3] Quoted in Aspland, p. 268.
[4] Ibid., p. 198.

clash with the zeal of those whose methods were so consciously copied. Smith's act was but the final step in clearing the ring for controversy, far though this was from his intention. His own intention is clearly seen in the very significant formula adopted for the admission of his own congregation in Essex Street into the Deputies. In the December election of Deputies following the passage of Smith's act, Belsham, the minister at Essex Street, informed the Committee that being neither Presbyterian, Independent, nor Baptist, the congregation could not send representatives under any of the traditional designations, and requested that they be allowed to send them under the 'denomination of Protestant Non-Conformists'. To this the Committee agreed, if they would consent to do so 'without declaring that you are not of either of the Three Denominations'. And this was the solution, Smith himself being returned as one of their two Deputies.[1] (It was not necessary for the Chairman to be a Deputy, and Smith probably had not been one since 1805.) It has been said of this incident that 'the triumph of Unitarianism was unveiled and blatant . . .; and the name of William Smith was used of set purpose to grace it'.[2] Actually, this was neither the intention nor the significance of the event, as a closer examination proves.

Belsham took a rather peculiar attitude toward Smith's act, and as it was also Smith's attitude (indeed Smith, unlike Belsham, had been consistent in holding the assumptions that lay behind it) it is worth investigating. Belsham saw Smith's act, not as the beginning, but as the end of anything approaching a separate Unitarian sect. And the name of his chapel—quite the reverse of the general tendency—was changed from 'Unitarian' to simply Essex Street to mark the event! Belsham argued that, while in title the act appeared to be a mere relief act for Unitarians, both in form and in affect it was a relief measure for Dissenters generally. Every Anglican was still bound by law to be a trinitarian, but the whole of Dissent was now freed from the statutory obligation. It was now possible and proper, argued Belsham, for Unitarianism to act as an integral part of Protestant Dissent. 'It was', as Alexander Gordon has said in summing

[1] Minutes, 12 December 1813 and 17 January and 25 February 1814.
[2] Manning, p. 67.

up Belsham's attitude, 'their business and duty to prove themselves an influential ingredient in that larger whole'.[1]

The difficulty, of course, was that the larger whole became increasingly less disposed to accept Unitarians, and far from being considered a basic ingredient, they were looked upon as a foreign element. Heretofore Arians and Unitarians had long sat among the Deputies under the old designations. Now they were to do so without them. (Unitarians were, however, to continue to sit under the old names as well: on 28 January 1814 the Committee received a letter from William Vidler apologizing for having failed to inform them in an application for membership that his congregation in Parliament Court were 'of the Baptist profession'.[2]) What is really striking about the Essex Street formula is not its novelty, but the fact that it was woefully out of date. The time was not far off when the orthodox and the heterodox could no longer sit comfortably in the same body, and the signs of the impending breach were not long in showing themselves.

The first such sign, or so Aspland and his friends interpreted it, appeared in the case of John Wright of Liverpool. At the Committee meeting of 25 April 1817, Smith reported that he had received a letter from Wright, the latter having been arrested on a charge of blasphemy and being held under £400 bail. There were also charges against him for holding religious meetings in a place not properly registered. With the latter charges the Committee would have nothing to do, 'as it appears such place or room is occasionally used for other purposes, as an auction room etc., and as a certificate of Registration cannot be obtained . . . and from doubts which might possibly arise when the appeal is heard upon the construction of part of the clause contained in the last act of 29th July 1812, and in case the same should not be allowed the result might be attended with serious consequences to other places of religious worship. . . .' Presumably the Committee did not wish to induce too close an examination of places used for religious worship. The charge of blasphemy was different. The committee was of the opinion that the

[1] On Belsham's attitude, see Gordon, p. 298ff., whose account and phrasing I have followed very closely.
[2] Minutes, 28 January 1814.

charge must necessarily be quashed for informality, as it alleged only a certain tendency rather than citing the specific words used. But in case his assistance was needed, the Secretary was instructed to retain the eminent barrister James Scarlett.[1]

This assistance was subsequently withdrawn for reasons which do not appear in the Minutes. It is simply recorded that at the meeting of 30 May Smith informed the Committee that new information had arrived in letters from Liverpool, and, having considered the new evidence, they decided that it was not a case in which the Deputies ought to interfere.[2] The facts of the matter suggest the reason. In 1812 Wright had founded an 'Independent Debating Society' for working men which became noted for its extreme radical opinions. It had recently made itself particularly obnoxious by its outspoken support for the abortive march of the 'Blanketeers',[3] and the Liverpool magistrates had thereupon forbidden it to meet. Wright, whose brother Richard was a prominent domestic missionary of the Unitarian Fund, got around this at once by simply changing the society into one for religious discussion.[4] The Committee's informant was the Rev William Shepherd, a leading radical in Liverpool. Shepherd, representing the opinion of Unitarian merchants and manufacturers in Lancashire, doubtless had no desire to be confused with those of Wright's views. Perhaps the Committee shared this desire. But apart from this, the Committee, which had always sought to avoid involving the Deputies in political controversies—particularly controversies extraneous to the interests of Dissent as such—probably saw excellent strategic arguments against associating itself in any way with Wright's radical opinions, especially as it believed that the charges against him could not be made to stick.

The dropping of the matter, however, caused considerable

[1] Minutes, 25 April 1817.

[2] Ibid., 30 May 1817.

[3] In the winter of 1816–17 Lancashire was badly hit by a depression. A number of artisans set out for London to plead their case. Each carried a blanket; hence the name attached to them. The magistrates' stern measures, however, halted the march before it got very far.

[4] See David Paterson 'John Wright', *Transactions of the Unitarian Historical Society*, VI (1935–38), 29–43.

uneasiness among the Unitarian members of the Deputies (even though they too would in all likelihood have shared the prejudice against Wright's social and economic views), and attempts were made to make it clear that the Committee stood ready to defend sufferers in simple cases of persecution for religious opinions. At the general meeting of 30 January 1818 Edward Busk, a Unitarian barrister, presented a resolution from the floor which went to extraordinary lengths to make the situation clear. It was stated that at the time the Committee made its decision three out of the four charges against Wright had been quashed. It was also stated that the Committee was of the opinion that the fourth charge would be, as had in fact been the case. In view of these special circumstances Busk wished the Deputies to resolve that the decision on the Wright case should not be interpreted as establishing any general principle of non-interference in such cases. But this they refused to do.[1] It is true that at the general meeting on 29 May J. T. Rutt was able to get through a resolution that

it is a most important function of this Deputation . . . to assist individuals among them who may be aggrieved by unfounded charges of misconduct, in the public exercise of their Christian ministry.[2]

This, however, was sufficiently general not to be binding in particular circumstances. It seemed obvious—at any rate, to some Unitarians—that the majority of the Deputies were extremely reluctant, if not strongly opposed, to defending Unitarians in cases of prosecution for blasphemy.

Unitarians of this opinion began to take steps to protect themselves almost immediately after the Committee made its decision to drop the case. In July 1817 some of the younger and more radical Unitarians met at Aspland's house to form the Non-Con Club, 'to promote the great principles of Truth and Liberty as avowed and acted upon by the enlightened and liberal Nonconformists or Protestant Dissenters from the Church of England'. Among those present were Richard and Edgar Taylor, W. J. Fox, and John (later Sir John) Bowring.[3] And it was the same group who, during 1818,

[1] Minutes, 30 January 1818.
[2] Ibid., 29 May 1818.
[3] Aspland, p. 404.

laid plans for the Unitarian Association, which was to be devoted exclusively to protecting the civil rights of members of that sect. It had been decided that, as others apparently would not look after them, the Unitarians must look after themselves. Aspland in his arguments for a separate society cited the Wright case specifically: 'When Mr. Wright was under persecution, the Deputies were appealed to in vain.' And he cited, as well, the Wolverhampton case (1816–42) in which a Unitarian congregation were being sued as unlawful holders of their chapel property, which, it was argued, had been endowed for trinitarian worship;[1] Smith's act was beginning to bear its unfortunate fruit. A new intolerance, or so the Unitarians saw it, was growing within Dissent itself.

Some thought this intolerance ought to be ignored. Belsham was particularly opposed to any separate Unitarian organization. As he wrote to Aspland in November 1818:

If I wished Unitarians to become a powerful political sect, I should be a warm friend to that grand scheme of federal union, of which I heard so much in Lancashire. But as a friend to truth and liberty, which I think much impaired by such associations, I must dissent from them. . . . Nor can I approve of any plans for separating Unitarians from their fellow-christians more than is absolutely necessary.

We are the *salt* of the earth. But a lump of salt lying by itself will never fertilize the ground. It must be mixed and blended with the earth, in order to manure the soil and produce a copious harvest.[2]

Coming from a man who had labelled the beliefs of the vast majority of his Dissenting brethren 'idolatrous', Belsham's notions may seem strange. But, as has been seen, Belsham had his own justification for them. Coming, on the other hand, from William Smith, who shared them, such notions make more sense. Unlike Belsham, Smith had uniformly been true to the tolerant catholicity of spirit which provided their only reasonable foundation. As he had told the Commons in 1791, Smith had disliked Belsham's preamble: 'When he saw it in the book published by the Unitarians, he had disapproved of it, because he wished that decency of language might be observed as much as possible. . . .' All he would say in their

[1] Ibid., p. 416.
[2] Ibid., p. 413.

defence was that 'he did think that when the principles of the Unitarians were called blasphemous, they were not so unjustified in using the term idolatrous, as they would otherwise have been. . . .'[1] Such epithets, in Smith's opinion, only clouded the intellect in what should be its one pursuit—truth. This he made very clear in 1808. In that year the Unitarian Society published an 'Improved Version' of the New Testament, based mainly on the translation of Archbishop Newcome, with an introduction and notes by Belsham. Smith bought a large number for distribution to Dissenting academies, accompanied by the following remarks:

The writer of this notice may be supposed himself to have settled opinions; but he has ever been averse to the practice, too prevalent among all sects, of usurping to themselves epithets, in their very terms decisive of all controversy. Who but the infallible shall presume to arrogate to himself alone the title of orthodox or evangelical? Who, duly conscious of the weakness of his reason and the strength of his prejudices shall claim to be exclusively rational?

In arguing about the names which they appropriated to themselves, people were apt to forget the point of all disputation—or what ought to be the point.

The question still remains, as in our Saviour's time, 'What is the truth?' i.e. the true doctrine of the Gospel. That which is not cannot be either orthodox or evangelical. Nor is it possible that this truth of God as it is in Jesus, when ascertained, should not be found sufficiently rational and liberal for his creature man: rational, for, 'He that giveth understanding, shall not he know?'—and liberal (if indeed in such connection the word be at all allowable) for it is of the essence of that truth to 'make us free,' free from error, free from prejudice, free from uncharitableness.

Smith ended his remarks with an exhortation to his student audience to 'scrutinize' their beliefs, 'with patience and reverence indeed, but without that servile fear which, as it paralyzes man's intellect, can surely never be pleasing to God who gave it. . . .'[2] Was Smith thinking of his own days at Daventry, when similar exhortations

[1] *Parliamentary History*, XXIX, 1395–6.

[2] Belsham quoted these remarks with high praise in his *Memoir of Lindsey*, p. 306.

had led to a weakening of his own orthodoxy? Perhaps he was, but the great lesson that he had learned at Daventry, and one which all his succeeding experience and reflection confirmed, was that there was one thing that above all other things was important—liberty. However appropriate his own use of the term, William Smith was in the deepest and most profound sense of the term 'liberal'. To Smith, all firmly held opinions were worthy of respect: against some he would argue, but he tried never to slander.

Smith's life had taught him tolerance and urbanity, and these qualities were, of course, a large part of the explanation of his success with so many different sorts of people. Zachary Macaulay, in a letter quoted earlier, wrote of Smith's daughter Patty:

She objects with considerable force to the kind of graduated scale which the Saints are in the habit of applying to all that come within their reach. She admits at the same time that things are terribly wrong in the circle in which she is chiefly called to move; and she loves the devotion[s] of the Church of England, and the conviction of some of her ministers.[1]

The Smith children, like some others, had definite opinions of their own, but in this case Patty was probably reflecting her father's views, and certainly his outlook. There can be no doubt that her opinions were formed in her father's house, in more than the literal sense. At Park Street, Wilberforce rubbed elbows with Fox, and Belsham with Dean Milner. At Parndon, the family always attended Church, though usually the evening service which they found more congenial, and they were always ready to hear any preacher of note, whatever his theological views. A more cosmopolitan atmosphere would have been difficult to find. But all of its elements were important in Smith's life, part of his everyday concerns. Born and reared an Independent, educated a Rational Dissenter, in adult life a member of the fashionable Unitarian congregation founded by the ex-Anglican Lindsey in Essex Street, Smith also had points of contact, or at least a shared experience, with all of those various people with whom he associated. His had not been, and was not, the sort of life which bred narrow views.

But Smith was not entirely unique. At any rate, he represented

[1] Macaulay to Hannah More, 23 July 1816, Huntington Library, MY 673.

one of the two main traditions in Unitarianism, as Aspland represented the other. Smith represented the catholicity of eighteenth-century Dissent, particularly of the Presbyterianism of his youth. This was the older tradition, going back indeed to the earliest period of Presbyterianism. Aspland, on the other hand, represented a tradition that went back, among the Presbyterians at least, no further than Joseph Priestley. It is significant that Priestley began life as an Independent, and he brought its sectarian attitude with him into Presbyterianism. Aspland too came from orthodox Dissent, with its sectarian traditions, having been born and educated a Baptist. Similarly William Vidler and David Eaton, though they had had little formal education, both coming from humble backgrounds. These new Unitarians brought something besides their sectarian attitudes—they also brought their evangelical fervour and their evangelical practices.[1] The new Unitarians were in large part incomprehensible to older Unitarians like Belsham and Smith. In a real sense, the conflict was one between the old Unitarianism and the new, between older men and younger men. There were exceptions, like J. T. Rutt who was almost Smith's age, but it is hardly surprising that Priestley's biographer should have thrown in his lot with the new Unitarianism of the Unitarian Association.

There was another difference between the old Unitarians and the new; this was in their respective political philosophies. Smith and Belsham were Whigs—liberal Whigs, but Whigs nonetheless. For them, bitter experience had tempered early enthusiasm. Though the determinist (or necessarian) philosophy which they shared (indeed Belsham was its most eminent living exponent) with the new Unitarians undoubtedly made them optimistic for the future, it was a distant future. In practice, they remained devoted to the Whig ideal of tempered aristocratic government. Not so the new Unitarians. They came from a new generation which had not tasted defeat, and they were avowedly and proudly radical in their political opinions. Bowring and Thomas Southwood Smith (who was soon to

[1] See Bolam *et al.*, pp. 236–40. As is evident, I owe a great debt to H. L. Short who wrote the concluding section of the book. Though he does not go quite so far in drawing contrasts as I do, I think my conclusions are implicit in his work.

join their inner counsels) were a little later to be drawn into the radical circle which gathered around Bentham and are remembered among the master's most eminent disciples.[1] There were profound differences both religious and political between the old and the new Unitarians, and the traditions which they represented were to continue.[2]

Smith saw only one solution to both religious and political problems. Men could not be made rational and liberal by crash programmes. Education was the only answer. (It was, of course, an answer for all good Necessarians; Smith's difference from the radicals was one of emphasis.) Parliamentary discussion was one means of education. Public debate outside Parliament was another means which he valued highly, and put into practice at Norwich. But he was keenly interested in more organized schemes of education as well. Smith joined with his friend Brougham in the founding of the Royal Lancasterian Institution in 1808, and he helped to transform it into the British and Foreign School Society in 1814.[3] In 1820 he gave his support to Brougham's proposals for a public education system, which were violently opposed by most Dissenters because of the important role they gave to the Church. And it was undoubtedly Smith's influence which kept the Deputies negotiating with Brougham while the other Dissenting organizations, including the Unitarian Association, were publicly hostile to the whole

[1] Professor R. K. Webb kindly lent me his very important lectures delivered at Leicester in 1966. In these, the first formulations of his research on nineteenth century Unitarianism, he argues strongly against the idea of utilitarian radicalism's exclusive intellectual obligation to Bentham. Nineteenth century radicals drew from many sources; and as is evidenced by the fact that they were radicals before they became Benthamites, Bowring's and Southwood Smith's radicalism was based firmly in their Unitarianism.

[2] See Short, in Bolam *et al*. James Martineau may be said to have been a later representative of catholicity. The Unitarian Association, or British and Foreign Unitarian Association as it became in 1825, continued to represent a sectarian view. Short, like historians generally, over-emphasizes the political conservatism of Unitarians after 1830. As Professor Webb suggests, they were all Liberals. And the founders of the Association, Bowring, Southwood Smith, and W. J. Fox, were to continue to be radical by any accounting, both with regard to religious and broader issues.

[3] See New, p. 204.

scheme—which the Deputies never were.[1] Smith once again showed the stress which he placed on education by breaking a tie vote, with his casting vote as Chairman, in favour of the investment of £1,000 of the Deputies' funds in the new London University in 1827.[2] Had Dissent continued to have leaders with such broad views as Smith's the history of public education in the nineteenth century might have been very different.

Smith was bound to have opposed the disruption of the Dissenting body on intellectual grounds. And there were also strategic considerations which dictated unity. It was not only Belsham's point that the Unitarians could only 'fertilize' the other Dissenting sects by intermingling with them; more important to Smith, common civil disabilities demanded unity as well. All of Smith's bull-dog tenacity, all his considerable tact and diplomacy were, therefore, devoted to the prevention of disruption and discord. He refused to be provoked by the hostile actions of evangelical Dissenters against Unitarians (and he would certainly have deplored the provocative words and actions of some Unitarians).[3] Personal attacks left him equally unmoved. In 1827 he was strongly criticized by some of the more rabid London evangelicals for his defence of the Rev Robert Taylor, who was being prosecuted for his deist views, and it was demanded that Smith be removed as Chairman of the Deputies, as unfit to preside over the affairs of a Christian body.[4] Smith took no notice (and neither, it should be added, did the Deputies). It was not until 1832, when he retired as Chairman of the Deputies, that he spoke of his deep desire for unity. Then, in a long letter to the general meeting, he delivered an eloquent plea for what he, at any rate, thought were basic principles. He noted that some 'seemed to think that differences of opinion on controverted points of Theology were sufficient grounds of separation, even as to the common intercourse of life in civil affairs'. To him this was to ignore their whole history and everything for which they had fought:

[1] *Hansard*, n.s. II, 366–7; Minutes, 1820–1, *passim*.

[2] See the proceedings of the Deputies' meetings of December 1827, *Monthly Repository*, n.s. I (1827), 135–7 and 228–32.

[3] For these controversies, see Bolam *et al.*, pp. 245–52.

[4] *Monthly Repository*, n.s. I (1827), p. 121.

. . . What is the whole foundation of the right of Dissent on religious subjects of every kind, and in every degree, but the Right of Private Judgment, limited only to the conscience of the Inquirer, and by the duty of exercising that right with decent respect which the serious and weighty nature of the subject will dictate to every sincere examiner desirous only of discovering truth? . . . On what other grounds does Protestantism itself stand? And if this line be once over-stepped and Christians attempt to stigmatize each other on account of their differences, as unworthy of Christian fellowship, is not this, so far as it lies in their power, inflicting punishment for opinions, and with what consistency can they blame the Autos de Fé of Seville or Madrid! I cannot therefore, refrain from expressing my earnest hope that every Member of this old and respectable Body, in which the several Denominations of Dissenters have acted in cordial harmony for so long a period, will utterly discountenance all such inconsistent and uncharitable presumptions.[1]

Smith's tolerance was deep and genuine, and he consistently refused to be confined by the narrow boundaries of creed and sect.

This plea was made two years after the launching of the Lady Hewley's Trustees Case, in which Smith's old colleague on the Committee, the great Congregationalist manufacturer, Thomas Wilson, was a correspondent. The end result was to drive the Unitarians from the trust, and it was one of the more important factors in their secession from the Deputies.[2] But this did not happen until a year after Smith's death, in 1836. So long as he lived Dissent remained united. His ideas may have been outmoded, but they were strong and so was the personality behind them. Smith opposed any disruptive forces in Dissent; and in 1818 the projected Unitarian Association constituted such a disruptive force.

But the reservations of the elder statesmen had no effect on the younger radicals. The Unitarian Association was duly formed early in 1819, with forty-eight congregations among its first subscribers.[3] It was very much an organization of new men. Not strangely, Smith took no part in its founding and Essex Street was not among the congregations represented. Its activities were directed by its

[1] Minutes, 2 January 1832.
[2] See Manning, pp. 68–93, and Aspland, chap. 30.
[3] *Monthly Repository*, XIV (1819), 380.

London Committee, and that was dominated by the Non-Con Club —Aspland, the Taylors, Bowring, and later Southwood Smith. These men differed very considerably from the man Sydney Smith was to call the 'Head of the Unitarian Church'. Unlike William Smith, they were 'evangelical' Unitarians; they were radicals in their politics; and they were radicals in their approach to the problems of Dissent. Their line, as advanced in the *Monthly Repository* which they also dominated, was hard and uncompromising. Difficulties were almost bound to arise.

They did so immediately. The first project of the new Association was to be an easing of the marriage law, and they showed their radical tendencies by choosing as their Parliamentary champion, not Smith, but Alderman Wood. Belsham was appalled, urging upon Aspland in the same letter in which he protested against the Association itself that 'to appoint Wood to conduct an application to Parliament, would be to bespeak a refusal. Mr. W. Smith should by all means be engaged to bring the business before the House. He is looked up to as a veteran senator'.[1] Clearly, however, the Association had had enough of veteran senators and would have by-passed Smith if it could have done so. But its leaders had reckoned without their man. Before the Association had framed its bill, Smith had introduced one of his own.[2] Whether they liked it or not, the Association had a wily and unprovocative spokesman for its cause. As Henry Crabb Robinson reported of Smith's speech introducing the bill, 'it had the merit of raising a feeling favourable to the Speaker, and it was not so intelligible as to raise opposition. Lord Castlereagh did not pretend to understand it and Mr. Wilberforce spoke guardedly and with favour of the projected measure'.[3] This

[1] Belsham to Aspland, November 1818, Aspland, p. 413.

[2] According to the proposed bill the Dissenting couple would only have to present a written declaration to the officiating clergyman that 'we are Dissenters' in which case the service in the Book of Common Prayer would be limited to that part which begins with 'I require and charge you both' and ends with 'and thereto I plight thee my troth'. In other words the distinctly religious part of the ceremony was to be completely done away with (William Smith to Liverpool, 19 July 1819, Liverpool Papers, B.M. Add. MSS. 38,277, f. 358).

[3] Crabb Robinson Diary, 16 June 1819, Dr Williams's Library.

observation, by a shrewd observer, suggests that there may well have been craft even in the long, often rambling, speeches to which Smith treated the House. Perhaps Smith did not entirely object to the image of a bluff, rather vague, figure, 'with his hands in his pockets'. Certainly, there is evidence that elsewhere he adopted a very different style of oratory.[1] In any event, he was not to succeed in his objective now or later; bill after bill was wrecked because of the impossibility of meeting both Anglican and Dissenting scruples.[2] But, though he was never to succeed in getting a bill passed, he did succeed in establishing a title to the measure which he never lost. He remained the outstanding and pre-eminent spokesman of the Dissenting interest in Parliament. In 1827 Sydney Smith asked: 'How many Protestant Dissenters are there who pay a double allegiance to the King, and to the head of their Church, who is not the King?' He was able to answer the question to his own satisfaction by two more: 'Is not Mr. William Smith, member for Norwich, the head of the Unitarian Church? Is not Mr. Wilberforce the head of the Clapham Church?'[3] Whether Sydney Smith had accounted for all Protestant Dissenters is beside the point, but that it was still possible to couple Smith's name with Wilberforce's is some indication of the success with which he continued to handle the very delicate problem of leadership of the Dissenting interest.

Certainly it was to be no easy task, nor was Smith to have his own way on every issue. Hardly a question would arise in the crucial years ahead on which there was not violent disagreement among the Dissenters themselves. To preserve more than a semblance of unity would be impossible. All that could be done was to keep disagreement to a minimum, and to keep the several organizations in some kind of unison on common objectives. The task was to call for all Smith's tact, for all his political skill.

[1] According to the editor of the *Norwich Mercury* Smith's success at the polls could be attributed partly to his effective off-the-cuff speeches to popular audiences: 'The stile [sic] of Mr. Smith's speaking is particularly adapted to such an auditory. It is generally flowing, plain, clear, intelligible, full of good sense, and level to the understandings of those he addresses' (*Mercury*, 20 June 1818).

[2] A brief history of the measure during this period will be found in the *Monthly Repository*, n.s. I (1827), 367ff.

[3] Quoted in Brown, p. 369.

CHAPTER TWELVE

THE ORGANIZATION OF VICTORY

The eighteen-twenties saw the final, successful struggle for the repeal of the hated Test and Corporation Acts. Dissent once again became aroused to the issue, and enthusiasm was not to flag until the acts were abolished.

There were two main reasons for a revival of the question. The first was the fact that Catholic Emancipation became a major and continuing problem during the period. This naturally tended to concentrate the Dissenters' attention on their own closely connected grievance. It was probably not by accident that the first of the resolutions on the Test and Corporation Acts came at the Deputies' general meeting of January 1817, the first after the Catholic question had been revived in Parliament.[1]

But there was a more fundamental reason for the urgency with which the subject was approached during this period, a reason whose roots lay deep in the profound social and economic changes which England was undergoing, and one which would have brought the question to the fore again, no matter what course the Catholic question had taken. This was the fact that Repeal was not only a religious grievance; it was a class grievance as well, and clearly recognized as such by all parties. After the final victory Lady Spencer congratulated Lord John Russell on undertaking 'the renovation of your country's strength and the establishment of its power on a foundation which can never fail—the hearty concurrence and unanimity of all the intelligence, ingenuity, and enterprise of its population. . . .'[2] She referred, of course, to the leading elements

[1] Minutes, 31 January 1817.

[2] Spencer Walpole, *The Life of Lord John Russell* (London, 1891), p. 149.

of the middle classes, and Repeal, no less perhaps than Reform, was a middle-class demand for the recognition of their proper place in society and politics.[1] Perhaps the concentration of attention on Repeal is part of the explanation of the fact that Reform did not become a major issue before it did. In any case, the similar social and economic basis of the question is crucial in understanding the urgency and insistence with which it was pressed.

The agitation of the seventeen-eighties had had a similar basis; but by the eighteen-twenties the increase in numbers both of the middle classes and of the Dissenters, and the apparent connexion between those increases, gave Dissenting propaganda a new and blatantly open assurance. As the *Monthly Repository* confidently asserted in 1827:

> . . . In point of fact, we apprehend it will not be disputed, that throughout England a great part of the more active members of society, who have the most intercourse with the people and the most influence over them, are Protestant Dissenters. These are manufacturers, merchants and substantial tradesmen, or persons who are in the enjoyment of a competency realized by trade, commerce and manufactures, gentlemen of the professions of law and physic, and agriculturists, of that class particularly who live upon their own freeholds. The virtues of temperance, frugality, prudence and integrity that are promoted by religious Nonconformity and sectarian peculiarities assist the temporal prosperity of these descriptions of persons, as they tend also to lift others to the same rank in society.[2]

Religion and enterprise, it was claimed, had marched hand in hand to alter the whole basis of power in society, and the institutions of the country must be overhauled to meet the new reality. What the Dissenters called for was not only religious freedom, but social mobility.

Unlike opponents in the seventeen-eighties, their present opponents now argued that Dissenters already had what they demanded,

[1] As Professor Temperley remarked long ago: 'The significance of this measure as marking the influence of the middle classes and the tendency towards Reform is not easy to exaggerate' (*Cambridge Modern History*, vol. X [1907], 593).

[2] *Monthly Repository*, n.s. I (1827), 251.

in fact if not in theory; that the several laws passed to protect nonconformists gave complete security. As Peel contended in 1828: 'Dissenters were not practically excluded from municipal honours any more than from offices of state.'[1] So far as actual legal proscription went, Dissenting publicists, when pushed, were almost willing to admit this.[2] But as to practicality they made important distinctions. As the official *Statement* issued by the Dissenting Deputies argued:

It may be true, that under cover of indirect expedients, and still more under the protection of public opinion, Dissenters are often, without any actual annoyance, members of corporate institutions; that they occupy many minor stations. . . . It may be conceded also that the honours of a higher class, likely to be attained by them are small in number; and that few of them might even under the most liberal administration of the laws, appear in the magistracy, and fewer still advance to eminent public stations. . . . [But] honours, though ultimately obtainable by but few, are the objects of ambition, and stimulants to exertion, of all; and the fact is notorious, that Dissenters are not in the Magistracy, and in many other honourable offices, and that their known incapacity to hold with honour and consistency those more elevated posts, which every one wishes to be at least able to propose to himself or his children as attainable objects in the prosecution of his or their career, either leads to insincerity, or altogether deters the conscientious from exertion in those departments of public life, in which they can only purchase eminent success by a sacrifice of principle.[3]

It is difficult to see how the holding of the office of Lord Mayor of London, a position enjoyed by three Dissenters in the decade before

---

[1] *Monthly Repository*, n.s. II (1828), 274.

[2] They never did admit it, for the very good reason that it was not completely true. The old gap in the Indemnity Acts which prevented an unqualified Dissenter from standing for election in a corporation if he were challenged still stood. Lord John Russell said in introducing his motion in 1828 that he could give examples of places where elections had been 'nullified' in this fashion (*Hansard*, XVIII, 689). He did not do so, but cases are occasionally cited in Dissenting periodicals.

[3] *Statement of the Case of the Protestant Dissenters under the Corporation and Test Acts* (London, 1827) p. 12.

Repeal,[1] was any more compatible with conscience than the holding of the office of Lord Chief Justice would have been. Clearly, this was not the core of the problem. The difficulty, as it had long been, was that there was no disposition to appoint Dissenters to office. And it was this reluctance which gave them their most forceful argument. They believed that 'the public avowal of an unjust principle can never be without mischievous results. . . .' As the *Statement* went on to say:

. . . They feel that these laws lie, and are persisted in because they *do* lie, at the foundation of all the distinctions and preferences which meet them at every hour, in town and in country, in public and in private life, and mark them out as an isolated portion of the community; they know that the majority of the supporters of these laws cling to them for no other reason. . . .[2]

What Dissenters feared most was prejudice. Nor can it be doubted that this prejudice was very real. It was both social and religious, and it emanated from an acute struggle for power in English society. Both sides accepted the Test and Corporation Acts as a symbol; but it was the realities of the struggle that gave it its edge and its bitterness.

The result was not dissimilar from that seen in the more limited arena at Norwich. As their economic and social power became ever greater, the frustration of the Dissenters over the unseen, but nonetheless effective, barriers to advancement increased proportionately. And as their frustration increased, their approach became ever more radical. This growing radicalism can be seen in the unsuccessful attempts of a section of the Deputies, led by J. T. Rutt, to get that body to present an address to Queen Caroline in 1821.[3] And it can be seen as well in the approach adopted toward the new Repeal campaign.

Since 1817 the body of the Deputies had become increasingly restive. They passed a second resolution calling for action in 1819, and thereafter a year did not pass without a discussion of the matter.

[1] Matthew Wood, Robert Waithman, and Anthony Brown, (see A. B. Beavan, *The Aldermen of the City of London* [London, 1913], pp. 141–2).

[2] *Statement*, p. 11.

[3] Minutes, 26 January and 8 February 1821.

In 1820, the year after its foundation, the Unitarian Association also took up the hue and cry. In that year the annual meeting resolved that 'the Committee keep in view the proceedings of the Deputies of the Three Denominations on the Corporation and Test Acts, and . . . cooperate with them in any measure that may be practicable'.[1] In 1821, with Rutt in the chair,[2] it was resolved that 'this Association feels very deeply the absolute necessity of immediate measures being adopted towards the Repeal of the Corporation and Test Acts, and that it be recommended to the Committee to take every practicable means for reviving that question amongst all denominations of Dissenters'.[3] And in 1822, with Rutt once again in the chair, the Committee was instructed 'to convey to the Committee of the Deputies and the Committee of the Protestant Society, the strong and decided feeling of this Association, that the present period imperiously calls upon Dissenters of all denominations to concur and persevere in application to Parliament for a Repeal of the Corporation and Test Acts. . . .'[4]

The effect of all this agitation within the Dissenting body was at first very small. The Committee of the Deputies was consistent on each occasion in recommending that the time was not opportune, and, by a combination of cajolery and outright evasion, managed to avoid the demands for action. This was becoming increasingly difficult, however. In 1820, for instance, the general meeting in January had requested that the Committee 'report to an early special meeting of the Deputies, whether they consider the present an eligible opportunity for petitioning the two Houses of Parliament for the removal of the civil disabilities of Protestant Dissenters'.[5] The Committee waited three weeks before considering the matter, until the dissolution of Parliament was upon it, and then decided, for obvious reasons, that the time was not opportune.[6] The next

[1] *Monthly Repository*, XV (1820), 320.

[2] Rutt was a member of, and a Deputy from, the Hackney congregation where Priestley had once preached and where Aspland now preached. Not surprisingly, this congregation was one of those most pressing for action (see, for example, ibid., XIX [1824], 55).

[3] Ibid., XVI (1821), 375.   [4] Ibid., XVII (1822), 381.

[5] Minutes, 28 January 1820.   [6] Ibid., 18 February 1820.

general meeting in May did not even bother to ask the Committee's advice, simply resolving that the time *was* opportune and instructing the Committee to draw up a petition.[1]

The Committee was able to avoid any further action until 1823. But there were increasing signs of restlessness and distrust within the body of the Deputies. In 1823 the first general meeting broke into what can scarcely be termed anything else than open revolt. Their second resolution tells the story:

Resolved, that this Deputation is convinced from parallel cases in religious and political history that the end in view can be most effectually and honorably accomplished by active and unremitted efforts to enlighten the public mind and to concentrate and direct the temperate exertions of those who ought to co-operate in the cause and by earnest application to the Legislature at every possible opportunity urged on the broadest principles of truth and justice.[2]

The body of the Deputies had reversed a policy of more than thirty years' standing and had accepted the Unitarian Association's approach to the problem of reform. They had launched themselves on the policy of agitation.

Smith's reaction to this new turn of events was characteristically pessimistic. He warned the general meeting that tremendous difficulties stood in their way. It was his opinion that 'the apathy and indifference of the Dissenters under their grievances were not the least among them'. Further, he contended that the cause of religious liberty had made much more rapid strides in Parliament than in the country as a whole. In short, he made it very clear that he considered public opinion—significantly enough, even among the Dissenters— a most unreliable, and perhaps even a dangerous ally.[3]

From Parliament, he looked for better things, but not immediately. In a report drawn up for the next general meeting he explained the Committee's reluctance to act in the following terms:

Since the discussions of the Catholic question the Committee, though aware of the broad distinction between that case and their own, yet

---

[1] Ibid., 26 May 1820.   [2] Ibid., 10 January 1823.
[3] *Monthly Repository*, XVIII (1823), 121.

seeing also in how many points they were connected and how great an influence the decision of the one might have on the other have deliberately preferred rather to be vigilant than active. . . .[1]

The thrust of this is clear. The great question before Parliament was that of Catholic Emancipation. Once Parliament had made up its mind on this issue, it would also have made up its mind on Repeal; but not until then. Repeal was only a secondary consideration in the great political question of the day; and, as such, it would have to wait its turn.

There was considerable justification for Smith's position. As has been seen, Catholics and Dissenters were—in the latter case, theoretically at least— excluded from both national and local offices by the same statutes. And, as the debates of the eighteen-twenties were to prove once again, in the minds of both the defenders of exclusion and its opponents, the two questions were inextricably connected.

The High Tories, or the 'Protestants' as they were called because of their position on Emancipation, were opposed to the claims of the Dissenters both on the independent merit of those claims and, of greater significance, because they felt that to admit the Dissenters to full political rights would force the admission of the Catholics as well.[2] It was not so important that Catholics and Dissenters were excluded by the same statutes, for the Test Acts could be revised in such a way that Dissenters would be freed of their disabilities, while Catholics remained excluded.[3] But it was important that Catholics and Dissenters were excluded on the principle of the Anglican Constitution, which would be destroyed if the Dissenters' disabilities were removed. The Tory defenders of exclusion clung to the notion that Church and State were indissolubly bound and were, or ought to be, co-extensive. They conceded that the toleration of differing

[1] Minutes, 7 March 1823.

[2] See, for instance, Lord Eldon to Lady F. J. Bankes, n.d. April 1828, Horace Twiss, *The Public and Private Life of Lord Chancellor Eldon* (London, 1844), III, 37–8.

[3] It was the sacramental test (the taking of the sacrament according to Anglican rites as a qualification for office) which excluded Dissenters. A declaration against transubstantiation provided an extra safeguard against Catholics.

religious opinions had become an integral element of the Constitution, but, as Perceval and Liverpool had made clear in 1812, they resolutely denied that the undoubted right to toleration implied any right to political power. The State might choose to tolerate opinions which differed from those of the Established Church, but it could not admit religious dissidents to full citizenship without irrevocably destroying the theory that the two institutions were co-extensive.

Thus the 'Protestants' could not admit the claims of the Dissenters without also sacrificing the fundamental principle on which they based their opposition to Catholic Emancipation. If Dissenters were brought within the pale of the Constitution, the lines of exclusion would become much more difficult to draw, the arguments for it mainly those of expediency rather than principle.[1] Lord John Russell was right in rejoicing that the success of his Repeal motion in 1828 not only destroyed the Anglican Constitution, but shattered the main line of defence of a 'Protestant' Constitution as well.[2] It was to avoid just such a consequence that the so-called 'Protestants' opposed the claims of Protestant Dissenters as vigorously as they opposed those of the Catholics.

The 'Catholic' Tories took another view of the question. They were ardent for Emancipation, but equally determined, until the very last minute, that Repeal must not be considered until the greater question had been carried. To relieve the Dissenters first would, they thought, harm the Catholic cause by reducing the pressure against religious disabilities generally. Even worse, William Huskisson, who succeeded George Canning as the 'Catholic' leader, declared in the 1828 debates that he was certain that if Repeal were carried the result would be, among the great majority of Dissenters, 'an additional and more vigorous opposition to the Catholic Question'.[3]

[1] For a detailed consideration of what was left of the 'Protestant' position after Repeal see G. F. A. Best, 'The Protestant Constitution and its Supporters', *Royal Historical Society Transactions*, 5th series, VIII, (1958), 105–27.

[2] Russell to Thomas Moore, 11 March 1828, Rollo Russell, ed., *Early Correspondence of Lord John Russell, 1805–40* (London, 1913), I, 272.

[3] *The Test-Act Reporter* (London, 1829), pp. 133–4. The *Test-Act Reporter* was a periodical published monthly by the United Committee during the Repeal campaign of 1828. The several issues were published together in a commemorative volume the following year.

The Whig champions of the cause of religious liberty also laid heavy emphasis on the connexion between Repeal and Emancipation —and left no doubt whatever about which issue they considered more important. In the course of the debates on his Repeal motion of 1828, Russell bluntly asserted that he considered the Catholic grievances to be

so much greater than those of the Dissenters, that though, whenever the present question is brought forward (should it unfortunately fail now), I shall unquestionably vote for it, still I conceive that it never can be so brought forward without a strong wish and desire on the part of those who promote it to do justice to the Roman Catholics. I know not the effect which my declaration may create, but I keep my feelings on this subject no secret from the Dissenters. I said to that respectable body last year, 'I will bring your cause forward; but, if at any future time, I shall think its success injurious to the Roman Catholic Claims, I cannot undertake it.'[1]

The Dissenters looking to Parliament for relief saw three positions on their problem. The 'Protestant' Tories were opposed to Repeal in large part because they believed it would advance the cause of Emancipation. The 'Catholic' Tories opposed Repeal because they felt sure it would be detrimental to the Catholic cause. The Whigs were primarily interested in Repeal as a means of furthering Emancipation.[2]

There was, then, some point to Smith's belief that the Dissenters must wait until the greater question had been settled, at which time the admission of the Dissenting claims would follow easily and naturally. But Smith's eyes were fixed primarily on the Parliamentary situation. The radical activists in the Unitarian Association, on the other hand, placed their major stress on extra-parliamentary measures, rejecting both Smith's reverence for Parliament and his basic assumption that the Dissenters' case would be heard more favourably by Parliament than by the public generally. In 1827

---

[1] *The Test-Act Reporter* (London, 1829), p. 171.

[2] I am speaking of the Whigs as practical politicians. Their arguments for both measures were identical, being based on their ideal of religious liberty (see G. F. A. Best, 'The Whigs and the Church Establishment in the Age of Grey and Holland', *History*, XLV [1960], 103–18).

Aspland summed up what had been the Association's position from the beginning:

The Dissenters . . . should pledge themselves as men and as Christians, never to allow the question [of Repeal] to lie dormant, but to pursue their way to the Legislature through good and evil report; and if they refused to grant their rights, they should always hear of their wrongs. The Legislature might in that way be forced into the charity of the unjust judge, who did what was right, that he might no longer be troubled with hearing what was wrong.[1]

In the opinion of the Association's leaders, only constant and unceasing agitation could gain the Dissenters' goal.

Smith's ideas of tactics were, therefore, directly opposed to those advanced by the Unitarian Association and accepted by the Deputies in 1823; the two views sprang from different basic assumptions. Smith feared that public opinion was not actually liberal and therefore trusted Parliamentary manoeuvre more than agitation. The activists in the Unitarian Association and the Deputies distrusted the unreformed Parliament and hence saw no recourse but forceful extra-parliamentary agitation. True, the exponents of agitation were not entirely confident of existing public opinion. The Deputies' resolutions of 1823 stated the double aim of an active policy: 'to enlighten the public mind and to concentrate and direct the temperate exertions of those who ought to co-operate in the cause.'[2] But, if their assessment of existing public opinion was not completely different from Smith's, the activists were at least considerably more confident of its educability.

Though they differed fundamentally on tactics—a disagreement which was to become critical in 1827—on one crucial point the view of the activists and Smith's view were at one. Since the Catholic victory in the House of Commons in 1821 (the Lords rejected the bill), it was obvious that the Dissenters had to proceed on grounds favourable to the Catholics. Both Smith and the activists readily accepted these grounds. There was no question on either side that the Dissenters based their claims on the right of every man, as Smith

[1] *Monthly Repository*, n.s. I (1827), 535–7.
[2] Minutes, 10 January 1823.

said, 'to enjoy and profess his respective opinions, without being therefore subjected either to reproach or disabilities'.[1] And, in what was to be the official statement of the Dissenters' case, Edgar Taylor, the secretary of the Unitarian Association and a new member of the Deputies' Committee in 1823, emphasized the parallels between the Dissenters' and the Catholic cause and proudly proclaimed that the Dissenters came forward 'with a firm conviction that, in urging to the best of their ability their own particular claims, they are serving the general course of freedom and liberality'.[2]

On this basis of principle, and after a year of painstaking preparation, the Dissenting Deputies took steps in 1824 to launch a vigorous campaign. The issue of Repeal was to be brought immediately under 'the public consideration by an application to Parliament on the subject of the Corporation and Test Acts'. Petitions were to be presented to both Houses without delay. Members of Parliament were to be approached, and it was hoped that a motion for Repeal would be made. Immediate success was not expected, but it was to be made clear that it was the 'decided intention of the Body of Dissenters seriously to make and renew applications to the Legislature on the subject'.[3] The Dissenting Deputies had resolved on action, and there was to be no turning back—so they thought.

Such a plan was, however, dependent on the co-operation of the two other major Dissenting organizations, the Protestant Society, and the Deputies' clerical counterpart, the General Body of Dissenting Ministers. The Committee immediately approached the Protestant Society, whose Committee had been as consistent as the Deputies' Committee in opposing action, and the General Body of Ministers. The result was a decided refusal from the Committee of the Protestant Society and, after some hesitation, a similar response from the Dissenting Ministers.[4] No reasons were given, and no

[1] William Smith on Catholic Emancipation, 14 May 1805, *Hansard*, IV (1805), 110.
[2] *Statement*, p. 17. Written in 1824, the *Statement* was not published until 1827.
[3] Minutes, 19 May 1824.
[4] Ibid., 30 April and 28 May 1824.

record remains of an immediate comment. But in the December issue of the *Monthly Repository*, carefully tucked away under the heading 'Ireland', the editor voiced his anger. The Catholic Association had voted a £20 subscription to a not clearly identified society in London for the protection of religious liberty, and Aspland demanded,

Is the "Protestant Society" meant, of which Mr. Wilks is one of the Secretaries? If so, we presume the subscription will be returned; this Society, as a *body*, being known to be so inimical to the Catholic claims, that, rather than they should be granted, they would willingly continue, as Protestant Dissenters, under the oppression of the Corporation and Test Acts.[1]

And a letter from one of the society's founders, Dr John Pye Smith, to William Smith in November proves that the charges were justified:

I wish I could hold forth the prospect that our body was likely to agree in any petition for a great and comprehensive measure of emancipation from political exclusions, to both protestants and papists. But repeated and painful defeats at our meetings have taught me to despair of such an agreement.[2]

It was evident that the Dissenters could not make a united appeal to Parliament; they were not united on the crucial principle of religious liberty.

So, the Dissenting Deputies abandoned the forceful programme of the early part of the year. A series of conferences in the autumn with representatives from the Dissenting Ministers, the Protestant Society, and the Unitarian Association came to the conclusion that only the most limited action was possible. At their final meeting on

[1] *Monthly Repository*, XIX (1824), 758.
[2] J. Pye Smith to William Smith, 29 November 1824, Leigh-Smith Papers. In my article, 'The Strategy of "Dissent" in the Repeal Campaign, 1820–1828', *The Journal of Modern History*, Vol. 38, No. 4 (December 1966), p. 381, I said that this letter came from Pye Smith in his capacity as 'chairman' of the Dissenting Ministers. A search of their records at Dr Williams's Library has since shown me that they had no regular chairman, though Pye Smith did chair at least one meeting during this period, which is what confused me initially. The letter, as will be seen, makes a good deal more sense as referring to the Protestant Society.

3 December they decided to insert an announcement in the religious periodicals that the Deputies and the Ministers—there was no mention of the Protestant Society—intended to make an application to Parliament early in the next session, 'but that they have no intention to invite congregational petitions on this occasion'.[1] The Dissenting public was to be positively discouraged from taking part in the campaign. Even the most determined exponents of agitation could not fail to recognize that the problem of education was somewhat greater than they had anticipated. Worse was yet to come.

The Dissenting Deputies at their general meetings of December 1824 and January 1825 made no attempt to pass a resolution on Repeal. But, while the Deputies were quiet, others were not. Early in 1825 a motion for Catholic Emancipation was introduced into the House of Commons. A number of counter-petitions were filed, among them some twenty-odd from those who designated themselves, or were clearly recognizable as, Dissenters. This response occasioned some bitter remarks from prominent Whigs, particularly from Brougham, on the Dissenters' inconsistency. Smith roundly denied the charge, claiming that most of the petitions came from Methodists, 'who were sometimes confounded with the Protestant Dissenters, but did not in reality belong to them'. Of the great bulk of those who had traditionally borne the name 'Dissenter', he contended, 'speaking of them as a body, he believed that they were perfectly desirous that justice should be done to the Roman Catholics'.[2]

This was a clever defence, and a reasonably safe one, as very few members of Parliament made any pretence of understanding the sectarian differences within Dissent.[3] But an analysis of the petitions

[1] Minutes, 3 December 1824.

[2] *Monthly Repository*, XX (1825), 445.

[3] In March of the same year, after a conversation with Robert Peel on a Unitarian marriage bill, Smith had felt it necessary to send him a 'Book, and a Sermon, from which, united, you may learn more in an hour respecting Unitarians than from a week's search thro' all the controversy on the subject. This last I am sure you have not the time to go into: and if you feel any interest in the question, I think you will find my proffered aid not unsatisfactory' (William Smith to Peel, 26 March 1825, B.M. Add. MSS 40,375, f. 152). Clearly, such ignorance was not always a disadvantage.

themselves shows that Smith was far too optimistic in his assertion of the soundness of the older denominations on the Catholic question, and that some confusion on sectarian differences in Dissent was pardonable. On 18 and 19 April twenty-six petitions were presented by persons recognizable as nonconformists. Of these, thirteen came from London or the immediate vicinity: one of the thirteen was from an Independent congregation; seven were from Baptist congregations; three were from Calvinist Methodist congregations; and two cannot be identified. Of the thirteen petitions from outside London, six came from widely scattered congregations, of which only two carry a denominational designation, one Wesleyan Methodist and the other Baptist. The remaining seven all came from the Brighton-Lewes area. One is simply from 'Protestant Dissenters'; and of the other six, three were from Independent congregations, two were from Calvinist Methodist congregations, and one was from the Wesleyan Methodist societies.[1] Obviously, not only Methodists were to blame for the petitions.

A survey of the situation of Dissent in the strongly anti-Catholic area around Lewes indicates that, in any case, Smith's distinction between 'Protestant Dissenters' and 'Methodists' was not a very meaningful one. Only one clear fact emerges from such a survey. Apart from the Unitarians, who had not petitioned against Emancipation, all the Dissenting congregations in Lewes were products of the evangelical revival. Most had clear Methodist origins. But, whatever Smith chose to call them, they called themselves 'Protestant Dissenters', and in two cases bore the traditional designations of Independent and Baptist.[2] In Lewes, as everywhere else in the country, orthodox Dissent continued to batten on the evangelical

[1] My identifications are based on the *Journals of the House of Commons* (1825), pp. 314–15 and 320–1; a list of congregations in 'London Non-conformity in 1810', *Transactions of the Congregational Historical Society*, VI (1913–15), 126–35; Horsfield, *The History of Sussex* (Lewes, 1835), I 471, and the same author's *History of Lewes*, I, 302–8.

[2] Horsfield, *Lewes* I, 302–8. It is interesting to note that prominent London evangelicals associated with the Protestant Society played an active part in the affairs of Lewes Dissent. Among them was the Rev Matthew Wilks, the father of the Secretary of the Protestant Society and himself a regular member of its committee.

revival.[1] And in Lewes, at any rate, the evangelicals were anti-Catholic.

The reaction of the several Dissenting organizations to Dissenting anti-Catholic petitioning, which all recognized as a most serious development, provides further evidence on the state of opinion within Dissent. At its 1825 annual meeting the Unitarian Association unanimously passed a resolution, conveying from Unitarians to 'their fellow-Christians of the Roman Catholic persuasion their thorough disavowal and disapprobation of the Petitions lately presented by persons calling themselves Protestant Dissenters, against the repeal of those intolerant laws which disgrace their country's name'. The Dissenting Deputies were neither so specific nor so emphatic as the Unitarians in denouncing Catholic exclusion, but their statement of general principle indicated a similar sentiment:

This Deputation is anxious to disavow any concurrence in, or approval of, the petitions lately presented to Parliament (purporting to be from Protestant Dissenters), in reference to the claims of the Roman Catholics for relief from the operation of existing laws; and . . . it will continue at all seasonable opportunities, to urge upon the Legislature (as it hitherto has done), the impolicy and injustice of every sort of penalty or disability, civil or political, for conscience' sake.

The Dissenting Ministers, after a long debate and a week's adjournment, finally resolved that 'as a body' they disclaimed every sentiment of 'religious intolerance' toward Roman Catholics, and expressed a hope that Parliament would 'at length, deem it proper to take measures for the relief of all classes of his Majesty's subjects, who may lie under penalties and disabilities for conscience' sake'.[2]

On the surface, the resolutions of the Deputies and the Ministers

---

[1] Between 1812 and 1827 alone the increase in the numbers of Baptist and Independent congregations was remarkable. In 1812 there were 432 Baptist congregations; in 1827 there were 799. Corresponding figures for the Independents are 750 and 1051 (see Bogue and Bennett, IV, 327–32; Bennett, pp. 264–7). The number of Unitarian congregations was small in comparison. In 1819 the Unitarians themselves estimated only 300 (*Monthly Repository*, XIV [1819] 380).

[2] All three sets of resolutions appear in the *Monthly Repository*, XX (1825), 316–17.

appear pro-Catholic. But, in fact, they represent a compromise. The division which they were trying to obscure was still present three years later. In 1828 Aspland made a speech at the banquest celebrating Repeal in which he expressed his fervent wish for the triumph of similar principles in the solution of the Catholic question. In reply to this speech the Rev Joseph Ivimey, the pastor of the Particular Baptist congregation in Eagle Street, published a pamphlet, *The Roman Catholic Claims a Question not of Religious Liberty, but of Political Expediency*. He argued that it was politically inexpedient to emancipate the Catholics. Now, both the Deputies and the Ministers, as has been seen, had avoided a specific statement on the Catholic claims in 1825; both had denounced exclusion for '*conscience' sake*' and the Ministers had disavowed '*religious intolerance*'; but, if one accepted Ivimey's argument, the Catholics were not excluded merely for 'conscience' sake' and to oppose their claims was not 'religious intolerance'. Again, in 1829 the Ministers passed a resolution calling for the abolition of all religious disabilities, which, as their own were already abolished, could have only one meaning.[1] This was passed by a large majority, but a minority led by Ivimey resolutely opposed it. And after its passage Ivimey published another pamphlet castigating the Ministers for their action.[2] It was to prevent such an open breach in 1825, when its effects would have been disastrous, that the Deputies and the Ministers, who represented roughly the same congregations, moved so carefully. Only by the greatest tact and diplomacy were Smith and the other leaders of the London bodies able to maintain for the outside world the theoretical consistency of their position.

The Committee of the Protestant Society, on the other hand, made little effort to hide the inconsistency of its position on religious freedom. Its first resolution regretted that the petitions had involved the whole Dissenting body 'in the imputation of indifference or

---

[1] It is significant that this petition, as well as a similar one by the United Committee, appears to have been instigated by the Whig leadership as an important element in the campaign for Emancipation (Lord Holland to Lord John Russell, 26 December 1828, Russell Papers, PRO 30/22, 1A).

[2] Joseph Ivimey, *Dr Williams's Library, and the Debate on the Roman Catholic Claims* (London, 1829), cited in Aspland, p. 494.

hostility to those great principles of Religious Freedom, for which their forefathers contended, and to which they continue ever attached'. The second resolution declared that the Society had always contended for the fullest religious freedom, that is 'that religious opinions should not alone qualify or disqualify for Public Office'. 'Not alone' suggested a very serious qualification. And the last resolution gave an even more open hint of hostility. It stated:

This Committee can never be unmindful of the needless, oppressive, degrading, and unjust restrictions imposed by 'The Test and Corporation Acts' on Protestant Dissenters, nor cease to desire their repeal. But, being convinced that the concessions proposed to be made, by the depending Bill, will not give to the Roman Catholics in England or Ireland any political advantage over Protestant Dissenters in those countries, they will not, *as Protestant Dissenters*, interfere in any manner that may prejudice or prejudge the Bill, but will leave the measure to the Wisdom and Justice of Parliament.[1]

The *Monthly Repository* was contemptuous of these resolutions, 'which do not stand for much, as they bear two senses'.[2] The same might have been said of the resolutions of the Deputies and the Ministers, but they had carefully hidden the double meaning and even managed to suggest positive support for Emancipation. The Protestant Society's Committee had, in contrast, made its reservations clear. Indeed it had gone further, taking care in its last resolution that it could not be charged with support of the Catholic claims. It is difficult to avoid the conclusion that the Society, as a body, was opposed to Emancipation. John Wilks, the Society's Secretary and the dominant personality in it, certainly was.[3]

Recent work on the Protestant Society is, therefore, obviously wrong in contending that the stand of the Society on the Catholic

[1] *Monthly Repository*, XX (1825), 317. Italics mine.

[2] Ibid., p. 255.

[3] See his remark to the 1825 annual meeting of the Society on an alteration of the Marriage Act in the interest of Catholics, that 'here at least my sectarian feelings could not have influenced me' (ibid., p. 698). As will be seen, Wilks adamantly opposed any association between the Catholic and Dissenting causes in 1827, and John Wilks jr cast one of the two Dissenting votes against Emancipation in 1829 (division list, 30 March 1829, *Hansard*, n.s. XVI, 1011).

issue was identical with the stand taken by the Deputies.[1] In the Deputies a majority opinion preserved a position which suggested support for the Catholics. The thinly veiled anti-Catholicism of the Society's resolutions, however, indicates that, at the very least, a majority opinion in that body opposed the Catholic claims.

This raises the old question of the explanation of the division in Dissent on the Catholic question. Halévy saw it mainly as a division between Unitarians and trinitarians, and argued that there was something in the very creed of the evangelical revival which perpetrated anti-catholicism.[2] J. H. Hexter contended strongly against this explanation, holding that the division was on social and educational lines, with the wealthier and better-educated supporting the Catholics and the humble and illiterate opposing them.[3] Recent scholarship seems to be swinging back towards Halévy's position. G. I. T. Machin states: 'Enthusiasm often generates intolerance, and the products of the eighteenth-century revival were largely anti-catholic.' In his opinion, 'sympathy for unitarianism was perhaps a deciding factor in the matter' of attitude toward the Catholic claims; and he quotes Ursula Henriques to substantiate his view: 'The more sophisticated leaders of Dissent petitioned for Catholic Emancipation, while their trinitarian troops marched in the opposite direction.'[4]

I have discussed this question in detail elsewhere.[5] For present purposes, I shall sum up my position, perhaps clarify it, and add a few significant details. The superficial evidence is pretty overwhelming in supporting recent scholarship, more overwhelming

[1] Henriques, pp. 146–7. Henriques in her general study, is giving currency to views on the Society expressed by M. B. Whittaker, in his M.Litt. thesis already cited.

[2] Elie Halévy, *A History of the English People in the Nineteenth Century* (London, 1961), II, 218, 240, and 263–4.

[3] J. H. Hexter, 'The Protestant Revival and the Catholic Question in England', *Journal of Modern History*, VIII (1936), 297–319.

[4] G. I. T. Machin, *The Catholic Question in English Politics, 1820–1830* (Oxford, 1964), p. 7. This is an excellent study of the Catholic question, though, for reasons which will be obvious, I disagree with most of what Mr Machin has to say about Dissenting attitudes.

[5] 'Strategy', *Journal of Modern History* (1966), pp. 374–93.

indeed than has been recognized. The Protestant Society was undoubtedly the special and chosen representative of evangelical Dissent, and its nation-wide organization, including Calvinistic Methodists and seceders from the Wesleyan Methodists, allowed it to speak for them with considerable authority. And—what has not been recognized before—the Protestant Society was anti-catholic. On the other side, the Deputies, as they had been since their inception, were in a direct sense representative only of London, although they had always circularized country Dissent generally, represented the interests of all Dissenters, and claimed to speak for them and they were to continue to do so. There can be no doubt of the strong Unitarian influence within the Deputies. And they were undoubtedly, as a body, in favour of Catholic Emancipation.

But the superficial evidence is very misleading. In fact, the split in Dissent had nothing to do with creeds—there was nothing distinctive in the evangelical *creed* to distinguish it from any other trinitarian creed—and nothing to do with enthusiasm—except for anti-catholic enthusiasm, which pre-dated religious enthusiasm by two hundred years. Only in the sense that the evangelical revival had a special appeal for those classes which were already violently anti-catholic did it have any connexion with the question. The English lower classes had been strongly anti-catholic for centuries: they simply brought their bigotry with them into the revival.

I agree, therefore, with Professor Hexter that the division in Dissent was not in the real sense a religious one, but was rather founded on class and education. A closer look at the Deputies and their Committee will make the point clearer. It is quite true to say that Unitarian *influence* in the Deputies was strong, but this is very different from saying that they dominated by their numbers. In fact, they were a tiny majority. Of the ninety-seven congregations represented in the Deputies in the twenties, no more than a dozen could have been Unitarian. (In 1836 there were only eleven.[1]) They were, it is true, stronger in the Committee, but still very far from being a majority. Because of the fact that Unitarians did not sit as such, it would have been impossible to have made formal

[1] On the question of the Unitarian secession from the Deputies, see Aspland, chap. xxx, and Manning, pp. 68–93.

regulations about the proportions of Unitarians on the Committee, but some such attempt seems to have been made in practice. On the 1827 Committee, for example, I have been able to identify seven Unitarians, which suggests that the facts of the case had been recognized: as there were no longer any Presbyterians except in name, the Unitarians, whatever they called themselves, had been recognized as the third denomination and given a third of the seats on the Committee of twenty-one. Then, of course, there was William Smith, as Chairman. But Smith was balanced by Henry Waymouth, the Baptist[1] Deputy Chairman, and there was probably a similar balance maintained in the other official positions of Treasurer, Deputy Treasurer etc. As far as numbers went, the Unitarians were a distinct minority both in the Deputies and on their Committee. Their point of view could never have triumphed without strong trinitarian support.

Trinitarian support, therefore, was an absolute necessity, and there is every indication that it was freely given—indeed, more than that, that on all but theological questions there was but one point of view, at any rate on the Committee. Thomas Wilson, one of the correspondents in the Lady Hewley Trust case, certainly disagreed with the Unitarians on theological questions, but both he and Henry Waymouth joined Smith, and opposed John Wilks, in the strong support they gave to the new London University, both being members of its first Council. And there is no reason to believe that they did not give equal support on other issues, like the Catholic question. Indeed there is every reason to believe that they did. Save for John Wilks, who was a member of the Deputies' Committee as well as being Secretary of the Protestant Society, there is no indication that there was more than one opinion in the Committee on the great question of the day.

The liberal opinions of the Deputies' Committee would seem, then, to have had little to do with theological views. Their social position would further tend to confirm Professor Hexter's arguments. As part of their aggressive programme in 1823, the Deputies had stipulated, in an obvious attempt to introduce vigorous new blood,

[1] I am not sure whether Waymouth was a Particular or a New Connection Baptist. At any rate, he came from one of the trinitarian branches.

that at least three members of every Committee elected at the subsequent annual meetings should not have served in the preceding ten years. But, though this brought in some new members, and vigorous ones like Edgar Taylor, they were drawn from the same classes as their predecessors. The 1827 Committee, which is representative, had on it four bankers, three barristers, six solicitors, three merchants, three manufacturers, two printers, and a stationer. And they were men of distinction in their several fields. Benjamin Hanbury, who held a post in the Bank of England, is more notable as an historian of Dissent. Among the barristers were Charles Bompas, Serjeant-at-law, and James Baldwin Brown, LL.D., the biographer of John Howard and author of several distinguished works on the penal laws (his son was to be an eminent Congregational minister). The solicitors included the venerable Samuel Favell, a member of the Application Committee in the seventeen-eighties, who besides being a member of the United Committee in the twenties also steered a critical resolution in favour of Repeal through the Common Council. Besides Smith himself, among the merchants were James Gibson, whose obituary in the *Christian Reformer* identifies him as a sometime trustee and treasurer of several of the more important Dissenting charities. Thomas Wilson was a big ribbon manufacturer, one of the first directors of the London Missionary Society, and, as has been seen, one of the first Council of London University. Richard Taylor was a leading printer, an eminent naturalist, and a Common Councillor (as well as providing, like his cousin Edgar, a link with the Unitarian radicalism of Norwich). Thomas Pewtress was a member of a large and well-known firm of stationers in the City and was also a Common Councillor. Then there were Robert Marten, Deputy Chairman of the Commercial Dock Company, and William Brodie Gurney, shorthand writer and leading Baptist philanthropist. In short, the Committee was composed of men from the cream of the professional and business classes of London.

As Professor Hexter suggests, such people in society generally were growing increasingly liberal in their opinions. But for this particular group, and for the other Dissenters whom they represented, there is another explanation—education. And I would be more limited in the use of the term than Professor Hexter, and put particular stress on what may be called 'political education'. For these Dissenters had grown up in a very liberal school. The Independent Favell, like the Unitarian Smith, was a living tie with the days when 'rational' (and here I use the term in a non-sectarian sense) Dissent had first taken up the battle against religious intolerance. And younger men had, as it were, been educated at their knees in the same politically liberal views. Here we see the crucial significance of the tenacious catholicity of London Dissent. It was this that had allowed the growth and flowering of 'Unitarian' political ideas among all creeds and denominations of Dissenters. Trinitarian Dissent in London did not 'sympathize' with the Unitarians, it simply shared their political views.

Such views would undoubtedly have been much less common among the country evangelicals whom the Protestant Society mainly represented. Most of them came from different social classes and had not had the benefit of such a political education. Again, of course, as in the eighties, it is necessary to qualify. In large commercial and manufacturing centres where conditions similar to those in London were reproduced on a smaller scale, there were similar effects. In the election of 1826 when the Catholic claims were the major issue,[1] Smith was returned unopposed for Norwich, with the plaudits even of some of his former enemies, and Leicester Dissenters gave their vigorous support to the pro-Catholic candidates against the 'Protestant' candidates of the Corporation.[2] Even some undoubtedly 'country' Dissenters gave the Catholics strong support. In the county that I know best, Buckinghamshire, Dissenters split on the issue. In the large rural Parliamentary borough of Aylesbury, a meeting to petition against Emancipation on 25 February 1829 was countered by another of 'the friends of civil and religious liberty' the same day. The former meeting was composed entirely, so far as I can tell, of Anglicans, the latter was certainly overwhelmingly Dissenting in composition, including the Independent

[1] For a consideration of anti-Catholicism and the general election of 1826, see Machin, chap. iv.

[2] See R.W . Greaves, 'Roman Catholic Relief and the Leicester Election of 1826', *Royal Historical Society Transactions*, 4th series, XXII (1940), 199–223.

minister and prominent representatives from both the Independent and the Baptist laity (there were no Unitarians in Aylesbury at this time).[1] A few miles away in Buckingham, on the other hand, Dissenters, mostly Independents, had always opposed the Catholic claims and they petitioned against them in 1829.[2] Once again, at any rate in Aylesbury, the explanation seems to be one of political education. Lord Nugent, M.P. for Aylesbury since 1812, had always been a champion of the Catholics as well as of Dissent, and on this question (though not on all others) his Dissenting constituents seem to have been convinced by his arguments. In Buckingham, the Duke was strongly pro-catholic, while his son the Marquis of Chandos was a leader of the 'Protestant' party. The Marquis may well have adopted his views for political advantage, that is, that in this case ideas flowed upwards, not downwards. At any rate, the two constituencies were to continue to be divided on various Catholic issues for the rest of the century.

There is good reason to believe, however, that the Buckingham Dissenters were in the great majority in the country, and that the Aylesbury Dissenters were the exception rather than the rule. This is certainly strongly indicated in the position taken by the Protestant Society, which represented the opinions of country evangelical Dissent. Probably anti-Catholic views would have been in the minority in the London Committee of the Society. They were certainly not the views of the Unitarian Aspland or of the Independent Pye Smith. Indeed there was a very considerable coincidence of membership between the Committee of the Deputies and the Dissenting Ministers, on the one hand, and the Committee of the Protestant Society, on the other. As has been seen, John Wilks, who undoubtedly did share the anti-Catholic views of his country brethren, is another example. But the Committee of the Protestant Society had to face its annual meeting and it was largely dependent for funds on the small annual subscriptions of its several hundred

---

[1] Robert Gibbs, *Buckinghamshire Local Occurrences* (Aylesbury, 1878–82), III, 184.

[2] See the correspondence between the Rev E. Barling (Independent) and Sir Thomas Fremantle in 1827 and 1828, Cottesloe Papers, Bucks Record Office; Gibbs, III, 185.

member congregations up and down the country. The London elected bodies were under no such disadvantages. Though they corresponded with country Dissenters generally, they were responsible only to London congregations, and they had ample funds of their own.

The situation which the above analysis reveals boded ill for the success of Repeal. In the existing state of Parliamentary opinion the only hope of obtaining a favourable hearing for the Dissenters' grievances lay in using arguments that would advance the Catholic cause as well. But it was evident that probably a large majority of opinion in Dissent would not tolerate such arguments, and another outburst of bigotry such as the anti-Catholic petitions of 1825 would set the Dissenting cause back immeasurably.

Under these circumstances, it was probably as well for the Dissenters that all three groups in Parliament agreed on a postponement of the question of religious tests. The Catholic Emancipation bill of 1825, though it passed the House of Commons, was thrown out by the Lords on 17 May. In September, Canning, fearing great gains for the 'Protestants' on a cry of 'No Popery', persuaded Lord Liverpool to postpone the imminent general election until the autumn of 1826. He also persuaded the Whigs not to raise the Emancipation question during the 1826 session.[1] The Dissenters had already been warned off taking any action on Repeal in 1825. At the general meeting of the Dissenting Deputies on 27 May, Smith reported that their Parliamentary friends opposed action during the current session, a report which was calmly received by the Deputies.[2] Even the petitions agreed upon by the Deputies and the Dissenting Ministers the previous year were quietly forgotten. Nor, apart from the presentation of a petition by the Deputies, was any action taken in 1826.

Following the elections of 1826, however, both the Catholics and the Dissenters began to stir again. On 7 March 1827 Sir Francis Burdett's motion for Catholic Emancipation was defeated in the House of Commons by four votes (276 to 272), the first time that a Catholic measure had been defeated in that house since 1821. Only

[1] See Halévy, II, 225.
[2] Minutes, 27 May 1825.

two days later the Dissenting Deputies' Committee met to consider the advisability of taking action on the question of Repeal.[1] On 28 March, at the behest of the Committee, representatives of the Protestant Society, the Unitarian Association, the General Body of Dissenting Ministers, and the Board of Congregational Ministers met at the King's Head Tavern and unanimously resolved that 'no time should be lost in bringing the subject of the Repeal of the Corporation and Test Acts before Parliament'. Even Smith stated emphatically that in his opinion 'the present *was* a favourable moment for preferring their claims'.[2]

It would seem to have been a remarkably odd time for such unanimity and decisiveness. The defeat of the Catholic measure certainly did not augur well for Repeal, especially as it was well known that many members of Parliament who favoured Emancipation did not favour Repeal. Further, the country was in the middle of a ministerial crisis. Lord Liverpool had fallen into an apoplectic fit on 13 February, and his successor had not been chosen. Surely, if any time called for Smith's favoured policy of watchful waiting, this would appear to have been that time.

In fact, however, there were several considerations which made all sections of Dissenting opinion reject such a policy. Anti-Catholic elements in Dissent were becoming increasingly restive as more and more of Parliament's attention was devoted to the Catholic question, and none to Repeal. As D. W. Harvey, member for Colchester, said in the House of Commons on 23 March, many of his constituents were 'Dissenters who were *opposed* to the Catholics; and why were they to wait till persons succeeded to whom they wished no success?'[3] Doubtless such a feeling motivated the Protestant Society, pressing it for the first time toward decisive action. Also, with the Catholic cause suffering from its recent Parliamentary defeat, the Society's own cause could be advanced as much on its own merits as was likely to be possible.

Similar considerations, though for entirely opposite reasons, probably made the time seem favourable to pro-Catholic elements

[1] Minutes, 9 March 1827.
[2] See the report of the meeting in the *Monthly Repository*, n.s. I (1827), 377–8.
[3] Ibid., p. 303.

in Dissent. At no time—not even on the eve of victory—did the Dissenters initiate a campaign with an expectation of immediate success. The only consideration was that of the most opportune time to begin a public agitation of their question. With the fears of the anti-Catholics temporarily soothed, this seemed to be that time. Now agitation could be undertaken with the least possible danger of exposing the very fundamental division within the Dissenting ranks. Thus, for various reasons, the Dissenting leaders showed an unwonted unanimity in desiring action.

But there were definite limits to this unanimity. At the meeting on 28 March everyone was agreed on action, but on what grounds was it to be taken? The Unitarian Association, through its spokesman John Bowring, was as firm as ever in demanding that the campaign be waged on basic principles, that the Dissenters' claims should 'be urged only on the broad ground of denying the right or policy of the magistrate's making religious opinion or profession the ground or pretence of civil preference or exclusion'. The representative of the Board of Congregational Ministers agreed: 'There was, no doubt, some difference of opinion among Dissenters, but he believed it to have been much magnified, and he was desirous of putting the matter to the proof.' The spokesman of the Baptist Ministers also concurred: 'He believed the laity of his denomination did not go quite so far as the majority of the Ministers, but that this was the consequence of want of discussion and information.' John Wilks, however, strongly dissented from the prevailing view. When it was moved to make the resolution of the Unitarian Association that of the meeting, he proposed an amendment 'confining the application to the relief of Protestant Dissenters from the operation of the Test and Corporation Acts, instead of seeking the total abolition of the test imposed by them'. The sense of the meeting was overwhelmingly against any such restriction of the grounds of the appeal, and Wilks withdrew his amendment.[1] It is clear, however, that the division of opinion among the Dissenting organizations was sharp.

Nevertheless, it was decided to proceed, and Smith, who presided at the meeting, was requested to invite members of Parliament to attend the next meeting. By the time this meeting took

[1] Ibid., pp. 377–8.

place on 6 April a drastic change in the political situation had brought another division of opinion, this time cutting along different lines. The new situation which confronted the meeting was the distinct probability that Canning would become the head of the government and that the Whigs would come in with him. This possibility gave new point to Canning's often-stated determination not to consider Repeal while the Catholic question remained unsettled, and the Whigs refused to consider his position any obstacle to alliance.[1] This state of affairs was almost bound to bring into the open the dispute on tactics between the exponents of forceful agitation, on the one hand, and Smith who favoured negotiation and Parliamentary manoeuvre, on the other.

Such proved to be the case. During the course of the debate which preceded the arrival of the members of Parliament, Smith advised dropping plans for active measures. He apprised the meeting of the recent political developments, and warned that their Whig allies were not prepared to support Repeal measures at this time. For him, this settled the matter. Repeal would have to wait for a favourable shift in the political situation. The sense of the meeting was otherwise. As the Rev Mr Yockney of the Congregational Board had said 'he was anxious for proceeding, not so much from the expectation of immediate success, as to understand their position. If those gentlemen who were so zealous in support of the Catholic cause, deserted the Dissenters, we should then know how to rate the pretended friends of religious liberty'. The activist view won over that of the shrewd Parliamentary tactician. The meeting decided not to postpone the Dissenters' claims on any account.[2]

Smith's prediction of Whig reluctance to raise the Repeal issue proved to be highly accurate. Only ten members of Parliament

[1] Indeed, if the published correspondence is any indication, the matter of Repeal was considered so unimportant that it was never mentioned in the negotiations between Canning and the Whigs. At least I can find no mention of the question in A. Aspinall, *The Formation of Canning's Ministry, February to August 1827* (London, 1937). I may have missed a reference, but the basic point is valid (see Austin Mitchell, *The Whigs in Opposition*, chap. ix; Machin, p. 103).

[2] The proceedings of the meeting of 8 April appear in the *Monthly Repository*, n.s. I (1827), 378-80.

bothered to attend the meeting. None who subsequently entered the ministry were there. The only politicians of first-rate importance who attended were Lord Holland and Lord John Russell. And, though Russell urged action, Holland was equivocal. The Dissenters should determine their own time, he said, and it was the duty of every member of Parliament to assist at any time in redressing a grievance. But he added the very significant qualification that as to the '*mode* of agitating the question' he must act on his own discretion. There were only two possible modes of proceeding. One was to have a motion made in the Parliament, which would have required active support. The other was to present petitions, which required only statements of sympathy. The former would have involved an extremely embarrassing conflict of loyalties for the Whig party, and Holland was not willing to commit himself to it. But Lord John Russell was unanimously asked to move the question in the House of Commons,[1] and did in fact give notice of a motion that evening.

Three days later the associated deputations met again and resolved to form a United Committee, including the whole Dissenting Deputies' Committee of twenty-four members and delegates not exceeding six in number from the other societies.[2] The first meeting of the new United Committee took place on 20 April. It found that the Protestant Society had decided to act independently and to wage a separate campaign. Wilks's determination to disassociate himself from the Catholic claims doubtless explains this action. The Society's decision made the United Committee the exclusive preserve of the London organizations and the Unitarian Association. Claiming to speak for all Dissenters, and generally accepted by the politicians as speaking for them, the United Committee, in fact, spoke only for the most liberal elements.

The new Committee immediately began a vigorous press and pamphlet campaign and circulated materials and model petitions to Dissenting organizations throughout the country in preparation for an equally vigorous appeal to Parliament. But hardly was the campaign well under way when the Committee was brought face to

[1] Ibid.
[2] Minutes, 9 April 1827.

face with the problem of Parliamentary support which had previously been dismissed in such a cavalier fashion. On 3 May
Canning, in reply to a question from Robert Peel, stated emphatically
that he would under no circumstances consider Repeal before
Emancipation, and gave a definite pledge to oppose it.[1] As some of
the Whig leaders like Lord Lansdowne were already in the government, or negotiations for their inclusion well advanced,[2] and as most
of the rest of the Whigs were already giving the government their
support, there was no likelihood of any significant support for
Repeal. The Committee requested Smith, who had been unanimously elected Chairman, to invite their Parliamentary friends to
another meeting, which took place on 23 May. In contrast to the
previous meeting, the Whigs turned out in some force for this one.
This time six members of the House of Lords were present, and the
twenty-three attending from the Commons included Lord Althorp
and Brougham as well as Russell. Their advice was overwhelmingly
against making any motion in the current session. Apparently, only
Russell and John Smith, member for Midhurst and the seconder of
Russell's motion, wished to press forward.[3]

The United Committee therefore confronted the alternatives of
abandoning its motion or embarrassing its Parliamentary supporters.
If the Committee pressed forward with its motion, it was certain to
get many fewer than the formerly expected number of votes, and
perhaps make a very poor showing indeed. Faced with the bleak
facts of the situation, a majority of the United Committee swung
back to the moderate leadership represented by William Smith. At
a meeting on 27 May the Committee requested Russell to withdraw
his motion because of 'the difference of opinion entertained by their
Parliamentary Friends and amongst the Dissenters themselves as to
the propriety of proceeding . . . during the present session and an
unwillingness to risk the embarrassment of a Ministry from which
they anxiously hope for a more liberal consideration of the claims of
Protestant Dissenters'.[4] This decision was opposed by both the

[1] *Hansard*, n.s. XVII (1827), 591.
[2] For which Whigs entered the government, and when, see Mitchell, p.
200.
[3] Minutes, 23 May 1827; Aspland, p. 470.   [4] Minutes, 27 May 1827.

Unitarian Association within and the Protestant Society outside the United Committee.[1] But Russell chose to accept it as the official policy of the Dissenters, and withdrew his motion.[2]

In the existing situation, the United Committee's decision seems to have been politically sensible. There was more cause for hope with the Dissenters' Whig friends in power than out, especially if Emancipation were achieved and the main reservation of the Canningites about Repeal thus removed. But some saw little sense in existing politics and no hope in conforming to their realities. Aspland was bitterly critical of the Committee's action in his report to the Unitarian Association. He contended that 'more had been lost by it than could be regained in many successive years'. It was his opinion that 'the question could not be forwarded unless the Dissenters were firm, united, and resolute, and determined not to take instructions from Members of Parliament, but to exercise their undoubted right of giving them'.[3]

The activist view and Smith's which opposed it, were made even clearer the following year. The situation was entirely different. Canning was dead, and Wellington and Peel were in office in coalition with the Canningites. It was of the essence of the controversy that this made no difference whatever to the activists, but it made a great deal of difference to a politician like Smith. Aspland records an exchange with an 'aged Member' who could have been no other:

I spoke my mind very freely to —— as to his constant clogging our cause with doubts and fears. . . . He avowed . . . that this was not a fit time . . .; that we were wrong in petitioning, especially the Lords; that we should wait for a strong Whig Administration, who would grant us our claims quietly. Against this I argued and protested. . . . I told him I would rather not have our question carried than it should be smuggled through. The benefit of it would consist in its coming as a matter of open right, a concession to justice and liberty. I anticipated a long struggle, but the sooner we began the nearer would be the victory. Parliament and the country, and even the

---

[1] *Test-Act Reporter*, p. 80.
[2] Ibid., pp. 18–19.
[3] *Monthly Repository*, n.s. I (1827), 535–7.

Dissenters, wanted discussion to enlighten them. No Ministry would ever volunteer to give us our rights, and perhaps the Whigs least of all, who do not need the charge of being Dissenters to make them odious. And though we cannot *force* our question, we must make a show of strength to have it seriously considered by the Legislature and the Court.[1]

As always, Smith's eyes were fixed on the realities of the Parliamentary situation, while the activists believed that success was to be won only through extra-parliamentary activities.

Smith's objections to a new agitation for Repeal were overridden in the United Committee, and early in 1828 it began to prepare for another campaign. A crucial agreement on strategy was made between Russell and the Committee in the first week of January. The Catholic Association had proposed that Dissenters and Catholics unite for the advancement of mutual objects. Russell advised against any 'formal junction', and at its meeting on 7 January the United Committee announced that it had 'adopted and acted upon the principle of not forming any union with the Catholics'.[2]

This decision did not mean that the fundamental situation had changed. The Catholic question was still uppermost in everyone's mind. What Russell contemplated was simply that, if Repeal were to slip through, it would turn the flank of the opponents of Catholic Emancipation and weaken their basic position.[3] The Repeal campaign would be primarily an experiment in diversion.

It was a brilliant tactical move, and it served an important end of the United Committee almost immediately. At its next meeting on 14 January it received resolutions of the Protestant Society's Committee passed on the 11th. These stated that 'as the United Committee and this Committee now entertain the same sentiment and desire the same object with a similar fervour and intenseness it appears that they may both more successfully promote its attainment by co-operation than by separate exertions which may produce occasional collisions and perplex rather than excite the country friends with whom both Committees correspond'.[4] Now that the campaign for Repeal was to be conducted on its own terms, without

[1] Aspland, p. 272.   [2] Minutes, 7 January 1828.
[3] See above, p. 219.   [4] Minutes, 14 January 1828.

the inclusion of the Catholic grievances, the Society was ready to co-operate.

The United Committee moved swiftly to effectuate this union. On 16 January a delegation of five headed by Smith met with representatives of the Society. They agreed that

the Protestant Society or their Committee will not adopt any measures relative to the Repeal of the Corporation and Test Acts either by publication, correspondence, conferences with Members of Parliament or otherwise separately from the United Committee except that the Protestant Society are forthwith to address a circular letter announcing their juncture with the United Committee for the accomplishment of the object in view.

Henceforward the Society was to express itself only through its six members on the United Committee.[1] The former spokesmen of the anti-Catholic elements thus became a small minority on a committee ruled by the liberals of the Unitarian Association and the London organizations.[2]

A new problem soon faced the United Committee. At the end of January a deputation from the Catholic Association called upon Robert Winter, the Secretary of the United Committee, and suggested a joint public meeting of Catholics and Dissenters to discuss their common disabilities. Winter, refusing to take any action on his own initiative, promised to refer the matter to the Committee. Before this could be done, however, an article appeared in the *New Times* of 31 January alleging that the Dissenters had taken the initiative in approaching the Catholics to solicit their co-operation. On 4 February the United Committee answered the allegation, resolving that

this . . . Committee acting upon their own best judgment and on the recommendation of some of their Parliamentary friends have not thought it expedient to endeavor to unite their application to Parliament with that of the Roman Catholics but that they disavow the

[1] Ibid., 16 January 1828.
[2] The Deputies' delegation of twenty-four was equal to all the others combined. To this initial advantage, the Dissenting Ministers added six; the Unitarian Association six; and the United Presbytery of London six.

inference that their acting separately and individually proceeds from any hostility to the claims of that numerous and respectable body of petitioners.

The Committee sent a copy of the resolution to Russell and John Smith, 'with a request that they will take the earliest opportunity of giving publicity to the resolution by stating the purport thereof in their places in the House of Commons'. John Smith did so on the same evening.[1] When the firmness and directness of the Committee's action is compared with the embarrassing diversity of the 1825 resolutions, the significance of the new unified command is clear.

It proved possible to maintain a similar tone for the balance of the campaign. Throughout the 1828 agitation the petitions presented were either favourable to, or silent upon, the Catholic claims.[2] This was partly because the campaign was waged with as little direct connexion with the Catholic cause as possible. But it was also due in large part to the care and attention which the Committee lavished on tailoring the Dissenters' public image to meet the necessities of the occasion, and to assure that the tone and bias of feeling throughout the campaign should be its own.[3]

Victory came with a speed which no one had anticipated. But it came in a manner much nearer to that which Smith expected than that which the activists like Aspland envisaged. It was not primarily because of any show of Dissenting strength that Lord John Russell carried his Repeal measure in 1828. The politicians had not quailed before the Dissenters in 1827, and no one—least of all, the activists—expected them to do so in 1828. Repeal was successful for a variety of reasons, but mainly because the responsible leaders of all parties were at last agreed on the imminent necessity of Catholic Emancipation, thus removing the major obstacle to Repeal. Peel became indifferent. The Canningite leaders gave, at best, only half-hearted opposition to a measure they were willing to admit freely in principle.[4] The focus of Whig attention was likewise on

[1] Minutes, 4 February 1828; *Monthly Repository*, n.s. II (1828), 202.

[2] *Monthly Repository*, n.s. II (1828), 585.

[3] See, for instance, Robert Winter to William Smith, 8 May 1828, 'The Deputies Letter Book, 1826–1834', Guildhall MSS. 3085, pp. 90–1.

[4] See Norman Gash, *Mr. Secretary Peel* (London, 1961), pp. 460–5. Mr

Emancipation. Everyone looked beyond Repeal to another, larger issue.

Primarily, then, it was a shift in the Parliamentary situation rather than a forceful display of an organized public opinion that carried Repeal. A strong show of Dissenting opinion—of the sort the Committee produced—was doubtless of the greatest assistance in securing the final victory. But in Parliament too success did not come without some flexibility and tactical skill. The closest co-ordination with the Dissenters' Parliamentary friends was essential, and this required a willingness on the part of the Dissenters to trim their sails to the necessities of the Parliamentary situation. During the 1828 campaign the practice of large conferences with Parliamentary supporters was abandoned, and relations with Parliament were put entirely in the hands of a sub-committee of six headed by Smith. Sometimes they acted as a body and sometimes Smith acted for them. But in either case it was bound to have been Smith who played the dominating role. The fact that he was the only M.P. on the sub-committee, his long political experience, and the breadth of his personal contacts made it inevitable.

An initial success in the Commons came with surprising ease. On 25 February Russell moved a resolution that the House go into Committee on the question of the sacramental test. Peel opposed. Huskisson, however, was equivocal. He admitted that 'looking abstractedly at the Test Acts, I certainly should feel regret at their continuance on the statute-book'. His sole ground of opposition was that if the question should be carried at this time 'the Noble Lord will find—I do not mean to say among the well-educated part of the Protestant Dissenters, but among the greater proportion of that body—an additional and more vigorous opposition to the Catholic question'.[1] Secretly he and the other Canningite leaders were thought to favour Repeal.[2] In any case, the government, if not actually divided on the issue, was embarrassingly divided on its grounds for opposition. The House was not convinced, and a com-

---

Machin brilliantly traces the nuances and shifts of opinion on the Catholic question during the twenties.

[1] *Monthly Repository*, n.s. II (1828), 274.   [2] See Gash, p. 464.

bination of those who dismissed Huskisson's fears, and doubtless of some who hoped they would prove correct, united to carry the motion by 236 to 193.[1]

On 28 February Russell moved another resolution calling for the repeal of those parts of the Test and Corporation Acts which required the sacramental test for office (the declaration against transubstantiation which excluded Catholics was to remain in effect). This was carried without a division. The debate brought another advance of tremendous significance. Peel offered full government support if some satisfactory declaration safeguarding the Church were agreed to. With government support the bill was almost certain to pass. Without it, it was almost certainly headed for the same grave in the Lords which had claimed so many Emancipation bills. Everything depended on whether or not the Dissenters were willing to make a concession.

At the United Committee meeting of 3 March Smith reported on the results of conversations with Russell and Lansdowne. It was their opinion that the way must be left open for negotiation. And this the Committee agreed to.[2] It remained to work out some declaration agreeable to all parties. To this end, Smith had several conferences with Sir Thomas Acland, the original proposer of a declaration, and with Peel. The sub-committee as a whole was in constant communication with Russell, Althorp, and Holland. The final result was the passage of a bill through the Commons on 1 April, with a declaration appended which differed in no important respect from one proposed by the Committee itself as being least objectionable:

I, A. B., do solemnly declare that I will never exercise any power, authority, or influence, which I may possess by virtue of the office of —— to injure or weaken the Protestant Church as it is by law established within this realm, or to disturb it in the possession of any rights or privileges to which it is by law entitled.[3]

This was not a religious test, and it was to be taken by all candidates for office, not only by Dissenters. The Committee had consistently

[1] Twenty M.P.s voted for Repeal in 1828 and against Emancipation in 1829 (Machin, p. 113n).

[2] *Test-Act Reporter*, p. 450.

[3] Ibid., pp. 451–2; *Monthly Repository*, n.s. II (1828), 281.

stated its desire for unconditional Repeal and its reluctance to accept any new test; but as this one met the more important of its scruples, it accepted it.

The debates in the Lords took up most of the month of April. Wellington loyally gave the bill his support in the form in which it had been sent up from the Commons. But the High Tories did not give way without a fight. Several amendments were proposed to limit the bill as much as possible, and almost every one was fought to the last ditch. One proposed the inclusion of the statement 'I am a Protestant' in the declaration. This was defeated. But long and strenuous debates on the preservation of a 'Christian' Constitution finally induced the Duke to propose the inclusion of 'on the true faith of a Christian' after the word 'declare'. After a heated debate this amendment was passed. There could be no doubt that this reimposed a kind of religious test. It did not, as some of its supporters mistakenly supposed, exclude Unitarians. But it did introduce a new exclusion of Jews, and probably also of Quakers, who objected to any form of oath. This the United Committee deplored, but it did not reject it. And in this form the bill passed the Lords, and received the Royal Assent.[1]

The United Committee had kept a close and anxious watch on the bill throughout its passage through the Lords. Smith was his usual insistent and probing self, constantly conferring with Wellington as well as with the Whig leadership. Nothing had been left undone that could possibly have been done to secure the best possible terms. But there had never been a breach with Parliamentary support, never an unseemly inflexibility on principle which might have embarrassed the Dissenters' friends. Throughout there had been a willingness to bow to necessity and to compromise in the interest of the attainment of their primary objective. As Smith said in the House on 2 May:

This bill was introduced to set at rest a question between the Dissenters and the Church of England; and as one of a numerous body of Dissenters, I am satisfied with it. I am aware that they would have

---

[1] The declaration was to remain a qualification for office until 1863, when the Test Act was finally entirely repealed by the Statute Revision Act of that year.

been better satisfied with a simple repeal of the Test Acts without any declaration whatever, but as the great body of Dissenters do look upon the declaration as a test of religious opinions, and as it sets at rest the question between them and the Church of England, it is not in my opinion of any great importance whether it exists or not.[1]

It was this realism which had dominated the Committee during the whole course of the negotiations. It did not mean an abandonment of ultimate ideals. One of the last acts of the United Committee was to pass a resolution expressing 'their earnest desire for the entire abolition of all laws interfering with the rights of conscience and attaching civil disabilities to religious faith and worship. . . .'[2] And Smith's voice was soon to be raised for the Catholics and for the Jews as strongly as it had ever been for the Dissenters. All that the Committee's policy during the Repeal campaign meant was that it had accepted political reality and got all it could by adapting to it. This had been Smith's approach from the beginning.

In the celebrations following the great victory, Smith was fêted and lauded on all sides. But perhaps the praise which comes nearest to the mark was that of the United Committee which acknowledged the 'judicious mixture of zeal and prudence' which had characterized the activities of its sub-committee to Parliament.[3] Smith's zeal had sometimes been unjustly doubted. On occasion there is no doubt that he had been too prudent. But, when all is considered, there can be no question that he richly deserved the tribute which the Committee gave

to their respected Chairman, William Smith, Esq., M.P., for the zeal, ability, and urbanity which uniformly marked his conduct in presiding over their deliberations, and in conducting them to that successful issue which his unwearied exertions in Parliament, and in every sphere in which those exertions could promote the great cause of Civil and Religious Liberty, during so many years of a most consistent and honourable public life, have essentially contributed to secure.[4]

[1] *Test-Act Reporter*, pp. 429–30.   [2] Ibid., p. 483.
[3] Ibid.   [4] Ibid.

EPILOGUE

Personal disaster and public triumphs were to mark Smith's declining years. A life of luxury was replaced by one of relative penury, while one after another of the principles which he had so long championed in the political wilderness came to fruition.

In 1834 Smith lamented to Brougham that he could not take the lead in providing a public monument for Wilberforce:

Were I as rich as I once was, I should be much disposed to act at once and run the Risk of being approved and repaid—but my own carelessness and the obstinacy and Folly of the Knaves whom I was fool enough to trust, have clipped my wings till the Quills are left very bare, and I am reduced to, not what I would, but what I can afford—which, sorry I am to say it, is but little.[1]

Not much has been said of Smith's business activities, for the simple reason that there is not much to say. No man could have carried the political burdens which he carried and had an active career in business at the same time. But it is significant that Smith himself refused to recognize this fact, flinging himself into one disastrous venture after another, '*merely*', as his son Samuel bitterly complained, '*to make him fancy himself a man of property* and squander, till not a penny was left for any body'.[2] It was a shrewd, if a harsh and self-interested, judgement. It was not merely, or primarily, a lust for wealth that impelled Smith. The fact was that he could not do

[1] William Smith to Lord Brougham, 13 August 1834, Brougham Papers, University College, London, 43,332.

[2] Samuel Smith to Fanny (Smith) Nightingale, 17 November 1823, Verney Papers.

249

without that badge of respectability which, in his own eyes, a connexion with the active commercial life of the country gave him. His whole image of himself demanded it. Whatever the facts of the case, he had to identify himself with the interests of the class into which he was born and whose political interests he spent his life championing, and he could no more have withdrawn from commerce than he could have rejected his religious principles.

The already-mentioned crisis in the wholesale grocery in 1819 was the beginning of the end. Park Street and Parndon, pictures and books, the whole outer fabric of domestic life disappeared almost overnight. The Smiths with their two spinster daughters, Patty and Julia, moved into apartments over the business in Philpot Lane. It was a fine, large structure of the previous century, with a garden behind; but after the airy vistas of St James's Park, the City was oppressive. They were not to bear it for long, however, for in 1823 the firm staggered to its final dissolution. When everything was sorted out, Smith, whose income for the greater part of his life had been in the thousands, was left with a few hundred a year. The family moved first to a modest house in Upper Seymour Street and, with the close of Smith's Parliamentary career in 1830, to a house belonging to Ben in Blandford Square.

The disaster was not as great as it might have been, however. A large, loyal—and wealthy—family gathered round their ageing patriarch. There was a good deal of grumbling, but much more love and devotion. Ben, who grumbled most, also did the most. It was he who largely financed the uncontested, but still very expensive, Norwich elections of 1820 and 1826. W. E. Nightingale grumbled not at all, and did much. Smith was deeply devoted to his host of grand-children, some of whom—most notably Florence Nightingale and Barbara Leigh-Smith (Bodichon), the foundress of Girton—were to have distinguished careers in their own rights. And the monotony of life was considerably broken by rounds of visits to the country houses of his Smith, Nightingale, Nicholson, and Bonham-Carter children. Mrs Smith could give only her uncritical loyalty, but of that she gave without stint.

Neither financial reverses nor age—he was seventy-two when Repeal was carried and seventy-four when he retired from Parliament

—seem to have cramped Smith's public life overmuch. Throughout the Repeal campaign and beyond, his other activities continued to give evidence of a remarkable breadth of interest. Hardly had he got out of the ill-fated grocery, when his unquenchable enterprise attracted him to the Thames Tunnel Company, of which he remained Chairman until 1830. He was to be a very active Vice-Chairman of the British Fisheries until his death. He gave generously of his time and influence in the founding of the Greek Committee, to rouse English support for the Greek struggle for independence. He was also one of the founders of the Polish Committee, after the Poles' abortive revolt in 1830. It was not until 1832 that he finally stepped down as Chairman of the Deputies.

Smith also continued to the end to display that tolerance and lack of dogmatism which had always been so prominent in his character. In his later years, this was to be particularly noticeable in his attitude to social and economic questions. Smith naturally prided himself on being in a special sense a spokesman for commercial and manufacturing interests, and he took many of the conventional attitudes, supporting all measures to free trade and opposing workmen's combinations. But, though he considered himself a disciple of Political Economy and was a close friend of Thomas Malthus, a fellow-member of 'The King of Clubs' and his neighbour in Essex, he was no more rigid on this question than on any other. Like his Evangelical friends, he was appalled by conditions in the cotton factories and always supported regulatory measures. He was willing to go much further than this. In 1828, moved by the plight of Norwich weavers, he suggested that Parliament should appoint a committee of manufacturers and labourers to fix compulsory wage rates for hand-loom weavers—a step which would have been anathema to an orthodox Political Economist. He admitted that he had little hope that much would be accomplished by such a measure, but he thought it ought to be tried.[1] In 1830, at the request of some Methodist petitioners (another sign of the catholicity which he emanated), he introduced a bill for the abolition of the truck system, the payment of wages in kind. This brought Joseph Hume to his feet in violent opposition. Smith replied that

[1] *Hansard*, n.s. XVII, 1060–2.

throughout the whole of his life, he had paid as much attention as any man to the principles of measures brought before the House, and he did not think that it was any objection to a measure to say it was at variance with some principle of political economy. . . . He did not mean to treat the science with the slightest degree of disrespect; but he had never heard any principle advanced, except moral principles, (and he had some doubts whether they would not admit of some exceptions) he had never heard any principle of political economy advanced which was not subject to objection, and he had even heard of many which men were dogmatically told to follow, though they were not susceptible either of exact definition or proof.[1]

At the basis of Smith's lack of dogmatism lay a fundamental assumption which he shared with the Saints. He had eloquently expressed it in a debate on the Slave Trade in 1797: 'He derided the argument of expediency, and declared that no system of commercial policy should be allowed to exist for a moment, which was repugnant to moral duty.'[2]

As with his Evangelical friends, the cause of the slaves continued to be a pressing concern, ranking equally for Smith with Repeal. Throughout the twenties, he continued to play a critical part in advancing their interests. On 13 January 1823, Smith, William Allen, the great Quaker philanthropist, and T. F. Buxton met at Zachary Macaulay's, and, according to Allen, together 'laid the foundation for the London Society for the Abolition of Slavery in our Colonies, agreed on the persons who are to form the Committee', and made arrangements for the first meeting of the Society.[3] Not only was Smith one of those who launched the movement for Abolition, he was also to be one of its main Parliamentary advocates so long as he retained his seat in the Commons. Sir George Stephen, himself an active protagonist of the cause, emphasizes that from 1823 to 1830 it was a Parliamentary team, rather than one individual, which carried on the battle. The team was made up of Brougham, Buxton, Dr Stephen Lushington, and Smith. Each one, Stephen says,

[1] *Hansard*, n.s. XXV, 829. On the bill, and Smith's part in it, see Halévy, vol. III, 115n.

[2] *Parliamentary History*, XXXIII, 583.

[3] New, p. 283.

was an 'Ajax in battle'.[1] In 1830, when he at last yielded his seat for Norwich, Smith declared that in the cause of the abolition of Colonial Slavery, 'I would cheerfully expend my latest breath'. He very nearly did, rising from his sickbed during his final illness to attend a meeting at Buxton's.

Life did not ebb away from William Smith. Only death could quiet that restless energy. It came suddenly on 31 May 1835, three years after the triumph of Parliamentary reform and one year after Parliament had committed itself to the abolition of Slavery. Smith lived to see his most cherished objectives achieved.

How does one assess such a long and active career? According to the anonymous author of Smith's obituary notice in the *Morning Chronicle*:

Few public men at the commencement of their career have encountered more of the World's obloquy and no man has lived to vindicate a higher character or a purer fame.

. . . .

Mr. Smith's career is closed, but the impression of his toils and his virtues will remain . . .; his Country has already put its seal upon his faithful labours in the holy cause of liberty and the happiness of mankind.[2]

Doubtless the praise is rather too fulsome, as praise then was apt to be. Yet that England was a freer and more humane place when Smith died than it was when he was born cannot be denied. Nor can it be denied that Smith's long and patient labours had played a part in the transformation.

---

[1] See ibid., pp. 283 and 287.
[2] *William Smith, Formerly Member for the City of Norwich.*

BIBLIOGRAPHY

MANUSCRIPT MATERIALS

British Museum

    Bentham Papers.
    Fox Papers.
    Liverpool Papers.
    Peel Papers.
    'Register of the King of Clubs, 1798–1823.'

City of London Library, Guildhall

    Minutes of the Dissenting Deputies (including the minutes of the United Committee of 1827–1828), 1791–1832 (cited as 'Minutes').
    The Deputies' Letter Book, 1826–1834.

Huntington Library, San Marino, California

    Clarkson Papers.
    Macaulay Papers.

Public Record Office

    'Resolutions and Orders of the Society for Constitutional Information.'
    Russell Papers.
    Treasury Solicitor's Papers.

Other Public Collections

    Grey Papers, The Prior's Kitchen, Durham.
    Roscoe Papers, Liverpool Public Library.
    Whitbread Collection, Bedfordshire County Record Office.

William Smith Collection, Duke University Library, Durham, North Carolina.

Private Collections

Smith papers in the possession of Victor Bonham-Carter, Esq. (cited as 'Bonham-Carter Papers').★

Smith papers in the possession of Miss Katherine Duff (cited as 'Duff Papers').★

Smith papers in the possession of Philip Leigh-Smith, Esq. (cited as 'Leigh-Smith Papers').★

Smith papers in the possession of Sir Harry Verney, Bart. (cited as 'Verney Papers').

Smith papers and business records in the possession of Joseph Travers & Sons Ltd. (cited as 'Travers Papers').

★All three collections to be deposited in the University Library, Cambridge.

PERIODICALS AND NEWSPAPERS

The Eclectic Review
The Evangelical Magazine.
The Ipswich Journal.
The Iris. [Norwich.]
The London Chronicle.
The Monthly Repository.
The Norfolk Chronicle.
The Norwich Mercury.

CONTEMPORARY PRINTED WORKS AND PRINTED SOURCES

The Annual Register, 1771

Aspinall, Arthur, ed., *The Formation of Canning's Ministry, February to August 1827* (London, 1937).

Aspland, R. B., *Memoir of the Reverend Robert Aspland* (London, 1850).

Belsham, Thomas, *Fast Sermon* (London, 1812).

——, *A Letter to Lord Sidmouth* (London, 1811).

——, *Memoirs of the Late Reverend Theophilus Lindsey* (London, 1873).

Bennett, J., *The History of the Dissenters* (London, 1839).

Bogue, D., and Bennett, J., *History of Dissenters* (4 vols.; London, 1808–12).

Chambers, J., A General *History of the County of Norfolk* (2 vols.; Norwich, 1829).

Coleridge, E. H., ed., *The Works of Lord Byron* (7 vols.; London and New York, 1898–1904).

Collection of broadsides and handbills, Colman Library, Norwich.

Collection of broadsides and handbills, Norwich Public Library.

A Collection of State Papers relative to the War against France (Debrett; London, 1794).

A complete Collection of State Trials, compiled by T. J. Howell (33 vols.; London, 1809–26).

Debate on the Repeal of the Test and Corporation Act, in the House of Commons, March 28th, 1787 (London, 1787).

The Debate in the House of Commons on Mr. Beaufoy's Motion for the Repeal of Such Parts of the Test and Corporation Acts as Affect the Protestant Dissenters, on Friday the Eighth of May, 1789 (London, 1789).

The Debate in the House of Commons, on Tuesday, the 2nd March, 1790, on the Motion of Mr. Fox, for a Repeal of the Corporation and Test Acts (London: J. Walter, 1790).

Furneaux, Philip, *An Essay on Toleration* (London, 1773).

Hall, Robert, *Christianity Consistent with the Love of Freedom* (London, 1791).

HANSARD. *Parliamentary Debates.*

Heywood, Samuel, *The Right of Protestant Dissenters to a Complete Toleration Asserted* (London, 1787).

Horsfield, T. W., *The History of Lewes* (2 vols. in one; Lewes, 1824–7).

——, *The History of Sussex* (2 vols.; Lewes, 1835).

Journals of the House of Commons, 1825.

Laprade, W. T., ed., *Parliamentary Papers of John Robinson, 1774–1784* (London, 1922).

A Letter to a Member of Parliament Concerning the Repeal of the Corporation and Test Acts (London, 1739).

Lockhart, J. G., *Memoirs of the Life of Sir Walter Scott* (7 vols.; London, 1837–8).

Oldfield, T. H. B., *A History of the Boroughs of Great Britain* (London, 1792).

The Parliamentary History of Great Britain.

Pellew, G., *The Life and Correspondence of the Right Hon. Henry Addington, First Viscount Sidmouth* (3 vols.; London, 1847).

The Poll[s] for Members of Parliament, Norwich (several are referred to in the text; they are identified by publisher and year of publication).

Rogers, Samuel, *Recollections* (London, 1859).

Romilly, Sir Samuel, *Memoirs* (3 vols.; London, 1840).

Russell, Lord John, ed., *Memorials and Correspondence of Charles James Fox* (3 vols.; London, 1853–7).

Russell, Rollo, ed., *Early Correspondence of Lord John Russell, 1805–1840* (2 vols.; London, 1913).

Rutt, J. T., ed., *The Theological and Miscellaneous Works of Joseph Priestley* (25 vols.; London, 1831).

Sketch of the History of the Protestant Dissenting Deputies (London, 1813).

Smith, William, *A Letter to William Wilberforce, Esq., M.P. on the Proposed Abolition of the Slave Trade, under the consideration of Parliament* (London, 1807).

Southey, Robert, *A Letter to William Smith, Esq., M.P.* (London, 1817).

Statement of the Case of the Protestant Dissenters (London, 1827).

Stephen, Sir James, *Essays in Ecclesiastical Biography* (2 vols.; London, 1849).

The Test-Act Reporter (London, 1829).

Twiss, Horace, *The Public and Private Life of Lord Chancellor Eldon* (3 vols.; London, 1844).

Walpole, Spencer, *The Life of Lord John Russell* (London, 1891).

Wilberforce, R. I. and S., *The Correspondence of William Wilberforce,* (2 vols.; London, 1840).

——, *The Life of William Wilberforce,* (5 vols.; London, 1838).

William Smith, Formerly Member for the City of Norwich (Hastings, 1835).

Williams, J., *Memoirs of the Reverend Thomas Belsham* (London, 1833).

Worsley, Sir Richard, *The History of the Isle of Wight* (London, 1781).

Wyvill, Christopher, *Political Papers*, (6 vols.; York, 1794–1802).

SECONDARY AUTHORITIES

Barlow, R. B., *Citizenship and Conscience* (Philadelphia, 1962).

Beavan, A. B., *The Aldermen of the City of London* (London, 1913).

Best, G. F. A., 'Church and State in English Politics 1800–1833', Ph.D. dissertation, Cambridge University, 1955.

Black, E. C., *The Association: British Extra-parliamentary Political Organization* (Cambridge, Mass., 1963).

Bolam, C. G., Goring, J., Short, H. L., and Thomas, R., *The English Presbyterians* (Boston, 1968).

Bonham-Carter, Victor, *In a Liberal Tradition: A Social Biography, 1700–1950* (London, 1960).

Brown, F. K., *Fathers of the Victorians: The Age of Wilberforce* (Cambridge, 1962).

Butterfield, Herbert, *George III, Lord North, and the People* (London, 1949).

Christie, I. R., *Wilkes, Wyvill, and Reform* (London, 1962).

Chronicles of Cannon Street (privately printed for Joseph Travers & Sons Ltd.).

Clark, H. W., *History of English Nonconformity* (2 vols.; New York, 1965).

Coomer, Duncan, *English Dissent Under the Early Hanoverians* (London, 1946).

Courtney, W. P., *The Parliamentary Representation of Cornwall to 1832* (privately printed, London, 1889).

Cozens-Hardy, B., and Kent, E. A., *The Mayors of Norwich 1403 to 1835* (Norwich, 1938).

Derry, J. W., *William Pitt* (London, 1962).

Ernouf, Le baron Alfred Auguste, *Maret, Duc de Bassano* (Paris, 1878).

Forster, E. M., *Marianne Thornton: A Domestic Biography* (New York, 1956).

Garnett, R., *The Life of W. J. Fox* (London, 1909).

Gash, Norman, *Mr. Secretary Peel* (London, 1961).

Ginter, D. E., *Whig Organization in the General Election of 1790* (Berkeley and Los Angeles, 1967).

Gordon, Alexander, *Addresses Biographical and Historical* (London, 1922).

Halévy, Elie, *A History of the English People in the Nineteenth Century* (6 vols.; London, 1961).

Hayes, B. D., 'Politics in Norfolk, 1750–1832', Ph.D. dissertation, Cambridge University, 1957.

Henriques, Ursula, *Religious Toleration in England, 1787–1833* (London, 1961).

Holland Rose, J., *William Pitt and the Great War* (London, 1911).

Holt, R. V., *The Unitarian Contribution to Social Progress in England* (London, 1938).

Hunt, N. C., *Sir Robert Walpole, Samuel Holden and the Dissenting Deputies* (London, 1957).

——, *Two Early Political Associations: The Quakers and the Dissenting Deputies in the Age of Sir Robert Walpole* (London, 1961).

Jones, R. Tudur, *Congregationalism in England, 1662–1962* (London, 1962).

Knight, Frida, *The Strange Case of Thomas Walker* (London, 1957).

Lincoln, A., *Some Political and Social Ideas of English Dissent, 1763–1800* (Cambridge, 1938).

Machin, G. I. T., *The Catholic Question in English Politics, 1820–1830* (Oxford, 1964).

Manning, B. L., *The Protestant Dissenting Deputies* (Cambridge, 1952).

McLachlan, H., *English Education under the Test Acts, 1662–1820* (Manchester, 1931).

Meacham, Standish, *Henry Thornton of Clapham* (Cambridge, Mass., 1964).

Mitchell, Austin, *The Whigs in Opposition, 1815–1830* (Oxford, 1967).

Namier, L. B., and John Brooke, *The House of Commons, 1754–1790* (3 vols.; London, 1964).

Namier, L. B., *The Structure of Politics at the Accession of George III* (2nd ed., London, 1957).

New, C. W., *The Life of Henry Brougham to 1830* (Oxford, 1961).

Past and Present in an Old Firm (London and Aylesbury, 1907).

Roberts, Michael, *The Whig Party, 1807–1812* (London, 1939).

Rudé, George, *Wilkes and Liberty: A Social Study of 1763 to 1774* (Oxford, 1962).

Senior, Hereward, *Orangeism in Ireland and Britain, 1795–1836* (London, 1967).

Skeats, H. S., and Miall, C. S., *History of the Free Churches of England, 1688–1891* (London, 1891).

Sperling, C. F. D., *A Short History of the Borough of Sudbury in the County of Suffolk* (Sudbury, 1896).

Stephen, Lady, MS Life of William Smith to 1813.

Steven Watson, J., *The Reign of George III, 1760–1815* (Oxford, 1960).

Sutherland, Lucy, *The East India Company in Eighteenth-Century Politics* (Oxford, 1952).

Temple Patterson, A., *Radical Leicester* (Leicester, 1954).

Venn, J. A., *Alumni Cantabrigiensis,* (Part II Cambridge, 1947).

Webb, R. K., *Harriett Martineau: A Radical Victorian* (London, 1960).

Whitley, W. T., *Art in England, 1800–1820* (Cambridge, 1928).

——, *Artists and Their Friends in England, 1700–1799* (London, 1928).

Whittaker, M. B., 'The Revival of Dissent, 1800–1835', M. Litt. thesis, Cambridge University, 1958.

Wilbur, E. M., *A History of Unitarianism* (Cambridge, 1952).

Woolrych, M. W., *Lives of Eminent Serjeants-at-law* (2 vols.; London, 1869).

ARTICLES

Beard, Lilian, 'Unitarianism in the Potteries from 1812', *Transactions of the Unitarian Historical Society*, VI (1935–38), 14–28.

Best, G. F. A., 'The Protestant Constitution and its Supporters', *Royal Historical Society Transactions*, 5th series, VIII (1958), 105–27.

——, 'The Whigs and the Church Establishment', *History*, XLV (1960), 103–18.

Butt-Thompson, F. W., 'William Vidler, Baptist and Universalist', *Transactions of the Baptist Historical Society*, I (1908–9), 42–55.

Christie, I. R., 'The Yorkshire Association, 1780–84: A Study in Political Organization', *The Historical Journal*, III, 2 (1960), 144–61.

Courtney, W. P., 'The King of Clubs', in Lady Seymour, ed., *The 'Pope' of Holland House* (London, 1906).

George, M. D., 'Fox's Martyrs', *Royal Historical Society Transactions*, 4th series, XXI (1939), 133–68.

Greaves, R. W., 'Roman Catholic Relief and the Leicester Election of 1826', *Royal Historical Society Transactions*, 4th series, XXII (1940), 199–223.

Hexter, J. H., 'The Protestant Revival and the Catholic Question in England', *The Journal of Modern History*, VIII (1936), 297–319.

Hunt, N. C., 'The Quakers and Dissenters', *The Listener*, 20 October 1960.

Laprade, W. T., 'Public Opinion and the Election of 1784', *English Historical Review*, XXXI (1916), 224–37.

'London Nonconformity in 1810', *Transactions of the Congregational Historical Society*, VI (1913–15), 126–34.

Mitchell, Austin, 'The Association Movement 1792–93', *The Historical Journal* IV, 1 (1961), 56–77.

Montgomery, R. M., 'A Note on the Acts of Parliament dealing with denial of the Trinity', TUHS, VI (1935–38), 209–12.

Paterson, David, 'John Wright', TUHS, VI (1935–38), 29–43.

Powicke, F. J., 'An Apology for the Nonconformist Arians of the Eighteenth Century', TUHS, I (1917–18), 101–28.

——, 'The Salters' Hall Controversy', *Transactions of the Congregational Historical Society*, VII (1916–18), 110–24.

Stephen, Lady, *The Shores of Sheffield and the Offleys of Norton Hall*, reprinted from the *Transactions of the Hunter Archaeological Society*, vol. V, Part I (January 1938).

Sutherland, Lucy, 'The City of London in Eighteenth-Century Politics', *Essays presented to Sir Lewis Namier* (London, 1956).

DISSENT IN POLITICS
1780-1830

INDEX

Adams family, 4, 5, 8
Addington, Henry (Viscount Sidmouth), 103, 117, 148ff., 171, 172, 173, 174, 175, 177
Anglican Church, and society, xiv, 62
Anglican Constitution, 219–20
Anti-Jacobin, 75
Arianism, 36, 55, 200
Arminianism, 35, 36
Aspland, R. B., 158
Aspland, the Rev. Robert, 164, 168, 184–5, 197, 198, 199, 202, 203, 206, 210, 216n., 221, 227, 234, 241, 244
Atkinson, Richard, 14, 15, 16, 19
Aylesbury Quarter Sessions, 151, 160

Barlow, R. G., 46, 60
Beaufoy, Henry, 33, 44
Belsham, the Rev. Thomas, 7, 8, 9, 55, 69, 96, 108, 133, 157, 161, 163, 164, 168, 169, 174, 196, 197, 199–200, 203, 204, 205, 206, 208; attitude towards hot-gospellers, 166–7, 198
Bentham, Jeremy, 207
Benyon, Samuel Yate, 33, 34
Blasphemy, 193, 200–1
Bonham-Carter family, xi–xii, 32, 41
Bonham-Carter, Joanna Maria (Smith), xi, 54, 190
Bonham-Carter, John, xi–xii, 190
Bowring, John, 202, 206–7, and n. 210, 237
British and Foreign School Society, 207
Brougham, Henry, 109, 187, 224, 240, 252; education bill, 207–8
Buckinghamshire, magistrates, 160–1; Dissent and anti-Catholicism, 233–4
Burdett, Sir Francis, 140, 141, 142, 143, 235
Burke, Edmund, 61, 62, 63, 66

Buxton, T. F., 187, 252, 253

Camelford, 58–9
Canning, George, 219, 235, 238, 240, 241
Canningites, 241, 244, 245
Canterbury, Archbishop of (Charles Manners-Sutton), 181, 191, 192, 193
Carlile, Richard, 193
Caroline, Queen, 215
Carter family (see Bonham-Carter)
Castlereagh, Viscount, 210
Catholic Emancipation, attitude of Dissent, xv, 221ff.; connexion with Repeal, 130 and n., 170–1, 172, 173, 177, 183, 185, 212ff.
'Catholicity' of Dissent, 36–7, 203, 206, 233
'Catholic' party, 219–20
Catholic toleration act, 77
Chauvelin, Marquis de, 89, 90
Clapham, 6, 11, 12, 58, 59, 99, 103
Clarke, Mary Anne, 140
Clarkson, Thomas, 56, 57, 108, 115
Coape family, 9, 12
Coke, Thomas (Earl of Leicester), 143
Copenhagen expedition (1807), 137–8
Conventicle Act, 160, 164, 170, 174, 180–1, 182
Corn Laws, 134
Corresponding Society, London, 92, 97

Daventry, 7–8, 32, 36–7, 55, 96, 204, 205
Deists, 193
Dissenting academies (see also Daventry and Warrington), 36, 87
Dissenting Ministers, General Body of, 38, 40, 152, 168, 222, 223, and n., 226–7, 236

265